T0224980

Complication Management In The Cardiac Catheter Laboratory

Erhard Kaiser

Editors

Complication Management In The Cardiac Catheter Laboratory

 Springer

Editor
Erhard Kaiser
Private Practice for Internal Medicine and Cardiology
Frankfurt am Main, Germany

ISBN 978-3-662-66095-9   ISBN 978-3-662-66093-5   (eBook)
https://doi.org/10.1007/978-3-662-66093-5

This Springer imprint is published by the registered company Springer-Verlag GmbH, DE, part of Springer Nature.
The registered company address is: Heidelberger Platz 3, 14197 Berlin, Germany

For my family

Foreword I

Today, diagnostic cardiac catheterization as well as interventional catheter techniques have a high success rate and only a low complication rate. For diagnostic cardiac catheterization, this is 0.9% and for interventional catheterization 2% according to the last statistics of the BQS for North Rhine-Westphalia.

Thus, a cardiac catheterization is usually performed uncomplicatedly and quickly in stable patients. However, the quality of a surgeon only becomes apparent when unexpected or self-induced complications occur. The excellence, also of the entire catheter team, is then reflected in the management of such situations.

Dr. Erhard Kaiser, Frankfurt, and other co-authors therefore set out to describe complication management in the cardiac catheterization laboratory in detail and to identify possible solutions. The prevention of a complication begins, of course, with patient preparation and this also includes a correspondingly detailed anamnesis and information. Especially in this area, problems are found again and again when procedures end up in court.

In the cardiac catheterization laboratory, the authors distinguish function-related complications from complications caused by catheter placement. Of course, complications of coronary interventions occupy a large space. Complications from coronary wire placement, balloon catheter, and stent implantation are considered in a differentiated manner. Of particular importance and especially difficult to treat are thromboembolic complications, which are also discussed below.

Contrast-induced problems are another major topic, as is airway management up to and including cardiopulmonary resuscitation.

Particularly noteworthy is also the final chapter on error management with borrowings taken from aviation and certainly a highlight in this book.

Finally, educational and training situations in interventional cardiology in Germany are presented and follow-up care is discussed.

The book by E. Kaiser closes a gap in the German-speaking world since a summary treatise on complication management was missing until now. The clinical experiences of more than 20 years of interventional work in the cathlab in various hospitals and his own achievements as a trainer for catheter based procedures, but also in the committees of the ESC and the German Society of Cardiology, have strongly influenced the writing of this book.

I wish this book every success and I am pleased that a summary work on this important subject is finally appearing.

R. Erbel
Clinic for Cardiology
West German Heart Center
Essen, Germany
November 2012

Foreword II

Health care has transformed society with dramatic improvements in the prevention and treatment of all disorders. However, in key reports including "To Err is Human: Building a Safer health System" and "Crossing the Quality Chasm: A New Health Care System for the Twenty-First Century" the Institute of Medicine has laid out the challenges of optimizing the medical care system and the importance of addressing the fundamental truth that human performance significantly accounts for both success and failure in caring for patients.

This book is important because it presents not only what can go wrong during procedures, i.e. the long list of potential complications, but also addresses the human performance and system issues that must be understood to prevent, recognize, and effectively manage complications. This approach is a major departure from prior textbooks and reviews that have addressed complications. A wide range of information has been published on the various complications and management strategies; however, the present knowledge is not enough to produce change. Drawing on lessons from the aviation industry, the ability to create true and sustained change requires medicine to first perform an analysis of how things can suddenly go badly in the cardiac catheterization laboratory.

This textbook does not exist alone but is linked to the practical and interactive training courses developed by Dr. Kaiser. These courses highlight the human performance issues of not only individuals but also teams. Using many innovative training methods and technologies, his courses have established a unique and effective approach to improving human performance in health care. The use of simulation has been a major part of this shift in training paradigm.

Interventional cardiology has always been a field founded on solid scientific studies that have allowed us to understand the right treatment for the right patient. It has an extensive literature allowing us to classify the evidence, determine appropriateness, and to provide clinical guidelines in the management of patients with coronary, vascular, and structural heart disease. This book takes the interventional field into a new domain of improving how we deliver the care dictated by best practices. No matter how strong and persuasive the clinical trial data are to support the need for a procedure, the safe and effective performance of the procedure is a completely separate process. Dr. Kaiser and the authors of chapters in this book focus us on understanding complications in a way that will lead to safer and more effective procedures.

John D. Carroll
Professor of Medicine
University of Colorado Denver
Denver, CO, USA

Former Director, Interventional Cardiology
Cardiac and Vascular Center, University of Colorado Hospital
Aurora, CO, USA

Preface to the Second Edition

Interventional cardiology is one of the most rapidly developing medical disciplines. Interventional procedures on the beating heart, which would have been unthinkable in the past, have become routine procedures today, and there is no end in sight to the technical and methodological development. Nevertheless, not everything that is technically feasible must ultimately be done today and our patients should always be the focus and benefit from the procedures performed.

Against this background, complication management in the cardiac catheterization laboratory has lost none of its topicality and importance. On the contrary, the more complex our procedures become, the more likely it is that procedure-related complications will occur, and the greater the demands on the quality of the surgeons and cardiac catheterization laboratory teams must be. So learning and training together doesn't stop, it goes on and on.

With this in mind, we have given the book a complete overhaul, adding to and updating all the chapters.

May this book continue to contribute to the establishment of a constructive approach to errors and a functioning complication management in interventional cardiology.

Erhard Kaiser
Frankfurt am Main, Germany
June 2020

Preface to the First Edition

Today, interventional therapy in the cardiac catheterization laboratory plays a central role in the treatment of a wide variety of cardiovascular diseases. Procedures that would have been unthinkable years ago, such as percutaneous aortic valve replacement, but also complex coronary interventions, are now performed worldwide in large numbers and with good treatment success. Our great gratitude within the cardiology community is therefore still due today to the pioneers of interventional cardiology (Andreas Grüntzig and Werner Forssmann may be mentioned here only as representatives), who with their pioneering spirit and skill took the first steps from which we still benefit today.

Since we have long left the age of pure diagnostics behind us (discovery of X-rays, development of X-ray contrast media, and the first angiographies), we have been living and experiencing the age of interventional therapy in many ways on a daily basis. However, for the past 10 years, interventional cardiology has been increasingly, and quite rightly, focusing on patient safety, challenging us to rethink more than ever before. In particular, the younger generation of interventional cardiologists is now challenged to establish a culture of error in their cardiology departments, which still seems difficult in many places. This book aims to contribute to a change of mood in the respective departments.

I am proud and pleased to have found co-authors for this book who all represent this young and new generation of interventional cardiologists, who are fully committed to patient safety and who, in addition to their daily interventional work, have also shown great personal dedication to cardiology education and training as well as patient safety. The same pioneering spirit may also be attested to all of them again because with innovative training concepts, namely simulator-supported teaching, we manage today to operate a complication management that would also have been unthinkable in the past and is hardly inferior to reality today.

My wish with this book is to contribute to a constructive approach to errors and complications in interventional cardiology. May this book become a permanent thematic part of interventional training and become embedded in the essence of the current, but also of all future generations of cardiologists.

Erhard Kaiser
Frankfurt am Main, Germany
November 2012

Acknowledgements

I would like to expressly thank all the contributors to this book who, in addition to all their professional and private commitments, have managed to devote themselves to the teaching and further development of the subject of cardiology, thus helping young physicians and teams in their daily work in the cardiac catheterization laboratory and acting in the service of patient safety. My special thanks go to Ms. Kerstin Barton and Mr. Hinrich Küster from Springer Verlag for their competent and patient support.

Above all, I would also like to thank my wife Nataša and my daughter Carla Anja, who always give me the strength and peace for my work.

Contents

III   After the Cardiac Catheterization Laboratory

List of Editor and Authors

About the Editor

Erhard Kaiser, MD, FESC, FSCAI
- Specialist in Internal Medicine, additional qualification in Cardiology
- Interventional Cardiologist DGK®
- Special Cardiovascular Prevention DGK®
- Hypertensiologist DHL®
- Emergency Medicine
- Fellow of the European Society of Cardiology
- Fellow of the Society for Cardiovascular Angiography and Interventions
- Member of the Society for Cardiovascular Angiography and Interventions
- Member of the German Society of Cardiology
- Member of the German Society for Vascular Surgery and Vascular Medicine
- Member of the Working Group Interventional Cardiology of the German Society of Cardiology
- Founder and long-standing spokesman of the Simulation Working Group of the German Society of Cardiology
- Member of the Education Committee of the European Society of Cardiology 2006–2008
- Head of the CardioSkills Simulation Centre Frankfurt am Main
- Head of the Vascular Academy Frankfurt am Main (VASA)
- Chief Emergency Physician

List of Authors

Ralf Birkemeyer Herzklinik Ulm, Ulm/Donau, Germany

Tonja Gaibler Ulsenheimer Friederich Rechtsanwälte, München, Germany

Erhard Kaiser, MD, FESC, FSCAI Privatarztpraxis für Innere Medizin und Kardiologie, Frankfurt am Main, Germany

Torsten Konrad   CardioVascular Practice Konrad&Dahmen, Bad Kreuznach, Germany

Michael Markant, MD   Klinik für Kardiologie, Marien-Hospital Marl, Marl, Germany

Martin Müller   Anästhesiologie Notfallmedizin, Capio-Mathilden-Hospital Abteilung für Anästhesie Am Schlag 9, Büdingen, Germany

Jan Pollmann, MD   Medizinischen Versorgungszentrums Hanau GmbH, Hanau, Germany

Carsten Skurk   Charité Universitätsmedizin Berlin, Campus Benjamin Franklin, Berlin, Germany

Kai-Uwe R. Strelow, Dipl.-Psych., Dipl.-Volksw.   Rudolf Frey Lernklinik Universitätsmedizin Mainz, Mainz, Germany

Thomas Twisselmann, MD   Kardiologische Gemeinschaftspraxis am Tibarg und Hohe Weide, Hamburg, Germany

Before the Cardiac Catheterization Laboratory

Contents

Examination and Treatment Planning

Torsten Konrad, Erhard Kaiser, and Tonja Gaibler

Contents

© The Author(s), under exclusive license to Springer-Verlag GmbH, DE, part of Springer Nature 2023
E. Kaiser (ed.), *Complication Management In The Cardiac Catheter Laboratory*,
https://doi.org/10.1007/978-3-662-66093-5_1

1

1.1 Patient Preparation

Torsten Konrad and Erhard Kaiser

1.1.1 Introduction

The performance of a diagnostic cardiac catheterization or a coronary intervention requires not only a high degree of care in the performance of the examination, but also thorough procedural planning and preparation of the patient. This is easy if the operator already knows the patient from previous contact and he himself makes the indication for the examination. It can be problematic if the operator does not know the patient and has not made the indication for the procedure himself. In this situation, it is all the more important that the minimum standards in diagnostics and documentation are observed and that the operator has the patient's current documents and examination results available for inspection on the day of the procedure. If examination results that are important for determining the indication are not available on the day of the procedure or are completely missing, the indication for the procedure must be critically reconsidered and missing examination results must be obtained or the procedure postponed.

1.1.2 Standards for the Performance of Diagnostic Coronary Angiography and Elective Coronary Interventions

The establishment of a standardized procedure in the cardiac catheterization laboratory for the performance of diagnostic coronary angiography and elective coronary interventions is desirable and recommendable as it increases procedural safety, facilitates cooperation in the cardiac catheterization laboratory team and simplifies workflows. The medical basis for standardized procedures in the cardiac catheterization laboratory is provided by the treatment guidelines of the responsible professional societies (e.g. ▶ www.escardio.org, ▶ www.dgk.org). Furthermore, additional in-house therapy standards and procedural standards based on the guidelines usually apply, which may affect various areas of the cardiac catheterization laboratory work environment.

> **Areas in the Cardiac Catheterization Laboratory That Are Subject to Standardization**
> - Staffing
> - Technical equipment
> - Medication
> - Provision of certain devices
> - Pre-, peri- and post-procedural workflows

Standardized procedures or Standard Operating Procedures (SOPs) are usually stored in a manual for in-house quality management and can be viewed. This facilitates the training of new employees and the maintenance of established standards. So-called silent standards, which only reflect a common consensus and always leave room for interpretation, which can lead to misunderstandings, should be avoided.

For the performance of elective procedures and diagnostic coronary angiographies, an optimum of cardiological pre-tests is required, since the diagnostic procedures and interventions can always be planned.

> **Standards of Pre-procedural Diagnostics for Elective Surgery**
> - Physical examination
> - 12-Lead ECG
> - Basic laboratory: potassium, creatinine, small blood count, basal TSH, INR, PTT
> - Ischemia detection (ergometry, stress echocardiography, scintigraphy, MRI)
> - Color Doppler Echocardiography
> - Other preliminary findings relevant to the procedure

Further standards in the cardiac catheterisation laboratory should regulate the X-ray technique, the behaviour in routine cases as well as in emergencies and the embedding of the workflows in the overall workflow of the department.

On the day of the procedure, the patient should be fasting for at least 3–6 h. If the procedure is not scheduled until noon, the patient can have a small breakfast in the morning. Before the start of the procedure, the patient is given a venous access cannula so that medication or infusions can be administered at short notice if necessary.

1.1.3 Standards for the Performance of Emergency Interventions

Compared to the procedure for elective interventions, only an absolute minimum standard of preliminary information is required from the patient in emergency interventions, and in some cases it may even be dispensed with altogether. Since many emergency patients reach the cardiac catheterization laboratory via the hospital's chest pain unit, a current 12-lead ECG, if necessary with right ventricular leads, a point-of-care laboratory test, an ECHO if necessary, and the findings from the on-site medical examination are usually available. In case of vital indication, in extreme cases of an examination during ongoing resuscitation, for example in the context of a myocardial infarction, the procedure is started and further information on the patient is obtained in parallel.

> **Minimal Standard of Pre-procedural Diagnostics in Emergencies**
> - Clinically appropriate symptomatology/name/external patient history
> - Marker elevation in the point-of-care laboratory
> - 12-Lead ECG, if necessary with right ventricular leads
> - ECHO, if applicable

1.1.4 Selection and Preparation of the Access Route

Which access route to the arterial vascular system is chosen depends on the one hand on the type of procedure and on the other hand on the individual anatomical conditions of the respective patient.

The standard access route for coronary angiography is now the radial artery in most centers. Randomized studies have shown a reduction in bleeding complications, vascular complications and even a mortality benefit for this access route compared to the femoral artery (Ziakas et al. 2010). There is also the possibility of earlier mobilization. A problem with the access route via the radial artery is a pronounced tendency to spasm in patients with nicotinic abuse. This can force a change to a femoral access route.

On the day of the examination, the hair in the puncture region should be removed. According to the guidelines of the Robert Koch Institute "Prevention of postoperative infections in the surgical area" of March 2007, shaving of the groin should not be performed due to cutaneous microlesions and the associated increased risk of infection. Rather, hair should be removed with short hair clippers or depilatory cream. If there is little hair, hair removal is probably not necessary. An increased risk of infection has not yet been shown with hair that has been left on.

If skin irritation or mycosis is found in the groin region, an alternative access route should be chosen whenever possible. Mycosis must first be treated antifungally and should be completely resolved on the day of the examination.

After shaving, the patient is sterilely draped with the puncture area left out and then the puncture region is thoroughly disinfected. Before coronary angiography, the operator himself carries out hygienic hand disinfection in accordance with the exposure times of the substances used. During the examination, it is important to ensure the highest possible level of hygiene by using sterile gloves, surgical gowns, face masks and hair coverings.

1

> Due to a lower risk of complications, a radial approach should usually be preferred.

1.1.5 Examination Under Anticoagulation

When taking oral anticoagulants, a continued intake has currently been established on the basis of a clear study situation. Here, an INR value in the low therapeutic range should be aimed for. A pause of e.g. Warfarin with administration of low molecular weight heparin should be avoided if the bleeding/complication rate is clearly increased. Especially when taking anticoagulants, a radial access route should be preferred.

In the case of the newer oral anticoagulants such as dabigatran, rivaroxaban or apixaban, the morning dosage can be paused before the examination during elective coronary angiography. Studies are being conducted to determine whether continuous dosing also has advantages in this case. If the patient to be examined is undergoing dual antiplatelet therapy, both substances can continue to be administered and do not have to be paused before the examination (Jamula et al. 2010).

> Patients taking Warfarin should not be bridged with heparins due to the demonstrated increased risk of bleeding complications.

1.1.6 Use of Checklists in the Cardiac Catheterization Laboratory

The general efforts to standardize workflows in the cardiac catheterization laboratory can be supported by the use of checklists (Buerschaper and St. Pierre 2003). In particular, the technical equipment should be regularly checked for completeness and functionality with the aid of a checklist. However, cardiopulmonary resuscitation performed in the cardiac catheterization laboratory can also be standardized if the adherence to the resuscitation algorithms is performed and documented with the help of a checklist. General guidelines for the use of checklists in the cardiac catheterization laboratory are not available.

> **Example: Checklist Before Performing a Coronary Angiography**
> ‒ Complete medical history
> ‒ Physical examination
> ‒ Review of relevant previous findings such as laboratory values, previous coronary angiography findings, information on bypasses
> ‒ Special check of the coagulation status, the renal parameters and the thyroid values
> ‒ Taking anticoagulants?
> ‒ Planning of the access route: Radial possible? PAD present? Previous puncture problems?
> ‒ Oral antidiabetic drugs discontinued in time?
> ‒ Current ECG available?
> ‒ Proof of ischemia?
> ‒ Sober patient?
> ‒ Patient informed? Are there still questions?

1.2 Legal Aspects of Patient Information

Tonja Gaibler

1.2.1 Introduction

Medical advances in interventional cardiology have significantly increased both outcome quality and patient safety in recent years. At the same time, the risk of interventional complications has been reduced due to constantly growing medical experience and the introduction of stricter guidelines for interventions in the cardiac catheterization laboratory.

Despite this positive trend, doctors and patients must be aware that an optimal treatment result cannot be achieved in every case. A residual risk of complications remains.

The entitlement to perform a medical intervention, i.e. any action on the body or its functions, presupposes not only the indication in accordance with the rules of medical art and the error-free performance of the measure in accordance with the applicable standard, but also, of course, the patient's consent. Legally effective consent, in turn, requires the physician to have carefully informed the patient ("informed consent"). This—as well as the entire rights and obligations arising from the treatment contract (§§ 630a et seq. BGB)—has now also been expressly standardised by law since the so-called Patients' Rights Act came into force in February 2013 (§ 630d para. 1 sentence 1 BGB). The law provides for an obligation of the physician to explain in a comprehensible manner the diagnosis, the probable development of health, the therapy and the measures to be taken in this respect as well as to provide a detailed and comprehensible risk information (§§ 630c para. 2 p. 1, 630e para. 1, 2 p. 1 no. 3 BGB).

In this context, the information is a genuine medical duty and can therefore not be delegated to non-medical staff (Section 630e (2) no. 1 BGB). A decision of the Higher Regional Court of Karlsruhe (VersR 2014, p. 710), according to which even a student is allowed to provide information prior to a cardiac catheter examination in individual cases with a proven level of knowledge, is therefore considered "doubtful" in view of the statutory regulation (Pauge 2015, marginal no. 463). For reasons of liability law, this can only be discouraged. If the consent is ineffective because the doctor did not provide sufficient or timely information, even the indicated and correctly performed intervention constitutes bodily injury under §§ 223ff. StGB, §§ 823ff. BGB. If the patient would have decided against the intervention, even possibly, if he had been properly informed, he can derive claims for damages and compensation for pain and suffering from this. However, insufficient information is also relevant under criminal law. The criminal offences of negligent bodily injury or homicide, and in the case of deliberately neglected informed consent even of intentional bodily injury, are possible. Fortunately, criminal accusations are made

less frequently. Here, too, the public prosecutor's office or the court must provide evidence of insufficient informed consent. In the significantly more frequent civil law disputes, on the other hand, the evidence situation is more problematic, because here it is up to the doctor to prove that the information provided was correct (Section 630h (2) sentence 1 of the German Civil Code). This is precisely where the considerable potential for liability lies, because any doubt as to the correct, complete and timely provision of information is at the expense of the doctor and can lead to liability.

Civil and criminal proceedings are not mutually exclusive—they can each take place separately, in parallel or consecutively.

> Without legally effective consent and careful information of the patient by the physician, even the indicated and correctly performed procedure constitutes bodily injury. The doctor has to prove the correct information in the trial.

1.2.2 Contents of the Enlightenment

The purpose of the information is to give the patient a picture of the nature and significance of the medical intervention. The physician's duty to inform is now regulated in great detail in § 630e BGB. According to this, the doctor must inform the patient "about all circumstances essential for consent", which include "in particular the nature, extent, implementation, expected consequences and risks of the measure as well as its necessity, urgency, suitability and prospects of success with regard to the diagnosis or therapy". Reference must also be made "to alternatives to the measure (…) if several medically equally indicated and customary methods can lead to substantially different burdens, risks or chances of recovery". The risks to be informed about must therefore be related to the advantages of the treatment and must not be played down. The patient should be enabled by the information to understand the pros and cons of the intervention for himself and his life situation. He must therefore be able to assess the nature and severity, procedure and consequences of the intervention, foresee the expected benefits and possible harm of the intervention, know what the consequences of a refusal of the intervention would be for him, and be made aware of foreseeable extensions of the intervention and typically necessary follow-up treatments. Therefore, the treatment options must also be carefully discussed in the course of the information with regard to the findings that may then be found during the intervention. Otherwise—in the case of inadequate diagnosis or planning of the intervention—the doctor is liable if the need for an extension of the intervention only becomes apparent during the intervention and recourse then has to be made to the presumed patient's will because stopping the intervention would involve an increased risk, i.e. the extension is urgently required (Section 630d (1) sentence 4 of the German Civil Code; Pauge 2015, marginal no. 452). Of course, the patient must also know whether the intervention recommended to him is absolutely or only relatively indicated. Only when a self-determined decision can be made in knowledge of all the relevant circumstances (BGH NJW 1989, p. 1535) is legally valid consent to the intervention possible.

> In addition to the type and significance of the medical intervention, the patient must also be informed of the risks, foreseeable extensions of the intervention and alternative treatment options.

1.2.3   Risk Disclosure

The focus of the forensic information problem is the risk disclosure. Case law has repeatedly emphasised that what is required here is an explanation "in broad terms" (BGH NJW 1991, p. 2346; Martis and Winkhart 2018, marginal notes A 513, 535, 834ff.). The patient does not have to be provided with medical decision-making knowledge, the risks do not have to be presented in a medically precise manner and not in all conceivable manifestations (BGH VersR 2009, p. 257). Rather, a "general picture of the severity and direction

of the concrete risk spectrum" should suffice (BGH VersR 2017, p. 100).

However, case law has made such an abundance of individual decisions to the contrary that in practice the greatest caution is required here. Details, precise explanations and presentations are often not regarded as dispensable if this is the only way for the patient to gain a concrete idea of the significance and scope of the intervention. Recent decisions of the higher courts make it clear that very strict standards apply, especially in the field of interventional cardiology. In particular, high demands are placed on elective and diagnostic interventions without intrinsic therapeutic value, unless there is an urgent indication. Here the physician must present to the patient even remote possibilities of complications in an appropriate manner (OLG Koblenz VersR 2003, p. 1313: hemiplegia after angiography). If an intervention-immanent intervention risk materializes, about which the patient was not informed, the physician is liable, if the patient can make plausible that he would have got into a decision conflict at any rate, if he had known about the risk, thus he would have possibly refrained from the treatment at the time in question or in the institution in question (§ 630h Abs. 2 S. 2 BGB). In this context, the requirements for the plausibility of the alleged conflict of decisions are conceivably low; the liability risk of the physician is correspondingly high.

> In the field of interventional cardiology, very high standards of information are required. This applies in particular to elective and diagnostic interventions without intrinsic therapeutic value.

1.2.4   Intervention-Specific, Typical Risks

In contrast to general surgical risks (e.g. infections, wound healing disorders, etc.), intervention-specific, typical risks always require information. A procedure-specific risk is a risk that is typically associated with the procedure in question, irrespective of its statistical incidence. Of particular importance are lasting stress, functional impairment of important organs (e.g. stroke, myocardial infarction), temporary or permanent nerve damage or paralysis, pain, the need for permanent rest and any follow-up treatment that may be required—to name just a few important aspects. In general, these are risks of which the patient is unaware and which, if they materialise, will have a lasting adverse effect on the patient's way of life—no matter how infrequently they occur (BGH 15.02.2000, VI ZR 48/99; BGHZ 144, 1ff.). The density of complications or risks is irrelevant (Martis and Winkhart 2018, A 521).

In this context, the patient's professional and private life and his or her recognisable decision-making preferences must be taken into account as part of the so-called patient-related information (Pauge 2015, marginal no. 386). In any case, the information must not be trivialising. Thus, in a decision for the information about the intervention-specific risk of blindness in a bypass surgery, the BGH considered the references in the information sheet to brain damage due to insufficient blood flow after circulatory disorders/embolism and thrombosis to be trivialising with regard to the risk of blindness that was not mentioned (BGH 29.09.2009, VI ZR 251/08; VersR 2010, p. 115).

Particular attention must be paid to so-called individually increased risks (e.g. due to a previous illness), as this aspect requires separate information. Thus the OLG Hamm (judgement of 15.06.2005, 3 U 289/04, NJOZ 2005, p. 4925) has affirmed an information error in the sense of insufficient risk information in the apron of a left and right heart catheter examination including coronary angiography, in whose consequence it had come to a kidney failure. Although the Perimed information sheet—according to the expert completely correct in terms of content—under the heading "Complications caused by contrast media" expressly referred to the risk of a "deterioration of renal activity up to renal failure requiring dialysis" in the case of pre-existing renal dysfunction, the patient had not previously been made sufficiently aware of his pre-existing, slight renal dysfunction (creatinine value 1.4 mg/dl), so that he did not have

to refer to the corresponding information in the sheet. The pre-printed question about a known pre-existing renal dysfunction had also remained unanswered. The proof of sufficient information under the aspect of the individually increased risk existing here could therefore not be provided.

> Irrespective of the frequency of the risk, information must always be provided about procedure-specific risks. Particular attention must be paid to intervention-specific, individually increased risks within the framework of patient-specific information.

1.2.5 Risk Medication Consent

It should not be overlooked that in the area of risk disclosure, problems also arise in the area of medication disclosure. In a decision of the Federal Court of Justice in 2000, a patient received amiodarone "on a trial basis" for the treatment of a cardiac arrhythmia in the sense of a change of medication (BGH NJW 2007, p. 2771). In the course of this treatment, she suffered hypoxic brain damage as a result of circulatory arrest. The BGH affirmed an information error, since over substantial side effects of the medicine had not been informed. The BGH literally states:

» The decisive factor for the duty to inform is not a certain degree of risk density, in particular not a certain statistic, but rather whether the risk in question is specifically inherent in the intervention and whether, when it materializes, it places a particular burden on the patient's lifestyle, so that, in principle, information must also be provided about such extremely rare risks.

It is also not important whether the drug should initially only be "tested". Rather, the patient should be fully informed prior to the first use in order to enable him to decide, in knowledge of the risk spectrum and free from the influence of an initial relief of symptoms, whether he wants to decide in favour of the trial at all or whether he wants to do without the drug from the outset because of the considerable side effects.

> The administration of medication also represents an interference with bodily integrity and requires consent.

1.2.6 Treatment Alternatives

In recent times, the provision of information on treatment alternatives has proved to be of considerable practical relevance to liability. In particular, it is often not possible to prove that the information provided was correct due to a lack of sufficient documentation. Particularly in hospitals, special liability risks lurk, which can be traced back to the structural conditions there: For example, the indication is often made during a consultation by a specialist, senior physician or head physician. The physician, who then carries out the informed consent after the admission of the patient, clarifies naturally particularly the planned intervention, however no more possible treatment alternatives and documents also nothing for this. If the information about the possible alternatives was not already properly documented by the doctor who gave the indication, it is difficult to prove later that the information was correct in this respect. For the patients or experienced patient lawyers it is however often a simple one to determine in principle treatment alternatives coming into consideration afterwards and to reprimand in this respect an insufficient clearing-up. The missing documentation represents in this respect in the practice of the legal processing thus a completely substantial liability risk. The Cologne Higher Regional Court (MedR 2017, p. 56) has also aptly stated in this regard:

> The Senate, which has been dealing with medical liability cases for years, can say from its experience that it is precisely the information about treatment alternatives that is documented less frequently than the information about surgical risks.

As a general rule, the choice of the correct method of treatment is a matter for the doctor (Martis and Winkhart 2018, A 1220 with further references; Pauge 2015, marginal no. 397). If there are "several equally medically indicated and customary methods" available

that "may lead to substantially different burdens, risks or chances of recovery" (Section 630e (1) sentence 3 BGB), the physician must inform the patient about these "genuine" alternatives. This applies, for example, if an invasive intervention in the area of the coronary vessels can be avoided by a conservative wait with medication—even if only temporarily—or if a surgical revascularization of the affected coronary vessel can be equally considered as a genuine treatment alternative instead of the interventional cardiac catheterization. Thus, in a recent decision, the KG Berlin also affirmed liability because a patient in the case of an only relatively indicated EP procedure with ablation therapy had not been informed about the non-invasive treatment alternative of a drug therapy that could be considered. This had been available within the "standard treatment corridor" in the specific case. Since the indication for the EP procedure had largely depended on the patient's wish, further information about the conservative treatment alternative would have been required here (KG, judgment of 13.03.2017, 20 U 238/15, BeckRS 2017, p. 115705).

Furthermore, in addition to the treatment alternatives, the significance of an existing or non-existing cardiac surgical backup for the emergency of an immediate surgical intervention must be explained to the patient in order to enable him to choose treatment elsewhere, if necessary. The omitted reference to the "suboptimal surgical backup" in the given case was at least met by the OLG Hamm with great reservations, although the plaintiff patient was a urologist and he was also aware that there was no cardiac surgery in the hospital in question (OLG Hamm 23.11.2009, 3 U 41/09; BeckRS 2010, p. 10751).

Through the required complete medical instruction, the patient must therefore also be put in a position, from the point of view of the possible treatment alternatives, to exercise his or her right of self-determination independently and to decide where and in what form the treatment should take place. Also the question whether he wants to get involved in which risk at the present or a later time and whether a waiting, if necessary under acceptance of which risks, is possible, must be communicated to the patient, so that he can decide himself about the pros and cons of the respective treatment alternatives. As already stated, these high requirements, or at least their proof in individual cases, represent a very considerable liability risk.

> ❯ Of particular practical relevance to liability is the provision of information about treatment alternatives.

1.2.7 New Medical Territory

The physician may use a new method of treatment even if it is still in a trial phase, provided that a very careful and responsible consideration of the opportunities and risks justifies this for the patient in comparison with the established method and that safety precautions that take account of the novelty of the procedure have been taken and, if necessary, can be demonstrated (Pauge 2015, marginal no. 210ff.). However, as with the risk disclosure of drugs that are being investigated in trials or are not (yet) approved for the respective area of application (off-label use), it must also be explained in detail in the case of novel interventions that are not yet considered standard cardiological practice that this is a procedure with possibly as yet unknown risks and a lack of long-term experience. The requirements for consideration, organisation and also information are even higher in the case of a new, clinically insufficiently tested therapy in the sense of an "individual attempt to cure", if the standard method is not promising in the specific case, the prognosis of the alternative is clearly more favourable and the risk of failure is clearly outweighed by the expected chance of cure. In this case, the patient must be informed comprehensively and unsparingly about the novelty, possibly unknown risks, the comparison of chances and risks, and in particular the experimental or trial character (BGH NJW 2007, p. 2767; Pauge 2015, para. 2017). The high information requirements as well as the exact documentation of the patient's information and consent cannot be taken seriously enough here—this also in view of the threat of criminal relevance if the

patient's comprehensive information cannot be fully proven.

> ❯ In medical "uncharted territory", the uncharted character and possibly still unknown risks and the lack of long-term experience must be explained in detail.

1.2.8 Timing of Informed Consent

Recent decisions concerning the field of interventional cardiology make it clear that special attention should be paid to the aspect of informing patients as early as possible. Since these interventions regularly involve considerable risks and may have serious consequences for the patient's future life, case law tends to assume that the patient is being overtaxed if the time between the information and the intervention is too short. The decisive factor is always that the patient must not be put under pressure (BGH VersR 1992, p. 960), he must still have the possibility to decide inwardly freely. Thus it is said now in § 630e exp. 2 No. 2, the clearing-up must take place "so in time that the patient can make its decision on the consent well-considered". Informing the patient on the evening before or even on the day of the intervention itself is likely to overtax the patient here—unless the emergency nature prohibits a different procedure—and is often regarded as delayed (cf. OLG Hamm 23.11.2009, 3 U 41/09; BeckRS 2010, p. 10751; OLG Hamm 15.06.2005, 3 U 289/04; BeckRS 2005, p. 13062; OLG Frankfurt 24.02.2009, 8 U 103/08; BeckRS 2009, p. 10888; OLGReport Frankfurt 2009, p. 736). The information given to a patient who has previously received a drug for sedation is also ineffective.

Any medical information must be provided as early as possible so that the patient has sufficient time to weigh up the benefits and possible risks of the proposed measure. In principle, this requires—and this must not be forgotten—that information is provided at the time the date of the procedure is agreed (Martis and Winkhart 2018, A 1634). Especially in the case of elective measures, the patient must have sufficient time to weigh up the pros and cons before the intervention. The decisive factor here is always the circumstances of the individual case. For example, it must be taken into account whether, in view of the preliminary examinations that would have been necessary anyway, the information could have been provided earlier.

In the case of inpatient interventions with low or less drastic risks, an explanation on the day before the intervention is usually sufficient (Martis and Winkhart 2018, A 1635, 1656), and in the case of "normal" (according to the BGH) outpatient and diagnostic interventions even on the day of the intervention. However, in the case of major outpatient and diagnostic procedures with considerable risks (such as percutaneous coronary intervention—PCI), the information will no longer be considered timely on the day of the procedure (Martis and Winkhart 2018, A 1649), unless medical reasons prevent a longer reflection period between the information and the procedure. In view of the intensity of the intervention and the risk liability of cardiac interventions, the greatest importance should be attached here—as shown by numerous examples in the case law—to ensuring that the patient has sufficient time to think about the matter after hearing, perhaps for the first time, about the significant risks associated with the intervention. In any event, the patient should have the opportunity between the information and the intervention to discuss the matter with someone they trust before making a decision (Pauge 2015, para 445). However, if the patient is informed only the evening before the procedure, this may no longer be possible, for example if the patient wishes to contact his or her general practitioner.

Only the information about the anaesthesia is still possible the evening before according to the principles of the jurisdiction. In any case, of course, the information must be given before sedative medication impairs the patient's ability to receive it.

In practice, it sometimes proves helpful to explicitly ask the patient whether he or she requires a longer reflection period after a possibly delayed explanation. This is advisable in any case if the patient does not attach any importance to a longer reflection period and

explicitly wishes to be admitted only on the day of the intervention. If the patient denies the (sincere!) offer of further time to consider, this should be recorded in the information sheet and countersigned by the patient. On the other hand, the repeatedly read comment that the patient feels "sufficiently informed" is hardly helpful in the case of liability, since the patient, as a medical layperson, can usually not have a well-founded opinion on the question of whether information is actually sufficient.

In the area of tension between physician liability and economic efficiency requirement the LSG Rhineland-Palatinate expressed itself in a decision of 18.05.2006 (L 5 KR 149/05, MedR 2006, p. 740) clearly in favor of the requirements of the liability law. The decision literally states:

> The decision of the hospital doctor to wait 24 hours between medical information (…) about a left heart catheter examination with insertion of a stent and this intervention is justifiable with the consequence that the (…) hospital stay is necessary and the health insurance company has to bear the costs. (…) Under no circumstances can the doctor (…) be obliged to act (…), which can lead to not inconsiderable liability risks for him, solely because the health insurance fund thereby saves costs.

This is to be agreed with without reservation.

> Particularly in the case of elective procedures, medical information must be provided as early as possible, at the latest on the day before the procedure, so that the patient has sufficient time to think things over between the information and the procedure.

1.2.9 Emergency Informed Consent

In medical emergencies requiring immediate action, informed consent may be provided at short notice prior to the procedure. In such an acute situation, the extent of the information required may be very limited, and in some cases it may not be necessary at all if the treatment cannot be postponed. The extent of the information required is inversely proportional to the urgency of the intervention. If the patient is not in a position, due to his condition, to follow an explanatory discussion and responsibly weigh up the advantages and disadvantages, the presumed will of the patient is also sufficient for the medical procedure (§§ 630d para. 1, p. 4; 630e para. 3 BGB; Diederichsen 2010, p. 259).

> In an emergency, the requirements for information are inversely proportional to the urgency of the intervention.

1.2.10 Formal Criteria of Informed Consent

The information must be provided orally, i.e. always requires a personal doctor-patient discussion, but "in addition, reference may also be made to documents which the patient receives in text form" (Section 630e (2) no. 1 of the German Civil Code). However, an information sheet can never replace this discussion. The law expressly provides that "consents and explanations" must also be documented (Section 630f. Paragraph 2 BGB), which can, however, also be ensured by corresponding entries in the patient's file—without the use of an information sheet.

An information sheet and the patient's signature are not mandatory, but highly recommended. It should be borne in mind that in civil proceedings any doubt as to whether the patient has been properly informed is to the detriment of the doctor and can thus lead to liability. The advantage of using commercially available information forms, such as those from Diomed/proCompliance (◨ Fig. 1.1), lies firstly in the fact that the list of possible complications is as complete as possible and serves as a guideline and basis for the discussion, and secondly in the fact that it makes it easier to prove that the information has been properly provided. The use of these preprinted clearing-up sheets presupposes however also that the opportunity was given to the patient to read the often very detailed text in peace (OLG Hamm 15.06.2005—3 U 289/04,

BeckRS 2005, p. 13062). Also the missing (OLG Munich, MedR 2006, p. 431) and/or incomplete (OLG Hamm 15.06.2005—3 U 289/04, BeckRS 2005, p. 13062) filling out of the form forms a clear indication for the fact that it was not used in the concrete case and/or this passage was not discussed. In an important decision of 28.01.2014 (NJW 2014, p. 1527), the BGH for its part has now expressly emphasised that "the signed consent form (…)—both in a positive and in a negative respect—is an indication of the content of the informed consent discussion".

It should now also be borne in mind that, pursuant to Section 630e (2) no. 3 of the German Civil Code, the patient must be provided with copies of documents which he has signed in connection with the information or consent. This includes the entire sheet, not just the last page with the patient's signature.

In any case, it is advisable to add any special features, individually increased risks, possible treatment alternatives and, if applicable, further aspects of the discussion, such as the discussed urgency, necessity and prospects of success of the intervention, in the form of handwritten bullet points in the information sheet. The court assumes from such handwritten additions that the decisive doctor-patient discussion actually took place, thus preventing the frequently raised objection that the sheet was only handed over for signature, while a discussion did not take place at all.

On the other hand, caution is advised with "self-made" or blanket forms which do not document the content of the information. Such forms are inadequate, precisely because the content of the information that is disputed in the proceedings often cannot be proven by such a form.

Special care is also required in the case of "unreasonable" decisions by the patient. In these cases, it is advisable to document the specific risks of the unreasonable decision and the corresponding "persuasion work" performed by the physician.

The OLG Bamberg has in a judgement of 04.07.2005 (NJW-RR 2005, p. 1266) in the omitted reference to the urgency of a necessary clarification (here assumed, because not documented!) even a rough treatment error

Info **Card3**

Clinic/Practice:

Left heart catheter examination, if necessary with X-ray contrast examination
(coronary angiography, aortography, laevocardiography)

Please read and complete the questionnaire before the educational interview!

Dear Patient,

The heart consists of a **right** and a **left** half (cf. Fig. 1), which perform different tasks.

In order to clarify the cause of your complaints (e.g. chest pain, tightness in the heart area, shortness of breath, water retention in the legs), we recommend a **left heart catheter examination, if necessary with X-ray contrast examination**.

This examination can determine whether your symptoms are due to a disease or malformation of the heart (e.g. coronary artery disease, heart valve disease, congenital heart defect).

Only when the type and severity of the disease are known can a decision be made as to which treatment is indicated in your case (e.g. with medication or surgery) or should be planned for later. It can be but it may also turn out that your symptoms are not due to heart disease.

The examination is also performed in preparation for an already planned intervention on the heart (e.g. bypass surgery, balloon dilatation, valve replacement).

Left heart catheter examination and X-ray contrast examination

For the **left heart catheter examination,** after local anaesthesia of the puncture site, a thin catheter is inserted into an artery below the groin, in the crook of the arm or - rarely - above the wrist (see Fig. 2). Under X-ray control, the catheter is advanced into the left ventricle.

The catheter is used to measure the pressure conditions in the aorta and in the left ventricle and, if necessary, to take small blood samples in order to determine the oxygen saturation of the blood. From these values it is possible to determine draw conclusions about the function of the heart and the heart valves.

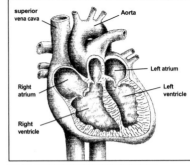

Fig. 1: Longitudinal section through the heart

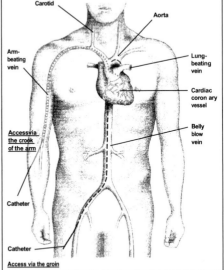

Fig. 2

Diomed educational system. 04/09 Editor: Prof. K. Ulsenheimer (Medical Law). Founding editor: Prof. W. Weißauer.
Author: Prof. G. Klein. Illustration: Atelier Gluska.
Copyright 2009 by DIOmed in Thieme Compliance GmbH - Am Weichselgarten 30 - 91058 Erlangen - Phone 09131 93406-49 - Fax 09131 93406-81.
www.diomed.de   Reproductions of any kind, including photocopying, are prohibited.   Order no. 06/ 033

Fig. 1.1   DIOMed information sheet

Information part for the patient

Additional findings can be obtained by **X-ray contrast examination.**
For this purpose, a contrast medium is injected through the catheter in order to make the coronary vessels (coronary angiography), the aorta (aortography) or the left ventricle (laevocardiography) visible in the X-ray image.

The spread of the contrast medium in the body may be accompanied by a brief feeling of warmth.

After the investigation:

If the catheter was inserted from the **groin**, the puncture site is closed by applying pressure for 10–20 minutes and then a tightly fitting pressure bandage is applied. If necessary, the arterial puncture site is closed by a special suturing instrument, by a collagen plug or other closure techniques after the procedure.
If the artery at the **crook of the arm was** opened by a small incision for the insertion of the left heart catheter, this may be sutured after the procedure; in the case of access above the wrist, the puncture site is closed by applying pressure for 10 – 20 minutes and then a pressure bandage is applied.

If additional examinations such as intravascular ultrasound, Doppler wire measurement or pressure wire measurement are considered, the doctor will inform you separately.

Risks and possible complications

In most cases, cardiac catheterization and X-ray contrast examinations are free of complications.

Patients with very narrow or deformed blood vessels may experience a **brief painful pulling sensation** when the catheter is advanced. Rarely, the catheter must be inserted through another vessel; very rarely, the **catheter** must be **surgically removed, e.g.** if it cannot be withdrawn due to loop formation.

Extra beats of the heart **(extrasystoles)** or slight cardiac arrhythmias that may occur during or shortly after the examination usually subside by themselves. Treatment with medication is rarely necessary. Even rarer are serious **arrhythmias that** require immediate electrical treatment (defibrillation).

There may be a **haematoma** at the injection site, which usually disappears by itself, as well as infections and local **hardening** or **discolouration of the skin. Infections that** penetrate into the heart and can lead to inflammation of the inner lining of the heart **(endocarditis) are** rare; they must be treated with antibiotics as an inpatient. **Larger bruises may have** to be surgically removed.

Nerve damage at the injection site, which can lead to a prolonged disturbance of sensation and sometimes to temporary pain, is also rare.

During insertion and advancement of the catheter, the **vessel wall,** the **heart wall** or one of the **heart valves** may be **injured** and very rarely perforated **(perforation);** surgical intervention and/or a blood transfusion may then be required.

Rarely, a **vascular aneurysm** or a **connection to the adjacent vein (vascular fistula)** can form at the puncture site of the femoral artery. If these complications cannot be eliminated by pressure treatment (compression), minor vascular surgery must be performed. Very rarely, venous thrombosis can occur as a result of the pressure bandage.

Also very rarely, blood clots **(thrombi)** can detach and block blood vessels. This can result in circulatory disorders, e.g. in the arms and legs, the lungs (pulmonary embolism) and in the brain (stroke, which can lead to temporary or, more rarely, permanent **visual, speech and hearing disorders** and **hemiplegia).** Extremely rarely, a heart attack can occur. In these incidents, for which we are prepared, treatment in the intensive care unit and drug dissolution or - in very rare cases - surgical removal of the clot may be necessary.
Usually an anticoagulant drug is given as a preventive measure, but this increases the risk of bleeding. After injection of heparin, a life-threatening disorder of blood clotting with increased clot formation and vessel occlusion (HIT II) can rarely occur.

In case of **allergy** or **hypersensitivity** (e.g. to X-ray contrast media, anaesthetics, drugs, disinfectants, latex), dizziness, itching, vomiting and similar minor reactions may occur temporarily. **Serious intolerance reactions** (e.g. swelling of mucous membranes) **and other life-threatening complications** (e.g. cardiac, circulatory or respiratory arrest) requiring inpatient treatment and **permanent damage** (e.g. organ failure, paralysis, visual impairment) are very rare.

◻ **Fig. 1.1**　(continued)

With a corresponding predisposition, iodine-containing contrast media can triggerhyperthyroidism (hyperthyreosis), which may have to be treated with medication

Contrast-induced renal dysfunction is rare. In the presence of pre-existing renal damage and diabetes mellitus, the risk of developing temporary renal damage (nephropathy) is much higher; however, permanent renal damage that may require dialysis treatment is rare.

The **radiation exposure** caused by X-ray contrast examination using modern technology is extremely low. The physician only orders the X-ray contrast examination if the expected benefit justifies the low radiation

The risks are increased if the heart is already severely damaged.

If the arm or hand artery has been chosen for the left heart catheter examination, the **blood vessel** may rarely become **constricted,** limiting the strength and fine mobility of the hand. A minor intervention can restore sufficient blood flow.

Please remember: the risk of heart disease not being detected and treated in time is generally much higher than that of cardiac catheterization.

Despite all the care taken in the production of foreign blood reserves, plasma derivatives and other blood productsrisks cannot be ruled out with certainty during their transmission/use, in particular infections, e.g. very rarely with hepatitis viruses (liver inflammation) and extremely rarely with HIV (AIDS) and possibly also with pathogens of BSE or the new variant of Creutzfeldt-Jakob disease or with previously unknown pathogensIncertain cases, a follow-up examination to exclude transmitted infections may therefore be recommended Please discuss whether and when this is the case with your doctor.

Please ask if you would like to know more.

Please be sure to observe!   **Unless otherwise ordered by a doctor!**

You can contribute to the success of the planned examination instructions below

Before the examination

Please inform us immediately if you are **diabetic** and are taking tablets with the active ingredient **metformina**, as there may be interactions with the X-ray contrast medium (including the risk of kidney failure). The attending physician will then decide whether and when these tablets must be discontinued or replaced by other agents.

- **Do not eat** or **drink anything** after midnight.
  Tell the doctor if you accidentally eat something during this period.
- Stop **smoking** at least 6 hours before the procedure.
- Please ask the doctor which **medicines** you are allowed to take or should take and which you must stop.
- contact lenses, removable dentures, rings, jewellery, artificial hairpieces and store them safely at Remove make-up and nail varnish!

After the investigation

you may be admitted to the ICU for monitoring.

Was the catheter inserted from the **groin:**
- If ordered to do so by a doctor, remain on strict bed rest; lie flat on your back and do not move the affected leg. Do not remove pressure bandage or sandbag yourself.
- To avoid postoperative bleeding, avoid physical stress (e.g. lifting, pressing) for one week after the examination.

Please continue reading on page 4!

◘ **Fig. 1.1**   (continued)

Information part for the patient 4

If the catheter was inserted from the **crook of the arm** or above the **wrist:**

- Rest the affected arm as directed by a physician.
- Have the dressing checked by a doctor after about 3 days.

Please inform your doctor immediately if bleeding from the injection site, chest pain or other heart complaints, fever (over 38 °C) or chills, drop in blood pressure or pain, blistering and/or a feeling of cold or numbness in the affected arm/leg occur during or after the examination!

Outpatient examination

If the procedure is performed on **an outpatient basis**, you will need to be collected by an adult companion, as your reaction may still be impaired by anaesthetics and/or painkillers. We will tell you when you are allowed to actively participate in road traffic or work on running machines again. You should also not drink alcohol or make any important decisions during this time.

The attending physician will give you more detailed information on home care and aftercare.

Signature of the doctor: ______________________

Diomed reconnaissance system. 04/09 Card3

Fig. 1.1 (continued)

1

Patient name and address:

> **Left heart catheter**   Doc **Card3**
> **Coronary angiography**
>
>
> **Questionnaire** (anamnesis)

Please answer the following questions carefully so that we can better prevent any risks. Please mark with a cross where applicable and underline or complete. If necessary, we will be happy to help you fill in the form.

1. Are you taking any medication? ☐No ☐Yes
Painkillers, anticoagulants drugs (e.g.
Marcumar®, Heparin, Aspirin®), sleeping
pills, laxatives, „birth control pills", diabetes
drugs (especially with the active ingredient
metformin)

or: _____

2. Do you have or have you had any of the
following conditions or signs of these
conditions?

Heart: angina pectoris, heart attack, ☐No ☐Yes
heart defect, arrhythmia, myocarditis

or: _____

Do you wear a pacemaker or an artificial ☐No ☐Yes
heart valve?
If you have a **pacemaker card**, please present it.

Circulation: High blood pressure, tendency ☐No ☐Yes
to low blood pressure

or: _____

Kidneys: Kidney stones, kidney ☐No ☐Yes
inflammation, dialysis, high creatinine
or urea levels.

or: _____

Blood: frequent nosebleeds, bruising even ☐No ☐Yes
without injury or after light touch,
coagulation disorder

or: _____

Metabolism: diabetes (diabetes), gout ☐No ☐Yes
If you have a diabetic card, please present it.

or: _____

If you are diabetic: Are you being treated ☐No ☐Yes
with metformin-containing medications?

Thyroid gland: hyper- or ☐No ☐Yes
hypothyroidism, goiter

or: _____

Allergy (e.g. hay fever, asthma) or ☐No ☐Yes
intolerance to food, medication, contrast
agents, disinfectants, plasters, latex,
iodine

or: _____
If you have an allergy card, please present it.

3. Did any complaints occur after previous ☐No ☐Yes
contrast agent examinations?

If so, which ones? _____

_____
If you have an X-ray passport, please present
it.

4. Have you ever had a cardiac ☐No ☐Yes
atheterization/coronary angiography/
aortography/laevo-cardiography?

If so, when and where? _____

Were there any complications? ☐No ☐Yes

If so, which ones? _____

_____

5. Do you smoke? ☐No ☐Yes

If so, what and how much? _____

6. Do you drink alcohol? ☐No ☐Yes

If so, what and how much? _____

7. For women of childbearing age:

Could you be pregnant? ☐No ☐Yes

◘ **Fig. 1.1** (continued)

<table>
<tr><td>

**Left heart catheter
coronary angiography**

</td><td>

Doc **Card3**

</td></tr>
<tr><td colspan="2">

Documentation

</td></tr>
</table>

Please tick the appropriate boxes, underline or complete the text in the spaces provided and sign.

Informative talk

☐ I have read and understood the information sheet. I was able to ask all the questions that interested me during the consultation. They were answered completely and understandably.

I have answered the questions about the medical history to the best of my knowledge.

☐ The separated info part or the ☐ a **duplicate of the bow**

I have received to take with me and to keep. I will follow the **instructions.**

Notes from the doctor _____ to the educational interview:
Name

Discussed were e.g.: Necessity of the examination, the procedure, advantages and disadvantages compared to other methods, risks and possible complications, risk-increasing peculiarities, possible side and follow-up interventions, behavioural instructions before and after the examination as well as (please also note any changes to the information section here):

_____

_____

_____

_____

_____

_____

_____

_____

_____

_____

Scheduled date of the investigation (date): _____

Consent

I have considered my decision thoroughly; I do not need another period of consideration.

☐ I consent to the left heart catheter examination, if necessary with X-ray contrast examination.

I agree to the elimination of pain, to unforeseeable changes or extensions of the planned procedure that prove to be medically necessary during the examination, as well as to necessary secondary and subsequent interventions.

If you object to certain individual measures, please indicate:

_____

Only in case of refusal of the investigation:

☐ I do not consent to the proposed investigation.
I was informed that this could delay and complicate the diagnosis and treatment of my illness, with the possible consequence of considerable health disadvantages.

_____	_____	_____
Place, date, time	Patient or carer/authorised representative/legal guardian*.	Doctor

*If one parent signs alone, he or she also declares that he or she has sole custody or that he or she is acting in agreement with the other parent.

◘ **Fig. 1.1** (continued)

1

seen. In view of the suspected diagnosis of a heart attack, the OLG Bamberg literally stated:

» If the patient refuses an urgently indicated examination that is suitable for preventing an impending heart attack, this must be documented.

In a more recent decision, the Federal Court of Justice (BGH) also stated in this sense that the failure to indicate the urgency of further clarification of a coronary heart disease—there within a period of several weeks—was to be regarded as a treatment error. Here, too, the omission of the urgency notice was assumed because, although the required measures were documented, it was not documented that the clarification should be carried out, although not immediately, but in any case promptly (BGH NJW 2016, p. 563). Since according to § 630f. Paragraph 2 BGB, clarification measures must also be documented, it is presumed pursuant to § 630h Paragraph 3 BGB that a corresponding clarification did not take place. This, too—and this does not require any further elaboration—represents a very considerable liability potential.

❯ "What is documented is considered done, what is not documented is considered not done". The use of "self-made" information sheets is not advisable.

1.2.11 Informed Consent by Telephone Permissible?

Only in the case of simple "routine interventions" can the physician also inform the patient about the risks of an upcoming intervention in a telephone conversation, provided that the patient agrees to this and the physician is still personally available for specific questions before the intervention is performed (BGH, NJW 2010, p. 2430). Even if the BGH has not defined precisely what is to be understood by a "routine intervention", the greatest caution is probably called for here in the field of interventional cardiology—this notwithstanding the fact that for the individual interventional cardiologist the intervention may well

present itself as "routine". According to the above-mentioned fundamental decision, invasive cardiological interventions should not be accessible to information by telephone, if only in view of the considerable risk spectrum.

❯ In the field of interventional cardiology, telephone information is strongly discouraged.

1.2.12 Safeguarding Information or Therapeutic Information and Economic Information

Finally, the safety information concerns informing the patient about the therapeutic behaviour with the aim of ensuring the success of the treatment. In addition to the required behavioral instructions and any information on the necessity and urgency of further clarifying measures, this also includes the organization of post-interventional checks after cardiological procedures, the necessity of which must also be pointed out to the patient. Particularly in the case of outpatient interventions, there is a risk of gaps in responsibility between the cardiologist carrying out the intervention and the referring physician, which in the worst case can lead to a situation where the post-interventional checkup with the necessary therapeutic informed consent (e.g. measures or activities to be recommended or omitted, further check-up appointments, adjustment of medication, resumption of employment, etc.) is not guaranteed. It is therefore advisable to carefully document the required behavioural instructions in this respect as well.

Economic information is now also required if the patient knows or must know that the treatment costs will not be fully covered by a cost bearer. The patient must then be informed of the anticipated costs in writing (Section 630c (3) of the German Civil Code).

❯ The necessary information about the therapeutic behaviour to ensure the success of the treatment is an integral part of the information.

1.3 Conclusion

Information errors are often the cause or at least the "second pillar" of a medical liability claim. Interventional cardiology in particular, as a sub-area of the most modern high-performance medicine, offers a broad "attack surface" here, which can only be successfully minimized by strict adherence to the requirements of liability law.

References

Buerschaper C, St. Pierre M (2003) Teamarbeit in der Anästhesie—Entwicklung einer Checkliste. In: Strohschneider S (ed) Entscheiden in kritischen Situ-ationen. Verlag für Polizeiwissenschaft, Frankfurt am Main

Diederichsen A (2010) Aktuelle Rechtsprechung des BGH zum Arzthaftungsrecht—Schwerpunkt: Notfall- und Intensivmedizin. GesR, May 2011

Jamula E et al (2010) Safety of uninterrupted anticoagulation in patients requiring elective coronary angiography with or without percutaneous coronary intervention: a systematic review and metaanalysis. Chest 138(4):840–847

Martis R, Winkhart M (2018) Arzthaftungsrecht, 5th edn. Schmidt, Köln

Pauge B (2015) Arzthaftungsrecht, 13th edn. RWS-Verlag, Köln

Ziakas AG et al (2010) Radial versus femoral access for orally anticoagulated patients. Catheter Cardiovasc Interv 76(4):493–499

In the Cardiac Catheterization Laboratory

Contents

Procedural Complications

Erhard Kaiser, Michael Markant, Ralf Birkemeyer, and Thomas Twisselmann

Contents

© The Author(s), under exclusive license to Springer-Verlag GmbH, DE, part of Springer Nature 2023
E. Kaiser (ed.), *Complication Management In The Cardiac Catheter Laboratory*,
https://doi.org/10.1007/978-3-662-66093-5_2

2.1 Puncture Site Related Complications

Erhard Kaiser

2.1.1 Femoral Access Route

■ **Topographic Anatomy**

A precise understanding of the anatomical conditions in the inguinal region helps in the arterial puncture of the common femoral artery and helps prevent malpuncture. The common femoral artery is in close topographical relation to the femoral vein and the femoral nerve. The common femoral artery is located lateral to the femoral vein and medial to the femoral nerve in a common vascular-nerve sheath (◘ Fig. 2.1).

Another important topographical landmark is the inguinal ligament (Poupart's ligament), which extends between the anterior superior iliac spine and the pubic tubercle (◘ Fig. 2.2). In the normally built patient, the inguinal ligament is palpable from the outside as a rough strand of connective tissue, since it is a condensed zone composed of various partly fibrous, partly aponeurotic structures (beginning of the fascia lata of the thigh, transverse fascia, fascia of the iliopsoas muscle, aponeuroses of origin of the oblique internal abdominal muscle and transverse abdominal as well as the aponeurosis of the oblique external abdominal muscle).

In addition, the inguinal skin fold is very easily recognizable from the outside. It is very important to note that the inguinal skin fold is not in topographical congruence with the inguinal ligament, but always caudal to it (◘ Fig. 2.3).

This results in three landmarks that can be easily used for correct arterial puncture of the common femoral artery:

— Inguinal skin fold
— Strong ingunal ligament
— Palpable femoral artery pulse

The correct puncture technique and the anatomically correct puncture site are decisive in avoiding puncture-related complications (Kacila et al. 2011; Rapoport et al. 1985; Marsan et al. 1990). Easily visible from the outside is the inguinal skin fold, but this is not in projection to the common femoral artery, but is located more caudally in up to 78% of cases. In contrast, puncture at the level of the

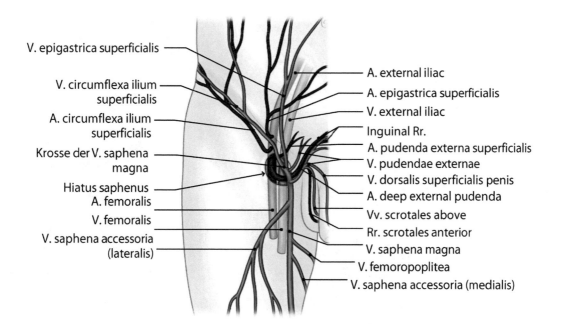

V. epigastrica superficialis

V. circumflexa ilium superficialis

A. circumflexa ilium superficialis

Krosse der V. saphena magna

Hiatus saphenus
A. femoralis

V. femoralis

V. saphena accessoria (lateralis)

A. external iliac

A. epigastrica superficialis

V. external iliac

Inguinal Rr.
A. pudenda externa superficialis

V. pudendae externae

V. dorsalis superficialis penis

A. deep external pudenda

Vv. scrotales above

Rr. scrotales anterior

V. saphena magna

V. femoropoplitea

V. saphena accessoria (medialis)

◘ **Fig. 2.1** Epifascial arteries and veins of the inguinal region of the right side

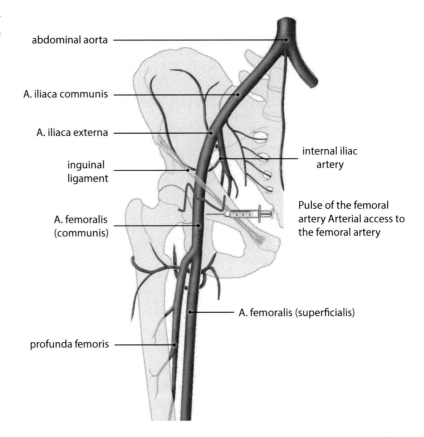

◘ Fig. 2.2 Overview of the arterial supply to the pelvis and leg

abdominal aorta

A. iliaca communis

A. iliaca externa

inguinal ligament

A. femoralis (communis)

internal iliac artery

Pulse of the femoral artery Arterial access to the femoral artery

A. femoralis (superficialis)

profunda femoris

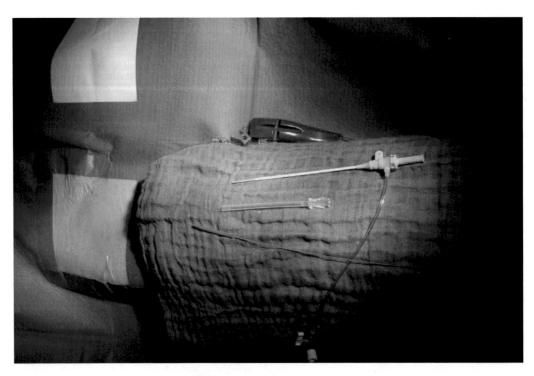

◘ Fig. 2.3 Puncture site before arterial puncture of the right femoral artery. (Thanks to R. Schräder)

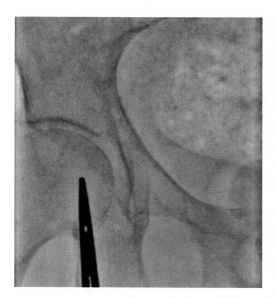

Fig. 2.4 Radiological marking of the puncture site over the femoral head

well-palpable inguinal ligament would always be too high (Garrett et al. 2005). The femoral artery to be punctured lies in projection on the femoral head, so that it is helpful to mark the puncture height, especially if large sheaths are to be inserted. It has proved practical to take a brief fluoroscopy and then mark the puncture height with the local anaesthetic needle, for example (**Fig. 2.4**). Particularly when using large-calibre sheaths, the exact puncture site should be found beforehand and then the artery punctured under ultrasound control and, if necessary, the first puncture made with a micropuncture set and then gradually dilated up to the actual sheath.

■ **False Aneurysm**

After arterial puncture of the right groin, clinical complaints may still occur on the day of the examination or on the following days, even though the puncture was completely benign at first glance. Patients then usually express pain at the puncture site or notice a small, palpable, painful swelling. Discoloration of the skin around the puncture site due to small or even larger hematomas is not uncommon, but is usually clinically insignificant.

In addition to these subcutaneously located and partially organized hematomas, it is important to distinguish clinically and sonographically the false aneurysm, which can also cause problems in the further clinical course. The false aneurysm is an outpouching of the blood vessel wall, which arises from an injury to the intima and media of the vessel. Initially, the adventitia always remains intact.

Morphologically, the false aneurysm is to be distinguished from the true aneurysm, in which all vessel wall layers are involved in the bulging of the vessel and there is no intimal and medial defect.

The diagnosis of a false aneurysm begins with palpation of the groin, which often, but not always, reveals a clearly palpable pulsation. With the stethoscope, a loud buzzing and hissing is auscultated. This should be taken as an opportunity to confirm the suspected diagnosis by duplex ultrasound. For this purpose, the punctured vessel is probed in two axes and, if pathological, a perfused aneurysm sac with turbulent flow is detected (**Figs. 2.5 and 2.6**).

Further diagnostics are usually not necessary. However, the imaging should be performed by a trained hand and lead to a clear statement.

The therapy of the false aneurysm consists first of all of a manual and very punctual compression on the aneurysm neck. This is done under ultrasound guidance. The compression should not be interrupted for 30 min and then a pressure bandage should be applied for 12 h.

In many cases, the false aneurysm can be successfully closed in this way. After removal of the pressure dressing, the findings are checked again by duplex ultrasound. Manual compression must be preferred to thrombin injection if there is no experience with thrombin injection. In all other cases, thrombin injection should be performed in the appropriate patient (Lönn et al. 2002; Danzi et al. 2005; Yao et al. 2008).

As an alternative to compression, the aneurysm can be closed layer by layer by injecting thrombin into the aneurysm sac, which is very comfortable and safe for the patient (Hofmann et al. 2007; Ferguson et al. 2001). Crucial to the safe feasibility of thrombin injection is the presence of a sufficiently narrow and long aneurysm neck. Aneurysms with very wide and short necks are rather not

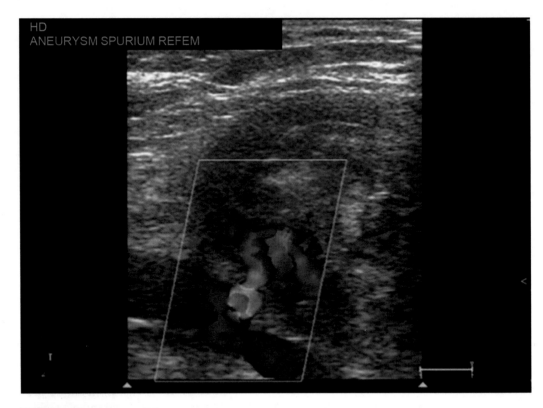

▫ Fig. 2.5 Pseudoaneurysm 1

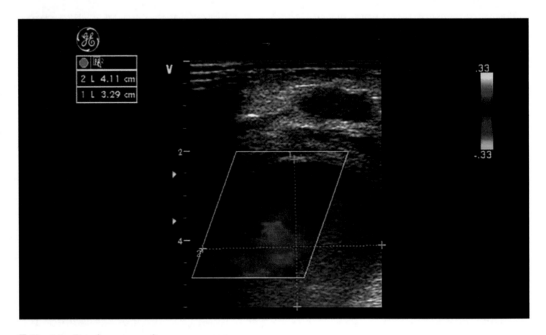

▫ Fig. 2.6 Pseudoaneurysm 2

recommended for thrombin injection (Luedde et al. 2007). In these, thrombin can easily inadvertently enter the femoral artery and occlude the vessel (D'Ayala et al. 2008; Bhat and Chakraverty 2007; Stawicki and Hoey 2007).

For the thrombin injection you need:
- Thrombin
- Saline
- 20 G cannulas of different length
- An insulin syringe
- Sterile conditions
- Duplex ultrasound

For the thrombin injection, the false aneurysm is visualized with the transducer and then entered laterally into the aneurysm sac with the cannula. From there, the aneurysm sac is then closed layer by layer under visualization by dropwise thrombin administration. Bolus thrombin injection is also feasible (Lewandowski et al. 2011). The success of the procedure is confirmed and documented by duplex ultrasound by arresting the turbulent flow in the aneurysm sac (◘ Fig. 2.7).

In our own patient population almost all false aneurysms could be closed by thrombin

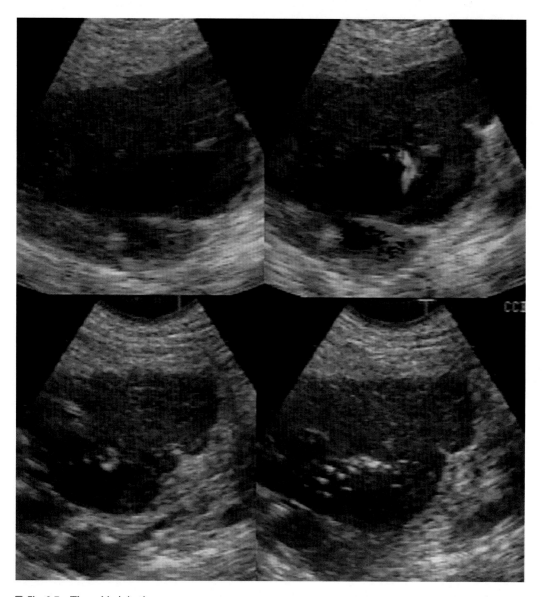

◘ **Fig. 2.7**   Thrombin injection

2

injection. Only in a few cases surgical suturing was necessary, especially when the primary thrombin injection was not successful. In these cases, a hidden vascular defect may play a role and be the cause of unsuccessful thrombin injection (Sheiman and Mastromatteo 2003). Also, concomitant antiplatelet medication and obesity play a role in the tendency to recurrence (Madaric et al. 2009). Nevertheless, if a hidden vascular defect is excluded, further thrombin injection can also be successfully performed (Edgerton et al. 2002). Complications of compression therapy, such as necrosis of the skin, are the absolute exception. If embolization occurs in the course of thrombin injection, intra-arterial lysis is also available as a therapeutic option in addition to immediate embolectomy and surgical therapy (Sadiq and Ibrahim 2001).

In addition to the avoidability of surgical therapy, the shortening of the patient's length of stay is another important advantage of thrombin injection. More important than the correct and timely therapy of the aneurysm spurium, however, is its prevention through the correct puncture technique.

■ **Arterio-Venous Fistula**

Similar to the pseudoaneurysm after arterial puncture of the groin, the arterio-venous fistula also appears clinically, but often much later in the time course. The incidence of arterio-venous fistula after cardiac catheterization is reported in the literature to be 0.22–1% (Sidawy et al. 1993; Kron et al. 1985; Kelm et al. 2002). The causes are either the simultaneous placement of arterial and venous sheaths or puncture error with puncture of the vein and artery without sufficient subsequent compression and persistent tissue defect. A puncture that is too deep is also associated with a higher incidence of arterio-venous fistulas (Altin et al. 1989). Other predisposing factors include anticoagulation with Heparin or Coumadin, puncture of the left-sided groin, arterial hypertension, and female gender (Kelm et al. 2002). Affected patients describe localized pain and swelling around the puncture site. Such complaints by patients should always be taken seriously. During the clinical examination, which has a high sensitivity and

specificity for the detection of arterio-venous fistulas, the findings can be confirmed and a loud buzzing can be detected by auscultation (Kent et al. 1993a, b). However, the suspected diagnosis of "vascular defect after arterial puncture" also automatically entails imaging by color-coded duplex ultrasound (Hruby et al. 1989; Neise et al. 1998). Here, the presence of an arterio-venous fistula reveals turbulent flow between the artery and vein. Many of the arterio-venous fistulas found close spontaneously within a year and without further intervention (Kent et al. 1993a, b). Regular duplex sonographic follow-up is appropriate with this approach (Perings et al. 2002). In addition, manual ultrasound-guided compression is an easy-to-perform and effective therapeutic procedure with subsequent reapplication of a pressure bandage (Zhou et al. 2007). If this non-invasive approach fails to close the arterio-venous fistula, endovascular therapy with percutaneous insertion of a covered stent is an option in addition to open surgical therapy (Ruebben et al. 1998; Thalhammer et al. 2000; Onal et al. 2004).

■ **Retroperitoneal Hematoma**

"Is arterial puncture dangerous?"—This question was asked by Platts and Ridgway more than 45 years ago, describing a case of retroperitoneal hematoma after puncture of the left femoral artery for dialysis purposes (Platts and Ridgway 1965). The answer to the above question today must be "yes and no". Yes, because in the worst case it can lead to a vascular defect that cannot be managed conservatively or to a retroperitoneal hematoma. And no, because in the hands of the skilled it represents an uncomplicated access route to the arterial vascular system. For correct femoral puncture technique, see earlier in this chapter. The incidence for retroperitoneal hematoma after arterial puncture is reported to be 0.45–0.74% (Maluenda et al. 2011; Farogue et al. 2005) (◘ Fig. 2.8).

The serious retroperitoneal hematoma must be distinguished from the superficial, subcutaneously located and clinically insignificant hematoma following arterial puncture of the right femoral artery. The superficially located, either flat or spherically encapsulated

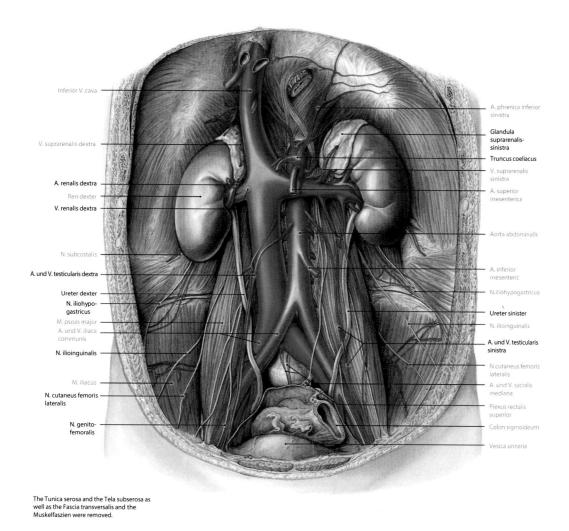

Inferior V. cava

A. phrenica inferior sinistra

Glandula suprarenalis-sinistra

Truncus coeliacus

V. suprarenalis dextra

V. suprarenalis sinistra

A. renalis dextra

A. superior mesenterica

Ren dexter

V. renalis dextra

Aorta abdominalis

N. subcostalis

A. inferior mesenteric

A. und V. testicularis dextra

N.iliohypogastricus

Ureter dexter

N. iliohypo-gastricus

Ureter sinister

M. psoas major

N. ilioinguinalis

A. und V. iliaca communis

A. und V. testicularis sinistra

N. ilioinguinalis

N.cutaneus femoris lateralis

M. iliacus

A. und V. sacralis mediana

N. cutaneus femoris lateralis

Plexus rectalis superior

N. genito-femoralis

Colon sigmoideum

Vesica urinaria

The Tunica serosa and the Tela subserosa as well as the Fascia transversalis and the Muskelfaszien were removed.

▣ **Fig. 2.8** Organs and pathways of the retroperitoneal space. (From Tillmann 2010)

hematoma causes a local pain in the area of the groin around the puncture site. On palpation, the pain can be elicited or intensified. In contrast, retroperitoneal hematoma presents clinically quite differently. Local discomfort in the area of the punctured groin may be absent altogether (Lodge and Hal 1993). The pain character is duller and is described as very strong, but occurs with a time delay, making early diagnosis difficult (Chan et al. 2008). The pain, which is then severe, is due to the peritoneal stimulus caused by bleeding in the retroperitoneal space. The pain is much more severe in intensity and localized in the flank or back region. Because the retroperitoneal space provides ample room for leaking blood,

patients are often noted for relevant hemoglobin drops and signs of incipient or manifest volume-deficiency shock. The combination of abdominal pain, flank pain or back pain and hemodynamic instability is highly suspicious for a retroperitoneal hematoma and must prompt adequate diagnosis and therapy.

The diagnostic tool of choice for verification of a suspected retroperitoneal hematoma is computed tomography (CT) or intra-arterial angiography (▣ Fig. 2.9). Orientational abdominal ultrasound and color-coded duplex ultrasound may be performed beforehand, but they should not delay the confirmatory computed tomography. In case of negative ultrasound findings

2

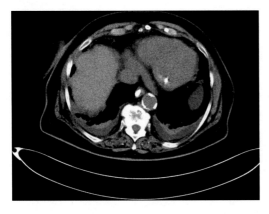

◨ **Fig. 2.9**   CT retroperitoneal hematoma

but urgent clinical suspicion of retroperitoneal hematoma, CT must follow in any case. Independent predictors for the occurrence of a retroperitoneal hematoma are too high arterial puncture, female gender, low body surface area and the presence of chronic renal insufficiency, whereas the use of GPIIbIIIa receptor antagonists and the use of closure systems had no influence on the occurrence of a retroperitoneal hematoma (Farogue et al. 2005; Tiroch et al. 2008). The investigation of an influence of the size of the arterial sheaths used leaves different results.

The therapeutic approach depends on the severity of the bleeding and the hemodynamic instability. Patients with retroperitoneal hematoma are hemodynamically monitored in the ICU with invasive arterial blood pressure measurement and measurement of central venous pressure. These measures help in volume management. If patient stabilization can be achieved by transfusion with red blood cell concentrates, crystalloid and plasma-expanding infusion therapy, and sufficient pain management, interventional or surgical therapy is not required. For patients who cannot be stabilized in this way, endovascular techniques with implantation of a stent graft or open suturing of the vascular defect are available (Chan et al. 2008).

■ **Dissections and Perforations of the Inguinal Vessels**

The vessel wall defects in the area of the arterial access path up to the aortic bifurcation can usually be traced back to the puncture itself as well as the insertion of sheaths, wires and devices. Hydrophilic or hydrophobic coated wires have a higher traumatic potential than non-coated wires. Whenever such a foreign body comes into contact with the vessel wall, vascular wall injury can potentially occur. The incidence of dissection of the arterial access pathway is 0.42–0.68% (Prasad et al. 2008; Muhs et al. 2005). This is even more the case when sheaths and devices with larger and very large diameters are used, such as those used in most interventions for structural heart disease. For example, in the early days of transfemoral percutaneous aortic valve replacement, iliac and femoral dissections were observed in about 10% of cases (Kahlert et al. 2009). Today, the delivery systems are much smaller, so that the complication rates have also been significantly reduced. The respective situation is particularly complicated by pre-damaged vessels, calcifications or severe kinkings in the area of the access path, since the passage of each curvature is accompanied by increased friction of the device on the vessel wall. Passage of vascular stenoses is also always associated with an increased risk of vascular dissection and rupture. The occurrence of local vessel wall dissection or vessel rupture does not necessarily imply a worsening of patient outcome (Hayes et al. 2002). During retraction of wires, catheters, devices and sheaths, the punctured vessel must also be subsequently checked for vessel wall defects, as dissections, ruptures or lacerations can also occur during retraction (◨ Figs. 2.10 and 2.11).

❱ Increased caution or a change of strategy is required if increased resistance is encountered when advancing sheaths, wires or devices. The position may not be intraluminal, but intramural or extravascular.

The therapy of vessel wall defects, be it complex dissections or relevant perforations or vessel ruptures, consists first of all in the application of an occlusive balloon to push back the dissection or seal the vessel wall defect. Dissections do not necessarily have to be stented. Stent implantation should be

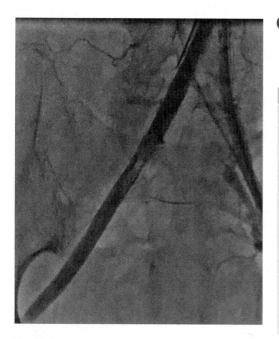

> For femoral access procedures, occlusion balloons of various sizes should always be kept in the cath lab's consignment stock.

Practical Tip

The correct puncture technique and the insertion of large-calibre sheaths can now be trained very elegantly on the CardioSkills SmartPuncture Simulator (◘ Fig. 2.12). The simulator has a vessel model with different vessel morphologies as well as pulsatile flow, so that punctures in complex anatomies and difficult circulation conditions can also be trained (▶ www. cardioskills.com). The "number needed to TRAIN" is 4, so in order to avoid one vascular access site complication four simulated cases need to be performed.

◘ Fig. 2.10　Iliac dissection

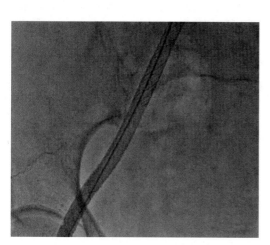

◘ Fig. 2.11　Iliac dissection after stenting

avoided, especially in the motion segments. Surgical repair of the vessel wall defect is the best option here. Outside of motion segments, stent implantation is the method of choice for dissections that threaten to occlude the vessel. If there is a relevant perforation, rupture or even laceration of the vessel, an occlusion balloon is first advanced over the intraluminal wire and inflated. Afterwards, it will have to be decided whether implantation of a covered stent is possible or whether the vascular defect must be surgically repaired.

2.1.2　**Radial Access**

Today, access via the radial artery should be chosen as the standard access route for coronary diagnostics and most coronary interventions. Compared with access via the groin with puncture of the femoral artery, access via the radial artery does not differ fundamentally, but it does differ in some points worth considering (◘ Fig. 2.13). In particular, the fact that the radial artery has a smaller diameter than the common femoral artery and is very prone to spasm in response to tactile stimuli has an impact on the clinical procedure when using the radial artery approach. In addition, special attention is required when the patient expresses pain, so as not to overlook an antegrade perfusion disturbance (spasm, see below).

■ **Topographic Anatomy**

The radial artery lies very superficially in the region of the carpus and is easy to palpate here. Together with the ulnar artery, it represents the metacarpal and finger perfusion via the deep palmar arch. The ulnar artery is also very superficial on the ulnar side in the carpal region and is easy to palpate (◘ Fig. 2.14).

2

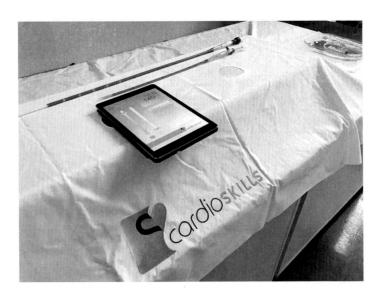

■ **Fig. 2.13** Puncture site radial artery

Further proximally, there is another good access route to the arterial vascular system via the larger calibre brachial artery. It runs along the medial upper arm, covered only by skin, subcutaneous fat and fascia (■ Fig. 2.15).

■ Spasm

The radial access route is now correctly considered by many interventionalists as the access of first choice for diagnostic cardiac catheter examinations, elective and also acute interventions and is now also recommended in the guidelines. The advantages of the ease of compressing the radial artery after the procedure and the rapid mobilization of the patient are offset by a pronounced tendency to spasm of the radial artery and brachial arteries in general. These spasms must be controlled with medication in some patients in order to make the examination via the radial artery possible and tolerable for the patient.

Due to its smaller vessel calibre, the radial artery is prone to pronounced vascular spasms, especially in smaller women. Spasms during the examination are by far the most frequent complication of radial access, especially at the beginning of the learning curve. They can be so severe that the catheter or sheath can no longer be moved and retracted. The use of force here can result in significant injury to the patient, such as a tear or eversion of the radial artery. In this situation, local or systemic vasodilating measures are often no longer successful and occasionally contraindicated, as many patients react vagally due to the strong pain stimulus. The most promising measure in this situation is therefore deep sedation or even anaesthesia of the patient. In my personal experience, all catheters and sheaths could be removed without injury.

Predisposing factors for a radial spasm are: the agitated or pain-stricken patient, a small radial diameter, a sheath that is too

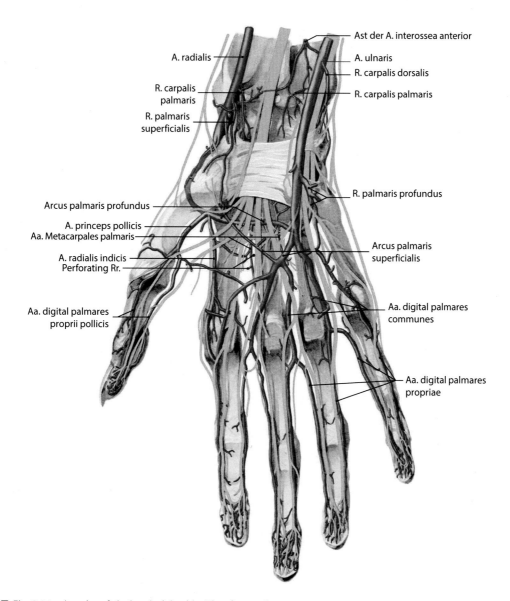

■ **Fig. 2.14** Arteries of the hand, right side. View from palmar

large in relation to the vessel diameter, pronounced radial loops or severe kinking in the vessel course, and frequent catheter manipulations, which are particularly necessary at the beginning of the learning curve.

Avoidance strategies can already be derived from this: sedation of agitated patients plays a very important role; in my opinion, even routine sedation is recommended for inexperienced examiners. The examination of very small patients at the beginning of the learning curve should be avoided or, if unavoidable, rather performed with a small sheath. Passage

of loops and kinkings is facilitated by the use of hydrophilic or thinner wires (0.018 in.) and visual control; however, the C-arm must often be rotated for this purpose; a forced approach is not recommended. The use of sheathless hydrophilic coated guiding catheters may improve the size ratio of the catheter to the vessel compared to a conventional sheath, but care must be taken to avoid increased catheter movement in the vessel due to movement of the sterile covered arm. The advancement of a guiding catheter in cases of spasm tendency or calcifications can be simplified by making the transition from

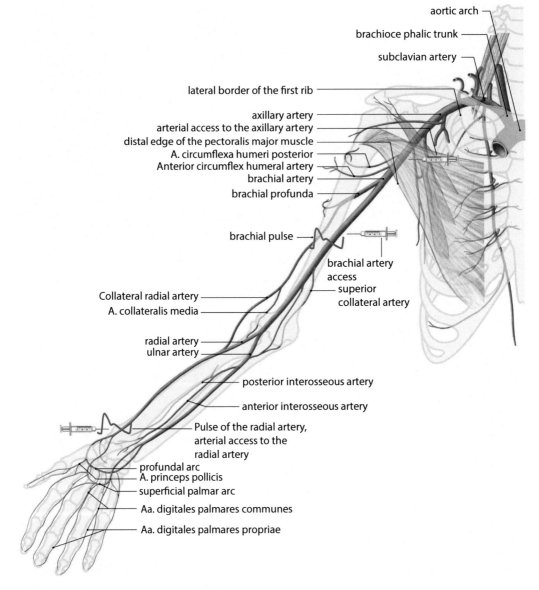

aortic arch
brachioce phalic trunk
subclavian artery
lateral border of the first rib
axillary artery
arterial access to the axillary artery
distal edge of the pectoralis major muscle
A. circumflexa humeri posterior
Anterior circumflex humeral artery
brachial artery
brachial profunda
brachial pulse
brachial artery
access
superior
collateral artery
Collateral radial artery
A. collateralis media
radial artery
ulnar artery
posterior interosseous artery
anterior interosseous artery
Pulse of the radial artery,
arterial access to the
radial artery
profundal arc
A. princeps pollicis
superficial palmar arc
Aa. digitales palmares communes
Aa. digitales palmares propriae

◻ Fig. 2.15 Arterial access routes on the right upper extremity

0.035 in. guidewire smoother, e.g. by inserting a slightly longer diagnostic 5F pigtail catheter into a 6F guiding catheter.

In addition, the local use of vasodilating substances naturally plays a central role, even if these do not always have to be given to all patients. In particular, nitrates and calcium antagonists are used here. Personally, the best experience has been with the slow administration of 0.3–0.5 mg nitroglycerin or 1 mg verapamil in 10 mL saline. The verapamil dose can be increased up to 5 mg. If the vessel is already spastic, it has proven use-

ful to rinse with 10 mL of isotonic saline after drug administration. This may be painful for the patient for a short time, but in personal experience it relieves existing spasms even better. With both substances, the blood pressure-lowering and possibly negative chronotropic effects must be taken into account. Particularly in fasting and agitated patients, pronounced vagal reactions may occur as a consequence of the administration of these drugs. In addition to sedation, intravenous pre- and post-hydration of the patient is helpful in this case.

❯ Vasospasms are the most common complication of the radial examination technique.
They occur especially in small arteries during the use of large sheaths and frequent
catheter manipulations. Agitated patients
in particular are predisposed. The use of
local vasodilating substances, appropriate
sedation and adapted material selection can
significantly reduce their frequency.

■ **Dissection and Vascular Injury**

Due to the small vessel calibre, the radial
artery can be dissected relatively easily during the puncture or insertion of the 0.0035 in.
wire. With good blood flow, the wire is then
inserted via the needle. In a non-spastic vessel,
virtually no friction can be felt. Resistance to
insertion of the wire must also always suggest
dissection. If a sheath is advanced in the dissection, it is usually very painful to the patient
and may cause permanent vessel occlusion or
hemorrhage. In addition to bleeding at the
puncture site, false aneurysms or AV fistulas
can occur in rare cases.

Bleeding complications of radial access
have some peculiarities: they can occur not
only at the puncture site but at any level on the
arm. The underlying mechanism is wire perforations of small side branches, especially when
using hydrophilic wires in a complex anatomy.
These hemorrhages sometimes become clinically visible with considerable latency. A fundamental problem of bleeding in the arm is
the limited space, so there is an increased risk
of compartment syndrome.

The primary treatment measure for bleeding is, of course, adequate compression treatment, e.g. with a blood pressure cuff and, if
necessary, antagonization of anticoagulation.
If, despite a perforation, it has been possible
to advance a catheter in the true lumen, this
can help to stop the bleeding from the lumen.
In this case, coronary intervention can also
be performed. After completion of the intervention, in personal experience, the bleeding
usually stops. Leeches may also be used to
treat pronounced hematomas. Rarely, surgical
relief of the hematoma is necessary.

The development of pseudoaneurysms
and AV fistulas after radial puncture is rare
but quite possible. In the event of painful

swelling around the puncture site or conspicu-
ous vein filling on the forearm, colour-coded
duplex ultrasound should therefore be performed.

❯ Dissections of the small radial artery are a
typical complication. Bleeding may occur
at the puncture site or by injury to side
branches at any level in the arm. It should
be noted that occasionally these bleeds
manifest with latency and bleeding into the
arm has the increased risk of compartment
syndrome.

■ **Vascular Occlusion and Hand Ischemia**

The incidence of radial artery occlusion after
sheath removal is reported in the literature
to be 3–10%. Predisposing factors are the
use of large sheaths in thin vessels and the
omission of periprocedural heparinization.
Heparin administration of 5000 IU is also
recommended for diagnostic studies. Many
operators prefer intravenous to intra-arterial
heparin administration because the acidic pH
can, at least theoretically, induce spasm. It
is suspected that the compression technique
after sheath removal also has an effect on the
rate of radial closure. Compression at the lowest pressure necessary to achieve haemostasis
is recommended.

Pronounced clinical symptoms as a result
of radial artery occlusion are very rare. The
frequency of discrete symptoms is controversial. In very rare cases, however, severe hand
ischemia may occur, affecting the thumb in
particular. This can lead to severe disability for
the affected patient. It has not yet been shown
that the performance of a pre-interventional
Allen test can reduce the complication rate,
which is why many operators do not perform
it at all. However, I still perform a modified
pre-interventional Allen test on every patient
due to liability considerations. The modifica-
tion consists of measuring the oxygen saturation on the index finger instead of looking for
paling and redness of the skin. In contrast to
a pathological Allen test, a drop in saturation
is only seen in very few patients overall.

If there is evidence of occlusion of the
radial artery, this should be confirmed by
duplex ultrasound. This may be indicated

by persistent paresthesia of the fingers, pain, and paleness. However, >50% of radial artery occlusions are probably asymptomatic. In the case of occlusion (in up to 10% of examinations!), therapy with a full dose of low molecular weight heparin should be considered. Significantly higher open rates of 86% after 4 weeks have been described with this than with observational therapy alone (Zankl et al. 2010). There is also evidence that in fresh radial artery occlusions, 1 h of compression of the ipsilateral ulnar artery can promote reopening of the affected radial artery (Bernat et al. 2011).

2.2 Aortic Complications

Erhard Kaiser

2.2.1 Epidemiology

The topic of this chapter is not the idiopathic diseases of the abdominal or thoracic aorta but the problems of the aorta which may result from catheter interventions. In this context we speak of iatrogenic aortic dissections and other complications explained by catheterization. Data from 2006 show that the incidence of iatrogenic aortic ascending dissections is about 0.04%. In the case of coronary interventions, the incidence is 0.12%, while in purely diagnostic procedures, the incidence is only 0.01%. In most cases, aortic dissections are found in the region of the right coronary sinus (Goméz-Moreno et al. 2006).

2.2.2 Complications in the Area of the Infrarenal Aorta

Iatrogenic aortic dissections in the region of the infrarenal aorta usually result from foreign body contact (0.0035 wire, diagnostic catheters, guide catheters, devices) with the aortic wall facing away from the puncture site. Especially the hard wires, large lumen sheaths, long sheaths and the guiding catheters bring a high risk of dissection to this anatomical area.

However, current larger devices, such as transfemoral aortic valves, can also be potentially problematic here (Kahlert et al. 2009). In addition to iliac or femoral dissections, pseudoaneurysms and retroperitoneal hematomas may occur (for the management of these complications, see ▶ Sect. 2.1). If the infrarenal aorta is injured, an occlusion balloon must be advanced quickly to seal the defect, especially in the case of perforations over the 0.0035 wire. If the balloon is left in place, immediate surgical repair of the defect is indicated. If the vessel wall defect is not vital endangering, i.e. circumscribed and covered, a prosthesis can be inserted endovascularly and the vessel wall defect can thus be covered.

2.2.3 Complications in the Area of the Landing Zone/Ascending Aorta

If dissections occur during coronary interventions, they may not only continue antegrade into the coronary vessel, but may also extend retrograde into the ascending aorta. Clinical experience shows that there is often uncertainty among operators as to how to proceed with these dissections, and in particular focal defects running circumferentially around the coronary ostium are not detected or are detected late. This is often due to inadequate fluoroscopy, suboptimal angulation, or contrast reflux into the aortic root, which may visually obscure the dissection. Therefore, the possibility of aortic dissection in this area should always be considered and increased attention should be paid to it. In particular, deep intubation of the coronary artery with the guide catheter is a maneuver associated with a high risk of dissection and should therefore be avoided (Meller et al. 1976). Guiding catheters that can also accidentally get into too deep a position in the coronary vessel primarily include the Amplatz catheter and the multipurpose catheter. The too deep guiding catheter position can result especially if balloon catheters or stents are advanced through the guiding catheter via an extra support wire. Nevertheless, it is important to keep in mind that dissections that continue retrogradely into the aorta can in principle also be caused by catheters that are actually not very aggressive. This also includes the Judkins right and Judkins left guide catheters, which are often used as standard guide catheters (Goméz-Moreno et al. 2006).

A distinction must be made between lesions that can be left in place and treated conservatively, those that require interventional treatment, i.e. closure of the entry to the dissection by means of stent implantation, and those that require surgical repair. A study and classification by Dunning et al. (2000) provides assistance. Dunning describes a classification (❏ Table 2.1) that can be used for decision-making when determining the therapeutic procedure on the basis of morphological criteria. Dunning stage I describes a focal dissection that extends retrogradely from the coronary artery and remains in the ostium (❏ Fig. 2.16).

In Dunning stage II, the dissection is extended retrogradely to the ascending aorta, but over a distance not exceeding 40 mm. Finally, Dunning stage III describes an extension of the dissection into the ascending aorta for a length exceeding 40 mm cranially (❏ Fig. 2.17).

While the dissections of stages Dunning I and Duning II can be treated well by closing the dissection entrance with a stent and then conservatively, the dissections of stage Dunning III must be surgically repaired (❏ Fig. 2.18). However, it should be empha-

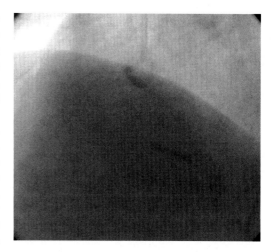

❏ **Fig. 2.16** Aortic dissection sinus valsalva/Dunning type I

sized at this point that any aortic dissection can develop further over time and must be followed up by imaging (TEE/CT). The clinical approach may then need to be adapted.

Dunning stage I and II aortic dissections generally have a good prognosis and can be treated by stenting and thus covering the dissecting orifice, followed by close clinical follow-up and imaging (Colkesen et al. 2007; Goméz-Moreno et al. 2006; Goldstein et al. 2003). Complex situations, such as the combination of left main dissection, aortic dissection, and pericardial tamponade, may also be amenable to interventional and nonsurgical treatment (Porto et al. 2005). In stage III, the subintimal perfusion may take on a greater extent and the dissect may grow into the aortic arch, so that surgical therapy may be necessary here (Yarlioglues et al. 2011; Tochii et al. 2010; Wyss et al. 2008). This is particularly true for a rapidly expanding dissection and for hemodynamically unstable patients.

In addition to clinical follow-up, accurate imaging of the ascending aorta must also be performed. For this purpose, computed tomography has proven to be a precise and informative imaging method (Tanasie et al. 2011). Transesophageal echocardiography can also be used to accurately localize the intimal flap and thus assess its progression (Alfonso et al. 1997).

❏ **Table 2.1** Dunning classification

Stage	Extension	Therapy
Dunning type I	Focal dissection, ostium, sinus valsalva	Conservative, stenting of the entry
Dunning type II	Ascending aorta <40 mm	Conservative, stenting of the entry
Dunning type III	Ascending aorta >40 mm	Surgical

2

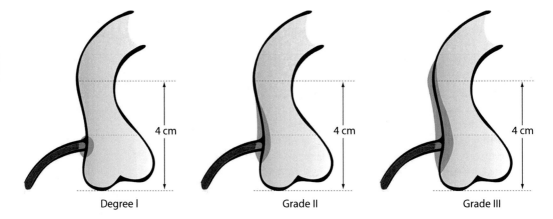

| Degree I | Grade II | Grade III |

○ **Fig. 2.17**   Schematic overview of Dunning type I–III aortic dissection

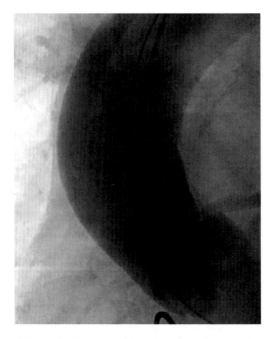

○ **Fig. 2.18**   Large ascending aorta dissection

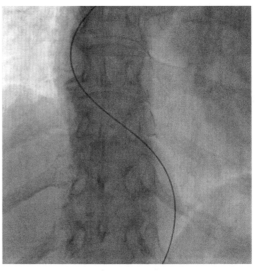

○ **Fig. 2.19**   Aortic kinking

2.2.4   Kinking of the Aorta

Aortic kinking, i.e. the severe tortuosity of the aorta, is not a complication in the true sense of the word, but it is a complication-prone situation in which increased attention is required. Very tortuous vessel sections can be stretched with stiffer wires or bridged by using long sheaths so that the steerability of the catheters to be used is maintained as far as possible (○ Fig. 2.19).

Practical Tip

Today, the correct handling of diagnostic and guide catheters can be trained very realistically on the endovascular VR simulator. Stenting of local dissections is part of the complication management training, which is e.g. also recommended in level 4 by the Working Group Interventional Cardiology of the German Society of Cardiology (▶ www.agikintervention.de, ▶ www.cardioskills.com).

2.2.5 Aortic Aneurysms

The presence of aneurysmal dilatations of the abdominal or thoracic aorta, like aortic kinking, is not a contraindication to left heart catheterization via femoral access. Nevertheless, it is important to plan the procedure well to avoid the risk of dissection, perforation or rupture during the passage of the aneurysms with wires, diagnostic or guide catheters and devices (◻ Fig. 2.20).

The abdominal aortic aneurysm is per se and untreated associated with a very high mortality (Nordon et al. 2011). Passage of the aneurysm should always be performed under fluoroscopy and never without a view of the aneurysm. If the procedure to be performed requires more frequent catheter and device changes, it is advisable to use a long sheath, such as a carotid sheath, to ensure safe passage through the aneurysm without frequent vessel wall contact.

2.3 Complications During Catheter Placement

Michael Markant

2.3.1 History of Medicine

More than 80 years ago, the first right heart catheter was performed in a self-experiment by the medical student Werner Forssmann (◻ Fig. 2.21) in 1929 (Forssmann 1929; ◻ Figs. 2.22 and 2.23).

In 1953, Sven-Ivar Seldinger performed the first left heart catheterization on one of his patients (Seldinger 1953).

The first selective coronary angiography starting from the brachial artery was performed in 1959 by Mason Sones (Sones et al. 1959) and then in 1967 starting from the femoral artery by Melvin P. Judkins (1967) (◻ Fig. 2.24).

◻ **Fig. 2.20** CT of an abdominal aortic aneurysm

2

Fig. 2.21 Portrait of Werner Forssmann

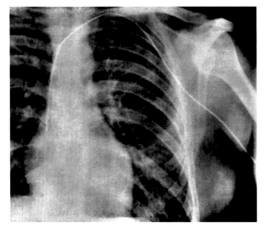

Fig. 2.22 X-ray image Werner Forssmann self-experiment

Subsequently, for decades, the femoral artery was chosen as the standard access route for left heart catheterization for very pragmatic reasons. Not only due to continuously improved catheter materials, but also due to clinical findings, the radial artery has gained in importance for diagnostic cardiac catheterization and for interventional treatment. The foundation for modern interventional cardiology was laid in 1977 by Andreas Grüntzig (**Fig. 2.25**) with the first percutaneous transluminal coronary angioplasty (PTCA) in Zurich (Grüntzig et al. 1979).

Fig. 2.23 Sven Ivar Seldinger

Since then, interventional cardiology has taken off on a triumphal march around the world and catheter-based treatment procedures are now the gold standard in endovascular therapy—and not only for coronary interventions. Through the establishment of

Fig. 2.24   Melvin P. Judkins

Fig. 2.25   Andreas Grüntzig

modern care structures, such as infarct networks, comprehensive endovascular care can be guaranteed today.

2.3.2 Dissections

Typical complications when probing the coronary vessels with a catheter are, on the one hand, dissections or possibly even perforations in the area of the coronary ostium, but on the other hand, cardiac arrhythmias and drops in blood pressure can also occur when probing the coronary ostium. Causes of dissection in the area of the coronary vessel are either direct injury to the vessel wall by the catheter or guidewire, a subintimal position of the guidewire, an excessively forceful injection of contrast medium or underlying media degeneration or severe calcifications of the aorta and coronary vessels (Yip et al. 2001b).

The frequency of dissections in the coronary ostium through the catheter is strongly dependent on the stiffness as well as the shape and size of the catheter and the handling of the catheter by the operator. Dissections occur much less frequently through a diagnostic catheter than through a guiding catheter (Perez-Castellano et al. 1998; Levenson et al. 2011). Increased risks of dissection exist with the use of such catheters that exert greater pressure in the region of the ostium due to their shape and stiffness, as well as with catheters that can enter deeply into the vessel due to their predetermined shape. Especially the Amplatz left guiding catheter (Yip et al. 2001a, b), but also an extra-backup catheter (e.g. XB, EBU or Voda catheter) and an Icari or Multipurpose catheter are associated with an increased risk of dissection.

Accidental catheter placement in a small side branch or in a heavily sclerosed or calcified vessel section can lead to increased dissection, so that plaque formation or calcification in the area of the vascular ostium greatly increases the risk of such a complication. In addition, forced catheter movements often result in dissections, especially in the case of an inexperienced operator or in difficult vascular conditions (Figs. 2.26, 2.27 and 2.28).

> The risk of dissection increases significantly with very stiff catheters or those that exert a great deal of pressure on the vascular ostium, as well as with technically difficult vascular intubations. The Amplatz guide catheter in particular is associated with an increased risk of dissection. Handling must therefore be carried out with care; it must be noted that a deeper intubation of the coronary vessel often occurs when the catheter is withdrawn.

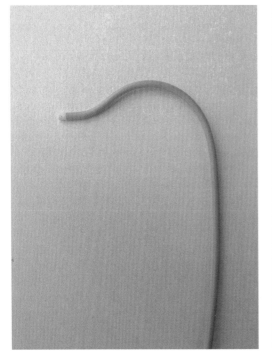

Fig. 2.26   Amplatz left (AL) guide catheter

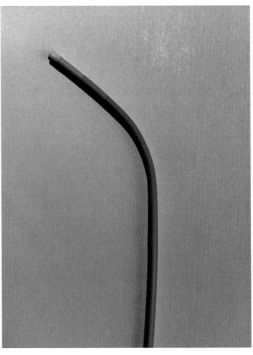

Fig. 2.28   Multipurpose (MP) guide catheter

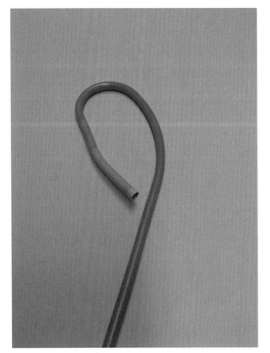

Fig. 2.27   Extra-backup (XB/EBU) guide catheter

> **Practical Tip**
>
> Today, the handling of different catheters and catheter shapes can be trained very realistically on the endovascular VR simulator.

As a complication of a dissection in the area of the coronary ostium, retrograde spread into the sinus valsalvae or the ascending aorta may occur. This is a fairly rare event: in diagnostic procedures, these retrograde dissections occur in 0–0.008% of cases, and in interventions in 0.06–0.15% of cases (Yip et al. 2001a, b; Masaki et al. 2005; Perez-Castellano et al. 1998; Dunning et al. 2000).

The report of the German Association of Cardiologists in Private Practice on Quality Assurance in Diagnostic and Therapeutic Invasive Cardiology shows that in Germany in 2009, coronary occlusion occurred in 0.09% of diagnostic cardiac catheterizations and in 0.36% of interventions, and dissection in the access pathway occurred in 0.06% of diagnostic cardiac catheterizations and in 0.11% of interventions, respectively (Levenson et al. 2011).

Comparative data from Spain showed a total of three dissections of the sinus valsalvae in 4970 PCIs, all of which resulted from retrograde propagation of a dissection of the right coronary artery (Perez-Castellano et al. 1998). Morphological and structural differences between the left and right sinus valsalvae appear to be responsible for the fact that dissections of the left coronary artery are significantly less likely to propagate into the aorta (Lopez-Minguez et al. 2006).

If a dissection has occurred and the patient remains stable and asymptomatic and there is no flow impairment in the coronary artery, therapeutic heparinization, possibly supplemented by the administration of a GPIIbIIIa receptor antagonist, can be performed without any problems (Perez-Castellano et al. 1998). If necessary, stent implantation must be considered on an individual basis, depending on the spread of the dissection (see also NHLBI dissection classification, ▶ Sect. 2.5.4), the size of the vessel and the observed progress of the dissection. If flow impairment or pectanginal symptoms or angina equivalent are associated with the occurrence of the dissection, stent implantation should be performed as a standard procedure to reattach the dissection membrane. If a guidewire must be re-advanced into the vessel when a dissection is already present, advancement of a microcatheter over the guidewire followed by careful administration of contrast through the microcatheter may be recommended to verify the location of the wire or microcatheter in the true vessel lumen. If the dissection membrane is short-stretch and involves the coronary ostium, stent implantation in the coronary ostium should be performed without delay. If the dissection membrane takes a fairly long course through the coronary vessel, it is best to stent and reattach the distal dissecting portion first and then stent the coronary ostium (Li and Cao 2011; Yip et al. 2001a, b).

If these measures fail to control the dissection and the patient becomes unstable, rapid aortocoronary bypass surgery must be initiated.

If contrast injection reveals a dissection in the area of the sinus valsalvae, further manipulations with guide catheter and wire as well as further dilatations should initially be avoided. However, the exact extent of the dissection should be quantified immediately by TEE, MSCT, or MRI (Perez-Castellano et al. 1998; Goldstein et al. 2003; Dunning et al. 2000; Bapat and Venn 2003; Darwazah et al. 2008; Maiello et al. 2003; Ghaemian and Jalalian 2010; Ochi et al. 1996). At the superior border of each aortic sinus, there is a clearly circumscribed circular collagen fiber-rich rim, which appears to prevent, but does not preclude, extension of the dissection beyond this region (Masaki et al. 2005). If the dissection extends more than 40 mm from the coronary ostium into the aorta, or if it is complicated by severe acute aortic valve regurgitation, hemopericardium, unstable circulation, or chest pain that is not well controlled with medication, acute cardiac surgery is required in most cases (Dunning et al. 2000; Yip et al. 2001a, b; Ochi et al. 1996; Takahashi et al. 2010) (◘ Fig. 2.17 and ◘ Table 2.1).

In the case of an isolated dissection in the area of the sinus valsalvae without further spread into the aorta, a purely conservative approach has proven to be sufficient (Yip et al. 2001a, b; Perez-Castellano et al. 1998). Local dissections in this area usually heal spontaneously within 4 weeks without consequences (Perez-Castellano et al. 1998).

If a dissection occurs, it is important to obtain an accurate picture of the clinical significance of the dissection, the flow impairment that has occurred in the coronary vessel, and the extent of the dissection. If there is evidence of spread of the dissection into the sinus valsalvae or ascending aorta on contrast administration, a TEE, CT, or MRI should be performed to accurately evaluate the extent of the dissection if there is any doubt (◘ Fig. 2.29).

2

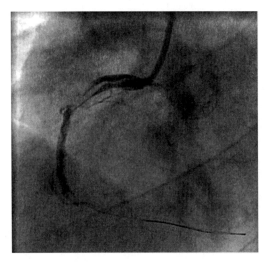

■ **Fig. 2.29** RCA dissection

2.3.3 **Arrhythmias and Hypotension**

Cardiac arrhythmias and blood pressure drops may occur during coronary ostium intubation, typically when ostium stenosis or vasospasm are present or during selective intubation of a small side branch. The typical case is intubation of a small conus branch of the right coronary artery. Prolonged dwelling of the catheter in the coronary ostium or administration of contrast in such a situation increases the likelihood of ventricular fibrillation (see also ▶ Sect. 3.5).

❯ Ventricular fibrillation may occur due to ostial stenosis, ostial vasospasm and selective intubation of very small side branches.

A suitable preventive measure to avoid vasospasm is the administration of glycerol trinitrate before the start of the procedure. In many centers, routine administration of 1–2 strokes of glycerol trinitrate sublingually is performed when blood pressure is stable (systolic blood pressure >100 mmHg). In addition, continuous invasive blood pressure monitoring during intubation of the coronary ostium is strongly recommended. In case of clinically relevant blood pressure drops, abnormal pressure attenuation or ventricularization of the pressure curve (normal

systolic pressure and very low diastolic pressure), the catheter should be easily withdrawn and placed in front of the vascular ostium if possible. Subsequently, the exact morphological situation at the coronary ostium should be verified by careful contrast administration. If ostium stenosis is confirmed, 100–200 µg of glycerol trinitrate should first be administered intracoronary and then the morphological situation should be checked again by means of contrast medium administration.

As a further precautionary measure, it must be ensured that a ready-to-use defibrillator is available before the start of the procedure in order to terminate any ventricular fibrillation that may occur immediately. In this particular situation, the current guidelines of the European Resuscitation Council (ERC) recommend deviating from the "1-shock strategy" and delivering up to three shocks in direct succession. This treatment strategy is likely to terminate ventricular fibrillation (see also ▶ Sect. 3.5). Prolonged cardiac massage resulting in a longer interruption of the procedure and the increased risk of bacterial contamination of the examination area can thus be avoided (Deakin et al. 2010).

❯ Routine administration of glycerol trinitrate sublingually is recommended to prevent coronary spasm, and intracoronary administration is recommended to treat spasm that has occurred, taking into account the circulatory situation.

2.3.4 **Perforations and Tamponade**

Vascular perforation through the catheter is a particularly serious complication with a potentially lethal outcome. It is diagnosed by extravasation of the contrast medium (see also ▶ Sect. 2.5). If pericardial tamponade occurs, the treatment of choice is immediate echocardiography-guided pericardiocentesis (■ Figs. 2.30 and 2.31) and, depending on the severity, long balloon inflation, implantation of a covered stent or immediate cardiac surgery (Shirakabe et al. 2007; Al-Mukhaini et al. 2011).

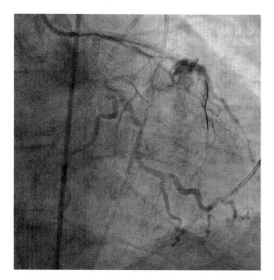

Fig. 2.30 Pericardial tamponade after RIA rupture, pigtail catheter lies in the pericardium

A retrospective study of all diagnostic and interventional cardiac catheterizations at the Mayo Clinic, Rochester, USA between 1979 and 1997 showed pericardial tamponade in 88 patients, which had to be treated by pericardiocentesis. In 99% of the cases this could be performed successfully. 3% of the patients subsequently developed a pneumothorax, 3% a tear of the right ventricle and 3% an injury of the intercostal vessels. A total of 18% of patients required subsequent thoracic surgery. No deaths resulted from the pericardiocentesis procedure itself. 9% of patients died due to injuries from the catheter-based procedure, 6% due to perioperative complications, and 6% due to underlying heart disease (Tsang et al. 1998).

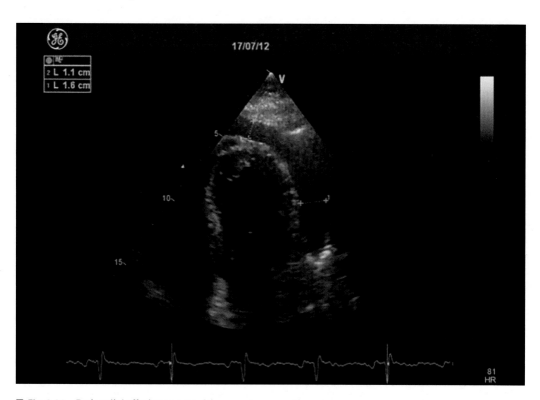

Fig. 2.31 Pericardial effusion not requiring puncture on echo

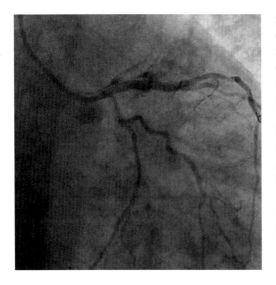

◘ Fig. 2.32 Proximal LAD rupture with extravasation

> Perforation or pericardial tamponade through the diagnostic or guide catheter is very rare. If the patient suddenly deteriorates clinically and a contrast extravasation occurs, this complication must be considered. The diagnosis is confirmed by echocardiography, which is performed immediately (◘ Fig. 2.32).

2.3.5 Selection of the Guide Catheter

Currently available guiding catheters vary in terms of their shape, size, internal diameter, stiffness, rotatability and advanceability. The most common sizes for the femoral access route are 5–8 French (F), although the larger diameter guide catheters (7–8F) often need to be used, especially for IVUS use, rotablation, bifurcation interventions and CTO interventions. The latter are characterized by greater stiffness and also require a larger sheath for access. In general, the use of a larger sheath is associated with an increased risk of bleeding. The use of a closure system (e.g. Angioseal, Perclose, Starclose) after the intervention can reduce the risk of bleeding.

For interventions via the radial artery, a 5F or, if an improved backup is required, a 6F guiding catheter is usually used. If larger catheters are required (e.g. rotablation, CTO

recanalization, bifurcation intervention), either a sheathless catheter (e.g. Eucath from the company ASAHI in 6.5F or 7.5F) or a 7F catheter without a sheath (e.g., with a 5F multipurpose catheter as an inner catheter) is recommended (Youn et al. 2011; Choi et al. 2013; Li et al. 2013). Because of the better compressibility of the radial artery, the sheath can be removed immediately after the intervention, eliminating the need for a closure system. Special compression devices are available.

The selection of the guiding catheter depends on the angle of the coronary vessel from the aorta and the localization of the lesion in the vessel. On the one hand, the catheter should not protrude too far into the vessel, and on the other hand, sufficient "backup" of the guide catheter should generally be ensured—this is particularly important in the case of very distally located stenoses or very tortuous vessels. In order to minimize blood pressure drops and arrhythmias caused by the catheter-related impairment of blood flow, the size of the vascular ostium should be taken into account when selecting the guiding catheter. Guide catheters with side holes should always be used for large guide catheters (7–8F) or coronaries with narrow calibres.

> Note: Use guide catheters with side holes when there is very little orthograde flow on the coronary vessel or the guide catheter leads to occlusion.

■ **Selection of the Guiding Catheter for Intubation of the Left Coronary Artery Starting from the Femoral Artery**

With a short main stem, note that depending on the secondary curve size of the catheter, either the left anterior descending (LAD) or the left circumflex artery (LCX) can be selectively intubated due to the different exit angles. A larger Judkins left catheter sits more securely and with better "backup" in the ostium of the LCX (e.g., 6F-JL-5), while a smaller one sits better in the ostium of the LAD (e.g., 6F-JL-4).

If a longer main stem is present, the LCX often extends from it at a rather steep angle. In this case, the backup of the Judkins catheter is typically not sufficient for distally located stenoses or tortuous vessel courses. In this case, guiding catheters with better backup are preferable, e.g. 6F-Left Amplatz-2 (-3) or 6F-Extra-Backup (XB- or EBU 3.5–4). However, these guiding catheters also have a higher risk of dissection at the ostium of the left coronary artery. In the case of the Amplatz catheter, this risk also exists above all when the catheter is removed. A safe way to remove the Amplatz catheter is to carefully advance the guidewire to push the catheter back out of the vascular ostium (◘ Figs. 2.33 and 2.34).

LAD Stenosis
- Judkins Left Guiding Catheter (JL 4–5)
- If there is no sufficient backup or no secure catheter position in the ostium: change to a more aggressive catheter with a better backup (XB 3.5–4 or AL 1–3)

LCX Stenosis
- Ostial stenosis: JL 4–5 guide catheter
- Distal stenosis: XB 3.5–4.0 guiding catheter
- If there is no sufficient backup or no secure catheter position in the ostium: change to an AL 1–3 guide catheter

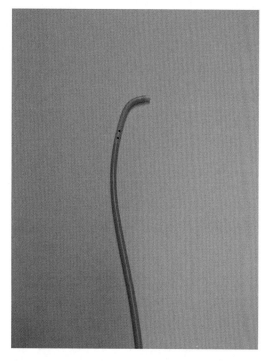

◘ **Fig. 2.34** Judkins right guide catheter

■ **Selection of the Guiding Catheter for Intubation of the Right Coronary Artery Starting from the Femoral Artery**

Various guide catheters can be considered for intubation of the right coronary artery. The standard guiding catheter in uncomplicated right coronary artery (RCA) anatomy is the Judkins right catheter (JR-4). If the proximal portion of the vessel points cranially, safe vascular intubation is possible with a 3D RC catheter. If the proximal vessel portion points steeply caudally, a Multipurpose catheter should be used. If more backup is needed, a Left Amplatz (usually AL-1) or an Ikari catheter (usually IR-1.5) is recommended. However, in cases of severe calcification or sclerosis of the proximal portion of the vessel, the risk of dissection is significantly increased by these catheters, as they can deeply intubate the vessel (even accidentally) (◘ Figs. 2.35 and 2.36).

If this tendency is evident, a Right Amplatz (usually AR 1–2) catheter should be used, which due to its shape usually does not intubate the vessel as deeply. Nevertheless, even with the Amplatz catheter, the catheter

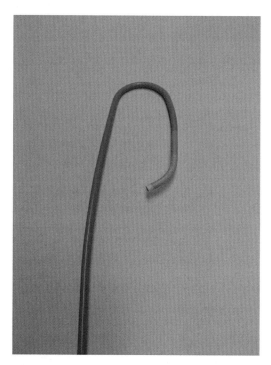

◘ **Fig. 2.33** Judkins left guiding catheter

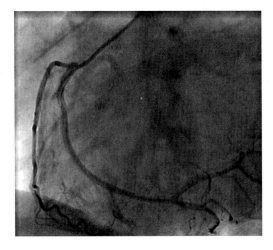

Fig. 2.35 Position too deep with Judkins right catheter

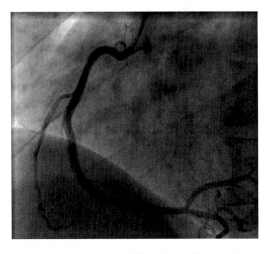

Fig. 2.36 Corrected Judkins right catheter position

can jump into a deep position in the coronary vessel, so that the placement should always be done carefully. In complex situations, an Extra-backup or Hockey-stick catheter is helpful as an alternative. Depending on the situation and experience, each operator should develop a strategy regarding guiding catheter selection.

1. Uncomplicated anatomy of the RCA: Judkins right catheter
2. Cranially pointing vessel outlet: First 3D RC catheter and, if no safe vessel intubation is possible, change to Left Amplatz catheter.
3. Steeply caudally pointing vessel outlet: Multipurpose catheter
4. Larger backup required: Initially Left Amplatz catheter and, if no safe catheter position possible, change to Ikari, Hockey stick or Extra backup catheter (e.g. XB-RCA catheter)
5. Ostial RCA, severe sclerosis and backup required: Right Amplatz catheter

When intubating an anomalously draining right coronary artery from the left sinus of valsalvae or an anterior vessel draining above the sinotubular line, a Left Amplatz or JL guide catheter are often appropriate to selectively intubate the coronary vessel (Yip et al. 2001a, b).

■ **Selection of the Guiding Catheter for Intubation of a Bypass Vessel**

For aortocoronary venous bypasses to the right coronary artery, a Multipurpose catheter is very well suited. The risk of accidental deep vessel intubation with the associated increased risk of dissection in the bypass must always be considered.

In general, venous bypasses to the left coronary artery can be well selectively visualized with a Right Judkins catheter or a Left coronary bypass catheter (LCB). A better backup can again be achieved with a Left Amplatz catheter (1 or 2).

The catheter of choice for intubation of the mammary artery bypass is the IMA catheter (■ Fig. 2.37).

■ **Selection of Diagnostic and Guide Catheters for Procedures Starting from the Radial Artery**

If the left radial artery is chosen as the access route for cardiac catheterization and intervention, the same catheters can usually be used as for the procedures starting from the femoral artery.

If the right radial artery is chosen as the access route, it must be noted that the catheter is at an altered angle in the ascending aorta, since it does not come from the aortic arch but from the right subclavian artery. This must be taken into account when selecting catheters: as a rule of thumb, a Judkins catheter can

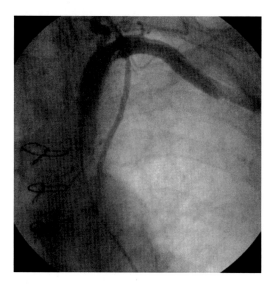

Fig. 2.37 Severe LIMA and subclavian artery dissection after intubation of the LIMA graft with an IMA catheter

be selected one size smaller. Alternatively, a "Barbeau" or "Tiger" catheter can be selected for a diagnostic examination, with which selective probing of both coronary vessels is possible without further catheter changes. It is recommended to probe the internal thoracic artery from the left radial artery either with an IMA catheter in 5F or 4F (slightly steeper angle) or with a special IMA catheter in 5F.

> In the case of a procedure from the radial artery, the same catheter shapes can be considered as for intervention from the femoral artery. In case of access via the right radial artery, the catheter may have to be used in a smaller size.

2.4 Complications of Coronary Wire Placement

Erhard Kaiser

2.4.1 Properties of Coronary Wires

To successfully perform a percutaneous coronary intervention, a well harmonized system of arterial sheath, guiding catheter, coronary wire and balloon or stent is required. Only

then is it guaranteed that the path through the coronary vessel can be taken and that there is sufficient backup and support, for example, to place a stent in a stenosis. The coronary wire plays a central role within this system, which will now be discussed in detail.

■ **Structure and Function of a Coronary Wire**
Nowadays, a coronary wire is a complex device and can no longer be compared with the devices of the early days of percutaneous coronary intervention, when, for example, Andreas Grüntzig still used a balloon fixed to a wire for his first intervention. In addition to guiding through the coronary vessel, the coronary wire allows in particular the passage of stenosis and the advancement of certain devices into the target region. The following wire characteristics are determined by the wire design:

- Forward thrust/controllability
- Rotational stability
- Flexibility
- Slipperiness
- Visibility
- Prolapse inclination
- Stability/Support

The wire materials used today are mainly stainless steel or nitinol. Nitinol wires are flexible, dimensionally stable and rather soft, whereas stainless steel wires are stronger and offer good support. This results in different fields of application for the various wire materials. As a standard coronary wire, a wire with moderate support and a soft tip should be chosen. If more support is needed, firmer wires (extra support wires) can be used up to very firm wires with hard tips for the treatment of chronic vascular occlusions. Furthermore, we distinguish coated wires from uncoated wires. A coating is particularly helpful in the case of a very tortuous course of the vessel or in the passage of heavily calcified vessel sections or highly calcified stenoses.

> The first choice wire should be uncoated, provide moderate support and have a soft tip. Only as a second choice are harder wires or coated wires used. The harder the wire and the coating it carries, the higher the risk of perforation and dissection.

2

2.4.2 Coronary Perforation by the Coronary Wire

Coronary perforations during coronary wire placement can occur at various locations within the coronary vessel. Whenever the coronary wire encounters resistance, there is a possibility that the wire tip will deviate and perforate due to increased forces on the wire tip during this maneuver. In most cases, perforation can be observed in the area of one end of the vessel or, if the wire is mislocated, in a small side branch of the main vessel. However, severe calcification of the vessel with plaques or severe tortuosity of the coronary artery can also lead to perforations. Especially when using hydrophilic wires, it is often difficult to feel resistance on the wire, so in this case there is an increased risk of perforation. It is therefore particularly important when using coated wires to always place them under visual control and to pre-bend the wire tip to match the vessel morphology and position of the target lesion in the vessel. This is the only way to ensure controllability in the direction of rotation and to avoid friction with the vessel wall as best as possible.

If the wire is perforated, the severity of the perforation may vary. The Ellis classification helps to classify perforations (see also ▶ Sect. 2.5). Type III perforation in particular, which occurs mainly in very complex vascular situations, especially type B2 and type C stenoses, chronic vascular occlusions and small vessels with a diameter <2.5 mm, should be taken seriously as it is associated with a pericardial tamponade risk of 63%. The risk of tamponade in type I perforations is 8% and in type II perforations 13% (Ellis et al. 1994).

If clinically relevant pericardial tamponade occurs as a result of the wire perforation, the defect must be immediately covered endovascularly and antagonization of the administered heparin with protamine must be performed. Prolonged balloon dilatation, implantation of a covered stent, or even targeted embolization of the coronary artery may be considered as measures to cover the defect. If the bleeding does not stop and the patient does not stabilize under these mea-

sures, he or she should be quickly transferred to surgical therapy. Even after completion of a supposedly uncomplicated procedure, if the patient's hemodynamics and clinical condition suddenly deteriorate, a delayed pericardial tamponade with compression of the right heart must always be considered and echocardiography must be performed immediately to rule out a relevant pericardial effusion (for pericardiocentesis in the cardiac catheterization laboratory, see ▶ Sect. 2.6).

2.4.3 Coronary Dissection by the Coronary Wire

The mechanism for dissection by the coronary wire is similar to the mechanism that leads to the development of perforations. Nevertheless, there are some peculiarities. Already during intubation with the guide catheter it is important to ensure that the true lumen has been intubated and that a false lumen has not already been created at the ostium of the coronary vessel, into which one can then easily get with the coronary wire and enlarge the dissection. Whenever increased resistance is felt at the wire, the correct wire position should be verified radiographically. In particular, if wire malposition and dissecting are suspected, balloons or stents should not be advanced over the malpositioned wire and inflated, as the increase in dissecting may lead to vessel occlusion. The wire tip should always be free, mobile as well as rotatable. If, on the other hand, the wire is trapped and stands up when manipulated or if a dissecting membrane is already visible, the position of the wire should be corrected or a second wire should be advanced in the true lumen (◘ Fig. 2.38).

If the coronary wire has to go a longer distance already supplied with stents, it is often helpful to use a wire with a small steel olive at the tip, the so-called Magnum wire (◘ Fig. 2.39). This has a high tendency to remain intraluminal, does not become entangled and brings a very low risk of dissection.

The strategy for chronic total occlusion (CTO) must be distinguished from the proce-

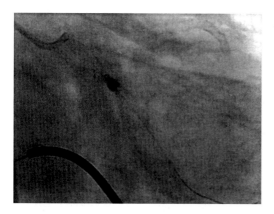

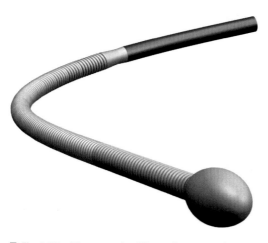

◧ **Fig. 2.39** Magnum wire (Biotronik company)

dure described above. In this case, the subintimal space, for example, is deliberately visited and dissected with a very strong wire in order to bridge the occlusion and then re-enter the true lumen with the wire behind the occlusion.

2.4.4 Wire Rupture in the Coronary Vessel

Rupture of the wire with loss of wire components in the coronary vessel is a rare complication (Stellin et al. 1987). Especially when using the so-called jailed-wire technique in the context of a bifurcation intervention, the soft tip may break off when the wire, which has been jailed to mark the side branch, is pulled back. Knowing this, coated wires should not be

jailed if possible, otherwise the coating may be detached from the wire during retraction and it may then embolize into the coronary vessel. Furthermore, the Magnum wire, with its steel olive at the wire tip, must not be jailed. If this wire is pulled back, the tip with the olive would most likely break off or the distal end of the stent would be damaged. If embolization of wire components occurs, an attempt can be made to retrieve embolized stents with a snare or to fix them with a stent, analogous to the retrieval of embolized stents (Eggebrecht et al. 2000). Other situations in which wires may rupture intracoronary are the passage of pre-implanted stents, the situation in the course of rotablation or during probing/passage of highly complex lesions (Foster-Smith et al. 1995).

2.5 Complications of Balloon Dilatation

Michael Markant

2.5.1 Introduction

The first balloon dilatation was performed in 1977 by Andreas Grüntzig and remained for almost a decade the only alternative to bypass surgery for the targeted treatment of stenosis of the coronary arteries. In 1986, the first intracoronary stents were implanted in humans by Ulrich Sigwart and Jacques Puel (Sigwart et al. 1987). In the 1990s, after the establishment of dual platelet aggregation inhibition, the proportion of stents in intracoronary interventions increased massively and is currently around 85% (Bonzel et al. 2008).

Since 1977, the material properties and also the shape of the balloon catheters have developed significantly, so that on the one hand the complexity of the procedures performed has increased considerably, but on the other hand the complication rate has decreased significantly. The first balloon catheter was made of polyvinyl chloride (PVC), a material with low compliance. Since then, there have been great advances in balloon profile, flexibility, compliance, advancement properties, and refolding properties after balloon inflation. Nowadays, a distinction is made between balloons with high ("compliant"), medium ("semi-compliant") and low compliance ("non-compliant"). The higher the compliance of a balloon, the more the balloon diameter increases with increasing inflation pressure. The common balloon materials are currently polyolefin, nylon, plastomer, polyethylene, polyester and urethane (King and Yeung 2007; Krakau 1999).

Special balloon catheters are available for the treatment of very hard, calcified coronary stenoses. An example of such a balloon catheter is the so-called cutting balloon. This is a "non-compliant" balloon with 3–4 integrated microsurgical blades, so-called atherotomes, attached longitudinally to its surface. This sets a "controlled dissection" in the stenosis area (Krakau 1999; Martin-Reyes et al. 2010; Ozaki et al. 2010; Park et al. 2010). As an alternative to dilatation with a cutting balloon, these very hard stenoses can be dilated with a high-pressure balloon or rotablated in the traditional manner. In all of the above cases, a very high risk of dissection must always be assumed.

2.5.2 Balloon Angioplasty Alone, POBA

Despite the dominance of stenting, there are still constant, and in some cases even increasing, indications for balloon dilatation alone. These include, in particular, side-branch dilatation in bifurcation procedures and the treatment of in-stent restenosis with an uncoated or, increasingly, with a drug-eluting balloon (DEB) (Scheller et al. 2006, 2008; Unverdorben et al. 2009; Fanggiday et al. 2008; Erbel et al. 1998) or, in individual cases, with a cutting balloon (Park et al. 2010). Typical domains of exclusive balloon dilatation are small vessel branches (diameter <2.0–2.5 mm), vessel segments in which stent deployment is unsuccessful, and situations in which prolonged dual antiplatelet therapy (acetylsalicylic acid plus ADP receptor antagonist) or triple therapy (oral anticoagulant plus acetylsalicylic acid plus ADP receptor antagonist) should be avoided.

2.5.3 Success Rate of Balloon Angioplasty

The evaluation of the success of balloon dilatation can basically be performed according to morphological and hemodynamic aspects. From a morphological point of view, success is defined as at least a 20% reduction in stenosis severity with a final stenosis grade <50%. If additional stenting is performed, a final stenosis grade <30% is required. From a hemodynamic point of view, the post-interventional freedom from symptoms of the patient and the improvement of the fractional flow reserve (FFR) (post-intervention >0.9) are expressions of the procedure success (Pijls et al. 2002).

The influencing factors that significantly determine the primary success rate of balloon dilatation alone are morphological and anatomical vessel characteristics (DiLuzio et al. 1998; Ellis et al. 1990; Maier et al. 2001). For example, a 1998 study showed a success rate of 77.9% in type A class (ACC/AHA stenosis classification), 73.9% in type B1 (1 characteristic from the B group), 54.0% in B2 (>1 characteristic from the B group), and 32.5% in C after balloon dilatation (DiLuzio et al. 1998). Additional predictors of success rate are patient comorbidities. In particular, diabetics (Ellis et al. 1990) and dialysis patients (Ahmed et al. 1994) have a lower primary success rate.

Comparison of procedure success rates shows a significantly lower primary success rate in the pre-stent era (1985–1986), 81.8%, than in the early stent era (1997–1998, stent percentage 70%), 92% ($p < 0.001$) (Williams et al. 2000).

The characteristics of the so-called type A, B, and C lesions are presented below (classification of the ACC/AHA; Ellis et al. 1990).

Type A lesions (high success rate [85%], low risk):
- Discrete, length <10 mm
- Concentric
- Easily accessible
- Non-angulated segment (<45°)
- Smooth contour
- Little or no calcification
- Not completely closed

- Not ostial situated
- No major branches involved
- No thrombus present

Type B lesions (intermediate success rate [60–85%], intermediate risk):
- Tubular (length 10–20 mm)
- Eccentric
- Moderate tortuosity of the proximal segment
- Moderately angulated segment (45–90°)
- Irregular contour
- Moderate or severe calcification
- Complete closure with an age <3 months
- Ostial localization
- Bifurcation lesion with the need for a double wire technique
- Thrombus present

Type C lesion (low success rate [60%], high risk):
- Diffuse (length >20 mm)
- Excessive tortuosity of the proximal segment
- Extremely angled segment (>90°)
- Complete vessel occlusion >3 months old or bridging collaterals or both.
- Impossibility to protect larger side branches
- Degenerated venous bypasses with friable lesions

> The success rate of balloon dilatation depends on morphological and anatomical vessel characteristics as well as clinical conditions. Its assessment is always morphological and hemodynamic.

Typical complications of balloon dilatation include prolonged angina, vascular dissection and perforation, emergency bypass surgery, myocardial infarction, vascular occlusion, vasospasm, hypotension, bradycardia, ventricular fibrillation, and intrahospital death (Dorros et al. 1983), and cerebral embolic complications (Table 2.2; Galbreath et al. 1986).

Compared with the early balloon dilatation phase (1977–1983), later (1985–1996) complication rates remained relatively high despite better materials and adequate experience, with increasing complexity and risk-taking by surgeons in the procedures performed (Srinivas et al. 2002; Alderman et al. 1996). Increased numbers of patients with chronic heart failure, unstable angina, three-vessel coronary disease, and left main stenoses, as well as diabetics, dialysis patients,

Table 2.2 Complication rate of balloon dilatation or stenting (2002) (Dorros et al. 1983; Galbreath et al. 1986; Srinivas et al. 2002; Wyman et al. 1988; Steffenino et al. 1988; Alderman et al. 1996; Holmes et al. 1988)

	1983 (%)	1990 (%)	1996 (%)	2002 (76% stent) (%)
Prolonged angina pectoris	7.9			
Myocardial infarction	4.8		2.1	0.8
Coronary vessel occlusion	4.7		9.5	1.5
Coronary vasospasm	4.2			
Vascular dissection	9.2		9	11
Emergency bypass surgery	6.8	5.9	10.2	1.9
Blood pressure drop	2.1			
Bradycardia	1.7			
Ventricular fibrillation	1.6			
Hospital mortality	1.1			0.9
1-year mortality	4.1			4.9
Cerebral embolic complications	0.2			

2

patients older than 65 years, and women have undergone coronary intervention (Maier et al. 2001; Lambert et al. 1988; Stein et al. 1995; Agirbasli et al. 2000; Ahmed et al. 1994; Little et al. 1993; Alderman et al. 1996; Holmes et al. 1988).

The stent era shows a reduction in complication rates compared with 1996 data (Srinivas et al. 2002), with the exception of in-hospital and 1-year mortality (Srinivas et al. 2002; Wyman et al. 1988; Steffenino et al. 1988).

In a 1990 study of 7246 coronary interventions, 5.9% of patients required bypass surgery during hospitalization because of a failed balloon dilatation attempt. 80.5% of these patients had persistent myocardial ischemia. The mortality rate during hospitalization was 1.4% in the operated patients (Talley et al. 1990).

When dilating with a drug-eluting balloon, the complication rate in the treatment of in-stent restenosis after 12–24 months in terms of myocardial infarction rate is 0–4%, the mortality rate is 3–4%, subacute occlusion has not been shown in any case so far, and stroke occurred in 0–4% of patients (Scheller et al. 2006, 2008; Unverdorben et al. 2009). In the treatment of bifurcation stenosis with subsequent dilatation of the main branch, a registry of 20 patients showed no vessel occlusion and no major complication after 4 months (Fanggiday et al. 2008).

Today, the ACC/AHA lesion classification (see above), especially in combination with other clinical parameters, allows an approximate estimation of the intervention risk (Ellis et al. 1990; Maier et al. 2001). The clinical parameters listed below are associated with an increased risk of complications.

Criteria (arranged hierarchically) for increased risk of major complication with PTCA (Maier et al. 2001):
- Acute myocardial infarction
- Expired myocardial infarction
- Unstable angina pectoris
- Angina pectoris CCS III–IV
- Concomitant valvular heart disease
- Significant CK increase
- Limited LV function
- Stenosis morphology

- Multi-vessel disease
- TIMI flow
- Vascular occlusion
- Calcification
- Proximal vascular segment
- Bifurcation lesion/double wire technique
- Multiple stenoses per segment
- Diffuse stenosis length
- Female gender
- Higher age

> Stent implantation leads to a reduction in complication rates compared to balloon dilatation alone. Certain patient groups, such as diabetics, women, patients >65 years, dialysis patients and patients with chronic heart failure, tend to have increased complication rates.

2.5.4 Dissections After Balloon Angioplasty

Dilatation of the coronary vessel is caused by stretching of the arterial wall and compression of the plaque as well as tears in the atherosclerotic plaque. However, this may also cause dissections in the vascular intima with immediate hemodynamic effects and the risk of acute vascular occlusion. In the pre-stent era, these dissections were the major cause of procedure-related morbidity and mortality (King and Yeung 2007; Dorros et al. 1983; Srinivas et al. 2002; Talley et al. 1990).

A distinction must be made between vessel dissection caused by balloon dilatation and so-called spontaneous dissection, which is observed with a prevalence of approx. 1.1% during diagnostic cardiac catheterization. Possible causes are plaque ruptures, heavy physical exertion and hormonal influences during pregnancy or contraception (Hering et al. 1998).

The correct choice of balloon size is crucial for a successful and less traumatic intervention. In general, the smaller the balloon, the lower the risk of dissection. For dilatation alone without subsequent stenting, a balloon diameter to vessel inner lumen ratio of 0.9–1.1:1 is recommended (Nichols et al. 1989; Roubin et al. 1988). The estimation of the inner vessel lumen is quite difficult in clinical practice, because diffuse vascular changes or vasospasm may lead to an underestimation of the true lumen. In the area of the right coronary artery, the rule of thumb is that the lumen is approximately 3.5 mm for a normal-sized vessel. In case of uncertainty, it is always possible to measure the stenoses exactly with the image processing software of the fluoroscopy system or, if necessary, to perform an IVUS (intravascular ultrasound) examination.

Another important criterion for balloon selection is its length. The balloon length should be such that it is possible to completely cover the existing stenosis. Multiple dilatations with a shorter balloon can lead to frequent dissections (Brymer et al. 1991). However, in very long lesions and diffusely altered vessels or very tortuous vasculature, it may be very difficult to advance an appropriately long balloon into the stenosis. In very rigid or highly calcified short-stretch stenoses, length-fitting balloons have the disadvantage of slipping out of the stenosis when inflated. In these situations, the use of a grip balloon, which has knobs on its surface, can be helpful. These fix the balloon in the lesion. To minimize the risk of vessel dissection in healthy vessel segments due to a balloon that is too long, predilation should be performed with a longer balloon of smaller diameter. Subsequently, the desired stenosis reduction can be achieved by using a shorter balloon with a suitable diameter.

The duration of balloon inflation should be 30–60 s for balloon dilatation alone, since a longer inflation time has not been shown to reduce the restenosis rate. Longer inflation times are only useful in the event of perforation or dissection occurring in the dilatation area if a stent is not to be used. Underlying studies have shown that the speed of inflation has no influence on the outcome (Ohman et al. 1994; Garrahy et al. 1991; Blankenship et al. 1999; Staudacher et al. 1991).

If a dissection occurs during balloon dilatation, it can take on very different dimensions and have very different consequences. A classification of the National Heart, Lung and Blood Institute (NHLBI; ▫ Table 2.3) divides dissections into six different types (Huber et al. 1991; Albertal et al. 2001).

▫ **Table 2.3** NHLBI classification of coronary vessel dissections

Type A	Local filling defect in the coronary lumen during contrast passage ("haziness")
Type B	Parallel filling defect in the coronary lumen during contrast passage (larger longitudinal tear)
Type C	Persistent contrast striae outside the vessel lumen (partial detachment of the plaque)
Type D1	Spiral filling defect with normal contrast medium outflow (spiral dissection)
Type D2	Spiral filling defect with delayed contrast medium outflow
Type E	Newly appeared persistent intraluminal filling defect (often thrombus)
Type F	Dissections leading to complete occlusion of the coronary artery (thrombus possible)

Huber et al. (1991) and Albertal et al. (2001)

Depending on the severity of the dissection, either no further therapy is necessary (especially for types A and B) (Huber et al. 1991; Albertal et al. 2001) or direct stent implantation (types C to F). Immediate aortocoronary bypass surgery is available as ultima ratio and still today a proven means for the treatment of endovascular unmanageable dissection. Nowadays, however, it is only very rarely necessary, since most dissections can be repaired by direct stent implantation (Preisack et al. 1998; Carlino et al. 2011; Darwazah et al. 2009).

In a 1989 study, 1346 patients with a vascular tear or dissection after balloon dilatation without immediate vascular occlusion had an ischemic complication, defined as angina, myocardial infarction, emergency bypass surgery, or death, in 9%. Predictors of an ischemic complication were dissection length, evidence of extraluminal contrast, and residual degree of stenosis after dilation (Black et al. 1989). Furthermore, an ischemic complication was more common in patients

2

who had unstable angina or total vessel occlusion before balloon dilatation (Black et al. 1989).

> The correct selection of balloon size and length as well as the duration of balloon inflation is crucial for the prevention of dissection following balloon dilatation. If dissection has occurred, the clinical status and angiographic assessment of the extent of dissection are crucial for further therapy.

2.5.5 Restenosis After Balloon Angioplasty

With regard to restenosis after dilatation, a distinction must be made between restenosis occurring immediately and restenosis occurring in the following weeks after the intervention. In the first minutes after balloon inflation, an elastic recoil (restoring force) causes a lumen loss of up to 50% in the dilatation area (Block 1990). The more the vessel is overstretched by the balloon, the more pronounced the recoil, suggesting that it is a more elastic phenomenon. Because of this phenomenon, control imaging of the dilated vessel segment should be performed after several minutes (5–10) of balloon dilatation alone (Kawaguchi et al. 2002; Daniel et al. 1996; Kuntz et al. 1993; Fischman et al. 1994; Ueda et al. 1991; Rozenman et al. 1993; Rensing et al. 1990; Mintz et al. 1996a, b). In the subsequent weeks after dilation, restenosis may occur by smooth muscle cell and myofibroblast proliferation and migration (neointima formation) and by lumen-reducing remodeling of the vessel wall (negative remodeling) (Block 1990; Majesky 1994). These two later mechanisms result in a restenosis rate of approximately 30% (12–50%) within the first 4 months. After more than 4 months, further restenosis occurs in only about 1–2% (Serruys et al. 1988; Glazier et al. 1989; Kaltenbach et al. 1985; Quigley et al. 1986; Luo et al. 1996; Lafont et al. 1995; Mintz et al. 1996b). In general, the rate of restenosis is dependent on clinical, anatomical, and procedural factors. It is increased in certain groups of patients, particularly diabetics and patients

Table 2.4 NHLBI classification of restenosis after balloon angioplasty

NHLBI 1	Increase in diameter stenosis of >30% from post PCI to follow-up examination
NHLBI 2	Increase in diameter stenosis of >70% from post PCI to follow-up examination
NHLBI 3	Lumen decrease to pre-PCI diameter stenosis values +10%
NHLBI 4	Loss of at least 50% of the initial PCI gain at the time of the follow-up examination

Serruys et al. (1988, 1993)

with chronic renal failure (Lambert et al. 1988; Stein et al. 1995; Ahmed et al. 1994; Block 1990). Furthermore, there is a principally increased risk of restenosis in balloon dilatation in the area of the proximal left coronary artery, the ostium of the right coronary artery and a venous bypass as well as in the reopening of chronically occluded vessels (Block 1990; Violaris et al. 1995).

It should be noted that the comparison of restenosis rates in different studies is limited because different definitions of restenosis are used. The most common definitions from the pre-stent era are the four definitions listed in Table 2.4 (Serruys et al. 1988, 1993).

> As a result of balloon dilatation, functional and morphological changes occur that can lead to restenosis acutely and within the following 4 months. In order to detect the acute changes, a control imaging several minutes after dilatation is useful. Clinical, anatomical and procedural factors influence the restenosis rate.

2.5.6 Vascular Occlusions After Balloon Angioplasty

Acute vascular occlusion is an event that occurred in approximately 4.7–9.5% of patients overall in the pre-stent era (Galbreath et al. 1986; Srinivas et al. 2002; Alderman et al. 1996; Detre et al. 1990; Lincoff et al. 1992). In a study of patients with unstable angina, the rate of acute vascular occlusion was 13% (Grassman et al. 1994). If thrombus is suspected, administration of a GPIIbIIIa antagonist or further heparin administration, possibly ACT-guided, should be considered. Predictors of acute occlusion during balloon dilatation include, in particular, diffuse vascular disease, eccentric plaques, severe calcifications, highly angulated segments, ostial lesions, bifurcation lesions, and the presence of thrombus (Tsang et al. 1998; DiLuzio et al. 1998; Grassman et al. 1994). Temporary occlusions in the sense of coronary spasm occur regularly and respond well to intracoronary nitrate administration. A special form is the so-called concertina effect (■ Fig. 2.40). This is an intimal pucker that is occasionally persistent and responds only with delay to vasospasmolytic measures. Vascular occlusion can also occur as a result of dissection. For further clarification of the cause, the application of a microcatheter and the careful administration of contrast medium via the microcatheter as well as the administration of heparin, GPIIbIIIa antagonists, glycerol trinitrate, adenosine or nitroprusside sodium via this microcatheter for therapy can be considered.

2.5.7 Coronary Perforation After Balloon Angioplasty

Coronary perforation is a very rare complication with a prevalence of 0.43% (Shimony et al. 2011). The severity of coronary perforation is divided into three types according to the Ellis classification (Ellis et al. 1994; ■ Table 2.5).

Predisposing risk factors for coronary perforation include treatment of complex lesions and more aggressive treatment strategies using rotablation, use of a cutting balloon, or even the use of laser angioplasty (Shimony et al. 2011; Quan et al. 2005).

Immediate clinical complications of perforation include hemodynamically effective pericardial tamponade and acute myocardial infarction, including death. The therapy required depends on the extent and clinical impact of the perforation. Pericardial tamponade occurs in 0.4% of type I perforations, 3.3% of type II perforations, and 45.7% of type III perforations (Shimony et al. 2011). Mortality is 0.3% in type I perforations, 0.4% in type II perforations, and 21.2% in type III perforations.

Therapy is based on the extent of the perforation. In type I and type II perforations, observation or prolonged balloon dilatation (average dilatation time 13 min) with continued ASA and heparin administration is usually sufficient. If a satisfactory treatment

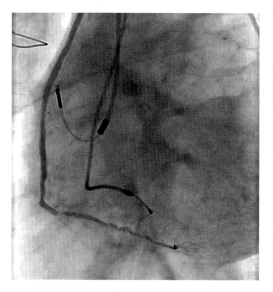

■ **Fig. 2.40** Concertina effect

■ **Table 2.5** Ellis classification of vascular perforations

Type I	Extraluminal crater without extravasation
Type II	Pericardial or myocardial KM staining without contrast jet extravasation
Type III	Extravasation through a free perforation (≥1 mm)

Ellis et al. (1994)
In addition, there is type III perforation into an anatomically preexisting cavity, e.g., the coronary sinus

result is not achieved despite these measures, implantation of a covered stent should be considered (Ellis et al. 1994; Shimony et al. 2011).

Type III perforation occurs mainly in very complex vascular situations, especially type B2 and type C stenoses, chronic vascular occlusions and small vessels <2.5 mm in diameter. In about half of the cases it is triggered by balloon dilatation alone, half by "compliant" and half by "non-compliant" balloons. In about 20% of cases it is caused by the guidewire itself and in 4% by rotablation.

Treatment options for type III coronary perforation include prolonged balloon inflation, which is performed for an average of more than 30 min, implantation of a covered stent, or targeted coilembolization. The success of these different treatment concepts varies considerably. While balloon dilatation alone has a success rate of only 55%, the implantation of a covered stent has a success rate of 85% and that of coilembolization is 100%. Rapid aortocoronary bypass surgery and suturing of the vascular defect is required in approximately 16% of type III perforations. If one of the aforementioned treatment modalities does not achieve an adequate treatment result, a combination of multiple treatment strategies (required in approximately 40%) is usually employed (Ellis et al. 1994; Shimony et al. 2011; Al-Lamee et al. 2011).

Overall, type III perforation is very rare in everyday clinical practice, but certain situations are associated with a very high risk of its occurrence. One risk factor is the unclear position of the wire (see ▶ Sect. 2.4).

❯ A relevant coronary perforation is a very rare event. In very complex situations and with unclear guidewire position, the risk for perforation is significantly increased. In case of uncomplicated dilatation and subsequent sudden clinical and hemodynamic deterioration of the patient, perforation with subsequent pericardial tamponade must be considered, echocardiography and, if necessary, pericardiocentesis must be performed immediately.

2.5.8 Need for Bypass Surgery After Balloon Angioplasty

Overall, the need for emergency bypass surgery has decreased over the past 30 years. Whereas in the pre-stent era bypass surgery was the treatment of choice for severe dissections, nowadays stent implantation can achieve an adequate treatment result in the vast majority of cases. In a 2002 analysis, the need for emergency bypass surgery was shown in 0.61% of patients for the period 1992–2000. The cause was extensive dissection in 54% of cases, perforation in 20%, and recurrent acute vascular occlusion in 20% of cases. As the rate of stenting increased during this period (1992: 5%, 2000: 56%), the need for emergency bypass surgery also decreased from 1.5% (1992) to 0.14% (2000) (Seshadri et al. 2002).

❯ The need for emergency bypass surgery has decreased significantly over the past 30 years due to the increasing possibility of stent implantation in the event of vascular dissection, occlusion, or perforation (implantation of a covered stent).

2.5.9 Dilatation of Ostial Stenoses and Bifurcation Stenoses

Ostial stenoses in the narrow sense are branch stenoses of the left and right coronary artery from the aorta. Sometimes the term ostial stenosis is also used for stenoses of the side branches of both coronary vessels. Balloon dilatation of ostial stenoses has been shown to have lower success rates (74% versus 91%), increased complication rates, and increased restenosis rates compared with non-ostial stenoses, in part due to increased elastic recoil in the aortic wall (Topol et al. 1987; Tan et al. 1995b; Mathias et al. 1991; Ten Berg et al. 1996). In the treatment of bifurcation stenosis, the exact extent of stenosis of the main and side branches is a predictor of the complication rate and the success rate of the procedure. To describe the stenosis localization in the main and side branch, the classification according to Medina is currently the most common (Medina et al. 2006).

Medina classification:

- Stenosis (1) or no stenosis (0) in the main branch before side-branch takeoff
- Stenosis (1) or no stenosis (0) in the main branch after side branch takeoff
- Stenosis (1) or no stenosis (0) in the side branch outlet

Examples:

- 1–0–0: Stenosis only in the main branch before side-branch takeoff
- 0–0–1: Stenosis only in the lateral branch.

The most common strategy in the treatment of bifurcation stenosis is stenting of the main branch followed by simultaneous dilatation of the main and side branches in the sense of a "kissing balloon procedure". If the side-branch outlet itself is already stenosed pre-interventionally, the risk of side-branch occlusion after stenting of the main branch is significantly increased. In this case, preinterventional "marking" of the side branch with a guide wire is recommended, especially for side branches >2 mm ("jailed wire technique"). This approach facilitates re-wiring of the side branch through the stent struts either with another wire or with the wire previously located in the main branch. If the side branch diameter is <2 mm, its occlusion should be accepted. Another way to avoid side-branch occlusion is to terminate the procedure without implanting a stent if a very good dilatation result was achieved (Pan et al. 2011; van Leeuwen et al. 1989; Nanto et al. 1990; George et al. 1986; Pinkerton and Slack 1985; Tamura et al. 2011; Godino et al. 2010).

2.5.10 Dilatation of Long Stenoses

The primary success rate of balloon dilatation is reduced in long stenoses (>20 mm) (Appelman et al. 1996; Tan et al. 1995a, b).

The restenosis rate correlates positively with the stenosis length (Anderson et al. 1993). A randomized controlled trial investigated the additional benefit of stent implantation after previous dilatation of long stenoses (>20 mm) with morphologically very good results ($n = 437$). After 9 months, there was no superiority in the stent group with regard to success and complication rates (Serruys et al. 2002). A more recent study compared DES implantation alone and DEB dilation, with or without DES implantation, for longer stenoses (>25 mm, mean 47 mm) in the drug-eluting stent and drug-eluting balloon era. In the DEB group, DEB dilatation alone was performed in 56% of patients with good primary outcome. In 36% of patients, DES implantation in the proximal portion of the stenosis was performed in addition to DEB dilatation due to very long stenoses. In 7% of the patients, DES implantation had to be performed subsequently due to dissection or an inadequate primary result after DEB dilatation. Both groups showed comparable primary success and complication rates and comparable complication rates in the clinical follow-up after 2 years (Costopoulos et al. 2013).

2.5.11 Dilatation of Bypass Stenoses

Balloon dilatation in venous bypass has a lower primary success rate than in native vessels and more peri- and postinterventional complications. Early complications include distal embolization, no-reflow phenomena, and myocardial infarction. In addition, restenosis is seen in >50% of patients. Interventional success in venous bypass is significantly higher after implantation of a stent than after dilatation alone (Savage et al. 1997; Platko et al. 1989; De Feyter et al. 1993; Agostoni et al. 2010; Lupi et al. 2010; Reeves et al. 1991; Weintraub et al. 1994).

Balloon dilatation in the area of the distal anastomosis of an IMA bypass is associated with a significantly lower restenosis rate than stent implantation (14% vs 80%, p 0.001) (Köckeritz et al. 2004).

2

2.6 Complications of Stent Implantation

Ralf Birkemeyer

2.6.1 Stent Loss

After the introduction of machine-crimped stents, stent failures occur much less frequently today than at the beginning of the stent era. The current incidence is only 0.3–0.9% in the sparse studies available on this subject, while older publications report an incidence of 1.6–8.3% (Brilakis et al. 2005). Nevertheless, any loss of a coronary stent still carries the risk of thrombosis or spasm in the coronary or embolic occlusion in the cerebral vasculature. The loss of coronary stents into the peripheral circulation—especially into the leg vessels—usually has no long-term consequences.

Stent loss typically occurs when the stent is advanced into a calcified and/or severely bent vessel segment or during retraction of a stent that cannot be advanced. This is further facilitated by poor backup of the guiding catheter. Regardless of coronary morphology, stents may also be lost during an attempt to retract the stent into a noncoaxially placed guiding catheter. Other typical stent loss situations include passage of a stent into an already stented side branch (bifurcation) and retraction of an already partially inflated stent. Usually the stent slipped off the balloon is still on the guidewire (☐ Fig. 2.41).

If the stent is lost at the distal end of the guiding catheter, the proximal stent meshes are usually bent open in a funnel shape. If the stent is lost during advancement or retraction in the vessel, other parts of the stent may also be bent open.

Interventional management of stent loss is primarily aimed at avoiding coronary occlusion or cerebral embolism. In principle, different strategies are available: retrieval of the stent into the guiding catheter, re-ballooning into the stent with subsequent implantation at the site of loss, or overstenting of the undeployed stent with a second stent. Surgical intervention is usually not indicated.

◼ **Stent Retrieval with Snares**
Retrieval of the unimplanted stent is in principle the most attractive solution, but in principle carries the risk that a stent lost in the coronary vessel may embolize in the aortic arch during retrieval. On the other hand, this is the obvious strategy if the stent has been stripped off the guiding catheter and is lying on the wire between the catheter and the main stem. The most common method of retrieving a stent is to grasp and retract it with a snare (☐ Fig. 2.42). Alternative retrieval devices

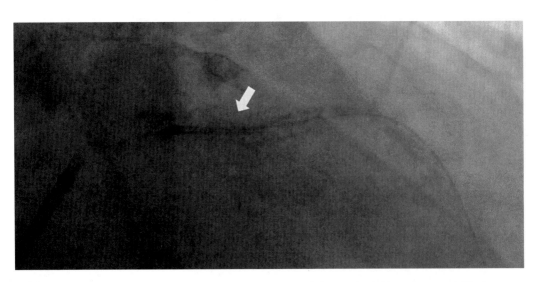

☐ **Fig. 2.41** Stent loss in the proximal LAD (during retraction of the non-pushable stent system). The lost stent still lies on the guidewire in a previously stented vessel section

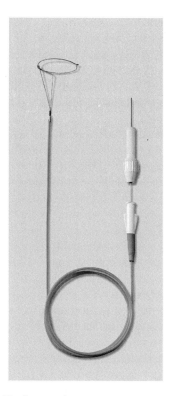

◘ Fig. 2.42 Snare catheter

◘ Fig. 2.43 Snares in various sizes (pfm medical ag)

include basket and forceps devices, but due to their size, these can only be used in the aorta.

Snares are available in various diameters (◘ Fig. 2.43). The choice of size is based on the diameter of the vessel in which they are to be used and the dimensions of the object to be grasped. Snares with a loop diameter of 2–5 mm are suitable for use in coronaries.

Fine sizing is achieved by partial retraction of the wire loop into the snare catheter. The object is grasped by pulling it tightly against the opening of the snare catheter with the loop. Grasping a stent in a coronary artery can be greatly simplified by inserting the snare over the guide wire, which is still in place. During insertion, the snare must be pulled back into the snare catheter so that it still slides well on the wire but is not damaged in the sheath or injures the vessel wall. To place the snare in the aorta or coronary artery over the stent, it is opened wider again. Care must be taken not to dislocate the stent distally during this maneuver. Preferably, the proximal portion of the stent is grasped (along with the guide-

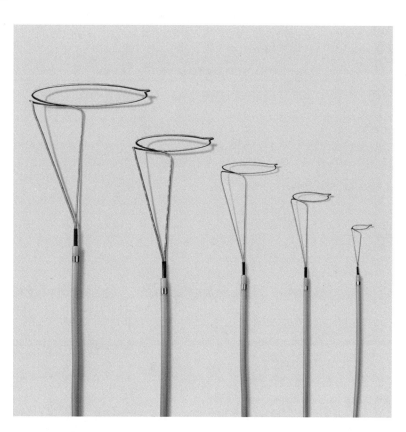

2

wire). The stent and guidewire are then slowly retracted with the snare to the distal end of the guiding catheter. Care should be taken not to pull the guiding catheter into the ostium in an uncontrolled manner, as this may cause proximal coronary dissection (◘ Figs. 2.44 and 2.45).

When the stent arrives at the distal end of the guiding catheter, resistance can often be felt, which may be due to unbending of the stent mesh or angling of the stent in the loop. It is not recommended to force the stent to retract into the guide catheter. Rather, the guiding catheter and the snare with the grasped stent and guidewire should then be retracted to the sheath in a common motion.

If the guide wire is no longer in the stent or if it is impossible to slip over the snare despite the wire being in place, an attempt can be made to push the guide wire already in place or a second guide wire through a stent mesh and repeat the maneuver over this wire.

Frequently, the withdrawal of the guiding catheter with the snared stent outside into the sheath is also associated with considerable resistance. Here, however, the attempt can be forced. Occasionally, the stent loses its integrity and can be retrieved "threadlike" (◘ Fig. 2.46).

Should the stent become detached from the sling during this maneuver and lie in the sheath below the valve, it can be retrieved there with a small clamp and thus gain access. If the stent embolizes distally in the leg, a decision must be made whether to leave it there or retrieve it. Salvage usually requires a crossover maneuver from the contralateral groin or a second antegrade puncture on the same side preferably with a larger sheath. If the stent can be retrieved with a snare and again not retracted into the sheath, an attempt can be made to remove the sheath together with the retrieved stent from the vessel.

An alternative to the snare is to advance a second guidewire parallel to the first into

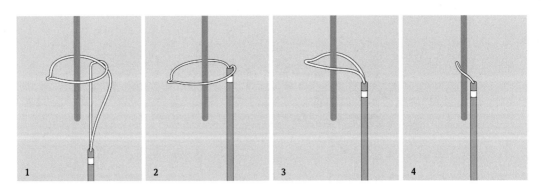

◘ **Fig. 2.44**   Snare handling level 1

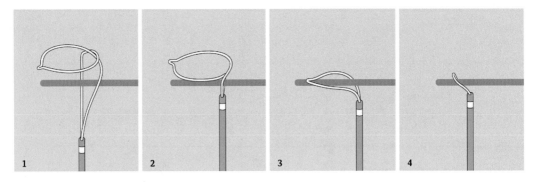

◘ **Fig. 2.45**   Snare handling level 2

Fig. 2.46 Drug eluting stents recovered by means of snare

the affected coronary artery and twist it with it. Simultaneous traction on both wires then mobilizes the stent. The disadvantage of this technique is that the twisting of the wires can unravel during the pulling movement and the stent embolizes.

Another alternative to the snare is to insert a small balloon (e.g. 1.5 mm diameter) into the undeployed stent and then inflate it in order to retract the partially deployed stent with the balloon. This maneuver is particularly promising when the stent is bent up proximally. A disadvantage of this interventional approach is the possibility that the stent can dislocate quite easily distally and, even if the maneuver is primarily successful, it will easily slip off the balloon again. If the stent is more bent up or slipped off the balloon during the maneuver described above, it may also be possible to slide a slightly larger balloon on the wire through the stent and deploy it distally. This then makes stent retrieval much easier.

Implantation of a lost stent at the site of loss also begins with the last maneuver described. However, after insufflation of the small balloon in the stent, no attempt at retraction is made, but the small balloon is replaced by a balloon of adequate diameter and the stent is then properly implanted. A fundamental limitation of this procedure is that a stent designed for small vessels that is lost in a large-diameter central coronary vessel cannot be adequately implanted even with a large balloon.

Overstenting a lost stent with a second stent is the ultima ratio. This is particularly necessary if the stent cannot be retrieved or threaded because, for example, the guide wire has become dislocated during the loss of the stent. In this case, it is recommended to pre-dilate the corresponding vessel section before the overstenting.

❯ Today, stent losses are rather sporadic events. Interventional management consists of either a retrieval technique, local implantation, or overstenting of the lost stent.

2.6.2 The Non-dilatable Stent

On closer inspection, of course, the correct diagnosis is a non-dilatable stenosis into which a stent has been advanced. This can occur when adequate lesion preparation has not been performed, for example, when a heavily calcified lesion is primarily stented. Leaving an undeployed stent in a stenosis can cause an acute increase in the degree of stenosis and thus ischemia, but more importantly it carries a significantly increased risk of stent thrombosis and also restenosis for the patient. Since both stent thrombosis and restenosis are associated with increased mortality, the situation of the non-dilatable stent is by no means only a "cosmetic" problem.

It follows from the above that a non-dilatable stent is usually avoidable by refraining from primary stenting whenever there is visible calcification. Furthermore, stenting should only be performed if the balloon used for predilatation was completely deployable (☐ Fig. 2.47).

If complete balloon deployment is not possible during predilation, other methods of lesion preparation must be used. These are essentially rotational atherectomy or a cutting or scoring balloon. The advantage of rotational ablation is that lesion passage with a special guidewire is the only technical requirement, which is usually possible. The calcified material is then removed from the proximal end as the drill head is advanced, i.e. the drill head creates its own path. In contrast, when using cutting or scoring balloons, these bulky devices must first be advanced into the lesion, which is often only possible with great difficulty or not at all. If this maneuver is successful, however, the stenosed segment can often be unfolded by dilating the stenosis several times and, if necessary, by subsequent high-pressure dilatation (☐ Fig. 2.48).

In principle, a stent should only be inserted if the lesion has been adequately prepared, i.e. is dilatable. If this is not the case, it must be decided whether the result of balloon angioplasty in conjunction with drug therapy is not

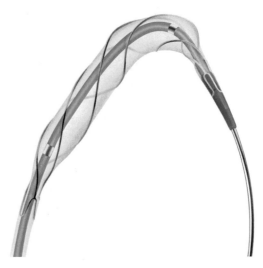

☐ **Fig. 2.48** AngioSculpt scoring balloon (Biotronik company)

☐ **Fig. 2.47** Non-balloon dilatable stentosis (high pressure balloon at 26 atm)

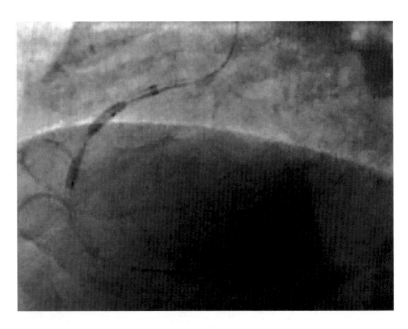

also sufficient. Alternatively, aortocoronary bypass surgery would be indicated.

If, nevertheless, a stent could not be deployed in a coronary stenosis, intensive efforts must be made to correct this result. If this is not possible, the indication for aortocoronary bypass surgery must also be made in individual cases.

The same measures that are otherwise used to prepare a calcified lesion can be considered as corrective techniques. First and foremost, this is post-dilation with a high-pressure balloon. With special balloons, dilatation up to 40 atm is possible today. However, it is important to bear in mind that this maneuver involves an increased risk of vascular rupture. Furthermore, it can be very difficult to advance a high-pressure balloon into the undeployed stent at all. Of course, the same is true for a cutting or scoring balloon. Rotablator deployment is the interventional ultima ratio. If it is possible to rotablate in the stent, a successful high-pressure dilatation can often be performed afterwards. However, rotablation in a freshly implanted, non-deployed stent generally leads to ablation of stent struts with strong heat generation, and there is a high risk of the drill head getting caught in the stent.

> A non-dilatable stent is the result of inadequate lesion preparation and can usually be avoided by a structured approach. In particular, rotational atherectomy has proven to be effective in the pretreatment of difficult-to-dilate stenoses. An undeployed stent carries an increased risk of restenosis or stent thrombosis. Therefore, a determined effort should be made to correct this inadequate primary outcome.

2.6.3 Vessel Rupture During Stent Implantation

The risk of coronary rupture is particularly present when balloon dilatation occurs within a circumferential calcific brace or, alternatively, in a vessel segment in which at least a major portion of the wall circumference is calcified. In this situation, under dilation, the balloon will expand where the wall exerts the least resistance, i.e., outside the calcific brace or in the region of the noncalcified wall. Significant shear forces will occur, favoring rupture. Rupture of the vessel is further promoted by bursting of the balloon, especially in the case of high-pressure insufflations in rough, calcified sections of the vessel, or by the choice of a balloon that is clearly too large.

Similarly, vessel rupture associated with stent implantation occurs primarily when adequate lesion preparation has not occurred and the stent must be deployed with very high pressure in a calcified lesion, or when there is a significant discrepancy between vessel and stent size, for example, at the distal end of a long stent implanted in a highly tapered vessel.

The management of vascular rupture does not depend on whether or not a stent has been implanted, but rather on the extent of the rupture. Whereas covered perforations usually present with moderate clinical symptoms, the much rarer free rupture into the pericardium often takes a dramatic course with the abrupt development of pericardial tamponade (◘ Figs. 2.49 and 2.50).

As a rule, sufficient cardiopulmonary resuscitation is impossible in the case of pericardial tamponade for mechanical reasons. As discussed in ► Sect. 2.5, type III perforations have a high mortality rate (>15%) and require rapid and structured complication management.

While in covered perforation the angiographic picture usually improves by itself (with or without balloon blockade of the affected vessel), free perforation often requires vessel repair.

The key to successful management of a free perforation is early detection and prompt balloon occlusion of the ruptured vessel. If the risk constellation is given, the vessel can be briefly injected with contrast medium under fluoroscopy after balloon deflation before the balloon is withdrawn. In this way, in the event of a rupture, the coronary artery can be blocked just a few seconds after the rupture. In any case, the retraction of the guidewire should be avoided after the occurrence of this complication. As soon as balloon occlusion has occurred, echocardiography should

2

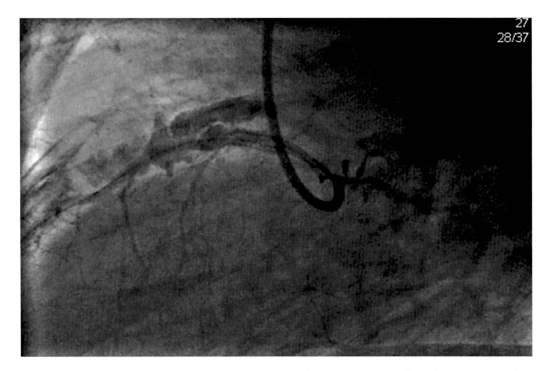

Fig. 2.49   Free perforation of the proximal LAD after stent implantation with outflow of the contrast medium into the pericardial space

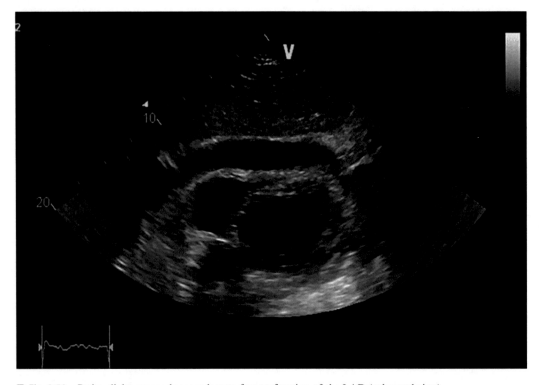

Fig. 2.50   Pericardial tamponade secondary to free perforation of the LAD (subcostal view)

be performed to look for pericardial effusion or tamponade, regardless of hemodynamics. If the pericardial effusion is hemodynamically relevant (obstructed filling/compression of the right ventricle), puncture should be performed immediately. The drainage of clear pericardial effusions that do not yet have echocardiographic relevance should also be considered, since in the course of an interventional repair the balloon occlusion must be removed, at least in the short term, and the patient may then still develop tamponade.

During balloon occlusion, it may be necessary to give the patient analgesic treatment for ischaemic pain (see also the comments on conscious sedation, ▶ Sect. 3.4.4).

It should also be borne in mind that haemodynamic instability in this situation is not always the result of tamponade alone, but may also be due to ischaemia. In this case, catecholamines may also have to be used (see also the comments on cardiogenic shock, ▶ Sect. 3.3.4).

The most elegant method of vessel repair is the implantation of a stent graft. When selecting the graft, care must be taken to ensure sufficient length (adequate landing zone proximal and distal to the perforation) and adequate diameter to achieve a sufficient seal. The major limitation of the first-generation graft was its bending stiffness, which limited its use predominantly to the proximal portions of the vessel and even there sometimes made passage impossible, especially when placed as a stent within a stent. In these cases, emergency surgery may have been necessary. The new stent grafts, which are much more flexible and thinner due to a different design, represent a significant advance in this regard. Whereas in the first generation coronary stent graft a membrane was fixed between two stents, in the modern stent grafts the membrane is applied directly to the stent in an electrospinning process. This allows the modern grafts to be advanced into almost all vessel segments and at least the smaller grafts can also be advanced via a 5F guiding catheter.

The situation is different for peripheral ruptures or perforations. As a rule, no stent graft can be used here. Prolonged balloon blockade with analgesic therapy and, if necessary, antagonization of anticoagulation with protamine administration can be attempted. Before antagonizing anticoagulation, however, the risk of thrombotic vascular complications should always be weighed, especially if foreign materials remain in the vessel for a long time afterwards. I personally tend not to antagonize anticoagulation in this situation. If balloon blockade does not have the desired success, a decision must be made whether to perform surgical vessel ligation or endovascular vessel closure. Bypass surgery is usually not an option for peripheral ruptures or perforations. If available in the cath lab, the affected end branch can be closed with coils. It should be noted that the commonly used "pushable" coils require a 0.0018 in. or even thicker microcatheter, which are not commonly used in interventional cardiology. Alternatively, a microcatheter or suction catheter can be used to carefully inject subcutaneous adipose tissue previously aspirated from the patient, a small blood clot, or other substances suitable for embolization into the vascular periphery. Some investigators also use the targeted injection of thrombin (off-label-use) in this situation. Of course, extreme care must be taken not to occlude proximal vessel segments. A ruptured smaller side branch can also be closed by overstenting with a stent graft, whereby care must be taken that the stent graft does not additionally close other larger side branches.

Patients with covered ruptures and patients with interventional closed free ruptures should still be closely monitored clinically and echocardiographically on the following days, as it is very likely that late, two-stage tamponades may occur.

■ **Performance of Pericardiocentesis**

It is advisable to standardize the performance of pericardiocentesis within a cardiology department and to keep appropriate puncture sets, which are also commercially available, to hand. This is the only way to ensure timely performance of the procedure in an emergency. Every interventional cardiologist must be able to perform pericardiocentesis independently.

Pericardiocentesis is usually performed from subcostal, but apical or in individual cases other atypical ultrasound-guided approaches are possible. In principle, pericardiocentesis involves the following steps: anesthesia and incision of the skin, anesthesia of the puncture channel up to the pericardium (in awake patients), insertion of a large-lumen puncture cannula up to the pericardial effusion. Then insertion of a guide wire into the pericardial space, introduction of a drainage tube via this and fixation of the same to the skin after removal of the wire.

In principle, subcostal or apical pericardiocentesis can be facilitated by positioning the patient in a semi-sitting position. However, this is often not done during emergency pericardiocentesis in the cardiac catheterization laboratory. In the preceding emergency echocardiography, the thickness and distribution of the pericardial effusion from subcostal or apical can be well estimated. As a rule, a subcostal approach is the best choice in the acute tamponade situation. After anesthesia, the skin is incised approximately 3–5 cm below the costal arch at the left xiphocostal angle. A spinal needle (25–27G), for example, can be used to anesthetize the puncture channel. Procedure: first vertical needle direction to a depth of 2–3 cm, then needle direction below the costal arch under aspiration in the direction of the left shoulder until pericardial effusion or blood is aspirated, in the forward and backward direction setting of local anaesthetic deposits. The direction of the puncture can be varied depending on the echocardiographic findings.

Subsequently, the puncture cannula is advanced in the same way under aspiration. When passing the parietal pericardium, a "give" is felt, when reaching the epicardial pericardium, cardiac motion is felt. The puncture needle should be at least 120 mm long and have an adequate inner lumen for the advancement of a 0.035 in. wire (18–19G). Pericardiocentesis needles with removable stylet are commercially available. When puncturing a tamponade after coronary rupture, the correct location in the pericardial space is sometimes not easily distinguished from a puncture of the right ventricle

without further imaging. The swab test and a Hb determination in the punctate cannot help here by their very nature. In principle, fluoroscopic or echocardiographic imaging should be used in this situation. In the first case, a 0.035 in. wire is advanced under fluoroscopy. This will move around the heart if positioned correctly. In the second case, echocontrast can be injected over the puncture needle under echocontrol (parasternal view); often even the tip of the puncture needle can be visualized in the pericardial space.

In principle, it makes sense to insert a drainage tube over a 0.035 guide wire during a tamponade in order to be able to aspirate any blood that continues to flow in the course. Often, the stitch canal is dilated over the wire with an 6F or 8F dilator and then an 6F–8F pigtail is inserted into the pericardial space as a drainage system. Unfortunately, the peripheral openings of the pigtail catheter clot easily, so that even if blood cannot be aspirated, tamponade can develop again. Therefore, the pigtail catheter must be flushed after each aspiration and in case of renewed hemodynamic instability, even with the drain in place, echocardiography must be performed immediately to exclude the possibility of renewed tamponade, especially since the hemopericardium can also chamber due to clot formation. We prefer a percutaneous 6F nephrostomy catheter to the pigtail because of the larger side holes, which is advanced via a peel-away sheath. The catheter is fixed with a skin suture after usually the first outflow from the sheath has already noticeably improved hemodynamics. The tip of the catheter should be positioned caudally in the pericardium under imaging so that it is at the lowest point in the seated patient. This allows complete suction of the hemopericardium. Usually, the drainage tube is connected to a drainage bag for this purpose and the drainage is left on drainage until the final repair of the coronary artery after a perforation.

In the further course, the drainage is flushed and clamped. A new suction is performed every 6 h if hemodynamic stability is maintained. The drain is removed when no more blood flows or less than 75 ml/24 h serous effusion is formed. However, if a larger

☐ **Table 2.6**   Composition of a pericardiocentesis set

Measure	Resources
Local anesthesia skin	e.g. 1% lidocaine solution/skin needle
Incision	Scalpel
Local anaesthesia of the stitch canal	e.g. 1% lidocaine solution/25–27G spinal needle
Pericardiocentesis	e.g. 120 mm 18G pericardiocentesis needle with stylet
Guide wire	e.g. 0.0035 J-wire
Dilatation of the puncture channel	e.g. 6F–8F dilator (peel away airlock if necessary)
Pericardial drainage	e.g. 6F–8F pigtail (if necessary nephrostomy catheter) plus collection bag with adapter for drainage (if necessary with sideport for suction)

amount of blood is still detected in the pericardial space by echocardiography, depending on the degree of coagulation and localization, further puncture or surgical evacuation is performed to counteract the development of constrictive pericarditis (☐ Table 2.6).

❯ Free coronary perforations are a rare but vital complication. The immediate threat to the patient lies in the development of pericardial tamponade and possibly in the occurrence of ischemic pump failure. The first goal of interventional management is therefore to secure hemodynamics by means of balloon blockade of the perforated vessel and, if necessary, the generous performance of pericardiocentesis. If spontaneous vessel occlusion does not occur after anticoagulation under balloon occlusion (possibly with anticoagulation), an attempt is usually made to seal the rupture site with a stent graft or, in the case of peripheral ruptures, to occlude the vessel by dropping coils or appropriate measures.

2.6.4   Edge Dissection

A common complication after stent implantation is marginal dissection. Although non-flow obstructing dissections are asymptomatic and often heal without sequelae, even small angiographically visible dissections are a significant predictor for the occurrence of subacute or early stent thrombosis. Therefore, after stent implantation, they should be looked for at least angiographically in two planes. Treatment of marginal dissection consists of implantation of another overlapping stent. If another stent with a smaller lumen is placed distally to the first implanted stent, it is recommended to dilate the transition zone with an adequately sized balloon to ensure apposition of the distal stent in the transition zone. With the more frequent use of OCT imaging, it has become apparent that very small edge dissections after stent implantation are the rule rather than the exception. This raises the question, which has not yet been conclusively answered, of the extent to which small edge dissections should be treated with another stent.

2.6.5   Closure of Side Branches

In particular, stenosed side branches can be occluded accidentally by overstenting. The extent to which this remains clinically asymptomatic or leads to myocardial ischemia with enzyme elevation depends on the size of the side branch and the collateralization situation.

As a result, a decision must be made prior to stenting as to which side branches should be retained or treated. It is recommended to protect size-relevant side branches before stenting by inserting a guide wire, which is also stented over. These wires are usually sufficient to maintain flow in the side branch and may also facilitate the advancement of another wire through the stent meshes into the side branch. There is controversy as to whether a relevant side-branch stenosis should be pre-stretched before overstenting or treated with a kissing-balloon maneuver afterward. The rationale for not pre-expanding is that the

2

side branch may be dissected and it may be necessary to insert a guide wire through the meshes of the main branch stent into the dissected side branch in the further course of the intervention, which is technically difficult and not always successful.

■ **Interventional Management**

In case of occlusion of a relevant side branch after stent implantation in the main branch, we stick to the stenting technique as long as the side branch does not show a high-grade ostial stenosis after the kissing-balloon maneuver. In case of flow obstructing dissections, we switch to a two-branch technique. Sometimes it is impossible to advance a second wire through the stent meshes into the side branch after stent implantation despite the presence of an over-stented wire in the side branch. In these cases, careful attempts can be made to advance a small balloon on the over-stented wire and use it to dilate the ostium to increase the chance of wire passage through the stent meshes. Then, of course, the overstented wire is removed and the main branch stent is re-dilated.

2.6.6 Distal Embolization and No Reflow

The term "no reflow" describes the situation in which, after adequate dilatation of an epicardial stenosis with complete elimination of the epicardial flow obstruction, there is no adequate blood flow in the dependent microcirculation. In the angiographic image, this may show up as stagnant or very slow-flowing contrast in the epicardial coronary artery (TIMI-0 or TIMI-I flow). However, significant microcirculatory disturbances may also be present with normal fast blood flow in the epicardial coronary (TIMI-III flow). In the angiographic image, this results in at least part of the dependent myocardium of the intervened vessel showing no blackening in the tissue phase or persistent blackening due to contrast leakage into the extravascular space (myocardial blush grade 0). On ECG, no reflow or slow reflow often correlates with persistent or newly occurring ST-segment elevations. Later, areas of microvascular obstruc-

tion (MVO) are found on cardiac MRI. The MVO areas may continue to grow even after successful primary PCI. No reflow after successful intervention worsens the patient's prognosis (Eeckhout and Kern 2001).

The no-reflow phenomenon occurs most frequently during primary PCI, but rarely during elective balloon/stent interventions in native coronaries. In contrast, it is also more common after rotablation of native coronaries and after interventions on old venous bypasses. The occurrence of the phenomenon during interventions on thrombus-containing lesions or old bypasses, especially after implantation of high-pressure stents, suggests that distal embolization of thrombus material or debris plays a crucial role. In addition, ischemic and reperfusion damage to the cellular structures of the microcirculation occurs in patients with acute coronary syndrome.

If it is not clear angiographically whether a no-reflow situation really exists or whether there is a persistent epicardial flow obstruction, e.g. due to a dissection, careful, selective injection of contrast medium into the vessel periphery beyond the treated epicardial lesion via a microcatheter or the wire lumen of an OTW balloon may help.

If distal embolization is the primary cause of no reflow, it is logical to use embolic protection to prevent it. This has led to the introduction of distal (e.g. filters) and proximal protection systems in venous bypass intervention (Baim et al. 2002) and the initial use of smaller, lower-speed drill heads (less plaque removal per unit time) in rotablation. The benefit of thrombus aspiration in primary PCI could not be proven in current studies (Lagerqvist et al. 2014).

Pharmacological treatment of no reflow has limited evidence from studies or registries. The importance of potent platelet aggregation inhibition, e.g. with abciximab (Koch et al. 1999), seems to be generally accepted. The advantage of intracoronary versus intravenous application could not be proven (Thiele et al. 2008). In addition, data exist on subselective intracoronary administration of individual vasodilators (verapamil, adenosine, and nitroprusside sodium) and epinephrine (Kaplan et al. 1996; Hang et al. 2005;

Fischell et al. 1998; Fischell 2008; Baim 2002). However, the value of these substances is controversial. We only have experience, albeit conflicting, with multiple bolus administration of adenosine.

No Reflow Checklist, Modified from T. Twisselmann (Eeckhout and Kern 2001; Niccoli et al. 2009)

Secure diagnosis:
- Determination of the TIMI flow degree
- Administration of intracoronary (i.c.) nitrate (ISDN 0.3–1 mg) to exclude epicardial spasm
- Determination of the MBG; this can also be reduced with TIMI-3 flow
- ST-segment analysis: complete regression of ST-segment elevations is a helpful, simple factor in assessing myocardial perfusion
- Angiographically, flow obstruction due to thrombus, dissection, spasm or similar must be excluded: in case of doubt "over-the-wire" balloon or double lumen catheter and selective distal injection and drug administration via this
- Consider thrombus aspiration, even if no visible thrombus is present.

Therapy: selective i.c. medication if necessary
- ASA, heparin target ACT 250–350 s, under GPIIbIIIa-AA 200–250 s
- GPIIbIIIa antagonists:
  - Abciximab: bolus 0.25 mg/kg, subsequent infusion 0.125 µg/kg/min
  - Tirofiban: bolus 0.4 µg/kg, subsequent infusion 0.1 µg/kg/min
  - Eptifibatide: double bolus 180 µg/kg, follow-up infusion 2 µg/kg/min
- The intracoronary administration of all GPIIbIIIa antagonists is "off-label". The benefit could not be proven in a larger study (Thiele et al. 2008). Adenosine bolus i.c. (up to 50 µg)
- Nitroprusside i.c. (50–200 µg)
- Nicorandil i.c. (0.5 mg) + 4 mg i.v., continuous infusion 6 mg/h
- Verapamil i.c. (0.25–2.5 mg)

Procedure:
- Keep ischemia as short as possible! Fast door-to-balloon time

Concomitant medication:
- Good blood glucose control during surgery reduces infarct size
- Administer statin therapy

2.6.7 Stent Thrombosis

Stent thrombosis, although a long known phenomenon, has gained considerable attention with the general safety debate on drug eluting stents (DES). As a direct result, uniform definitions of the different categories of stent thrombosis have been introduced by the Academic Research Consortium (ARC) (Cutlip et al. 2007). According to evidence criteria, a distinction is made between definite (autopsy or angiographically confirmed), probable (sudden death by day 30 after stent implantation or myocardial infarction in the service area of the stented coronary artery), and possible stent thrombosis (any unexplained death later than 30 days after stent implantation). The timing of stent thrombosis is considered acute up to 24 h after implantation, subacute from day 2 to day 30, late between day 30 and 1 year, and very late thereafter.

The majority of stent thromboses occur acutely or subacutely, regardless of whether a bare metal or a drug eluting stent was implanted (Mauri et al. 2007). Very late stent thrombosis was more frequently associated with first-generation Drug Eluting Stents than with Bare Metal Stents. The first long-term analysis from a first-generation Drug Eluting Stent Registry showed an annual incidence of 0.6% (Daemen et al. 2007). Current drug eluting stents no longer show a clustered incidence of very late stent thrombosis compared to bare metal stents (Kereiakis et al. 2011). Nevertheless, stent thrombosis is of course a very dangerous event for the individual patient and is associated with a high mortality rate (De la Torre-Hernandez et al. 2008).

2

Several studies have investigated the predictors of stent thrombosis (Iakovou et al. 2005; Airoldi et al. 2007; van Werkum et al. 2009). They show that patient-specific factors (compliance to dual antiplatelet therapy, smoking, diabetes, renal insufficiency, acute coronary syndrome, poor LV function), procedural factors (residual dissections, stent length, stent expansion, concomitant antithrombotic therapy), lesion characteristics (length, vessel diameter, bifurcations, thrombi), and stent-specific factors (surrounding inflammatory response, acquired malapposition, neoarteriosclerosis) all play a role. Data on recent DES models show that as little as 3 months of dual antiplatelet therapy can result in adequate long-term protection (Costa and Valgimigli 2018). The concept of individualized adjustment of treatment duration to the patient's unique situation and individual bleeding risk is gaining acceptance. When treating stent thrombosis, it is important to consider that initial ("white") platelet thrombi are present and the thrombus burden is considerable. The use of a GPIIbIIIa receptor antagonist in addition to the frequently still taken dual platelet inhibition should always be considered in stent thrombosis, taking into account the thrombus burden and the prognosis of the patient, insofar as the bleeding risk is acceptable. Usually, much clot material can be aspirated in stent thrombosis. Therefore, standard thrombus aspiration should also be considered in principle in this indication to reduce the risk of no reflow, even if the data are not clear.

After restoration of blood flow, it makes sense to investigate possible causes of stent thrombosis in the cardiac catheterization laboratory. Especially in the case of early stent thrombosis, it makes sense to inquire about the patient's compliance with dual platelet inhibition (if possible due to the degree of sedation), as well as to look for edge dissections or incomplete stent deployment or poor stent apposition. Especially in the context of acute coronary syndromes with an overall tendency to spastic coronary vessels, stents are occasionally implanted that are too small. In individual cases, the performance of an intravascular ultrasound examination may help to clarify the cause. The detection of a marginal

dissection will then usually lead to implantation of an overlapping stent, and the detection of insufficient expansion or malapposition will lead to high-pressure post-dilatation.

Many centers perform aggregation inhibition testing after stent thrombosis. Unfortunately, there are still no standardized recommendations for performing these tests. If a GPIIbIIIa receptor antagonist has been used, the extent to which it affects the test result must be considered. Evidence of clopidogrel resistance will certainly lead to conversion to one of the newer ADP antagonists. In principle, switching to a newer ADP antagonist without testing, especially if no mechanical causes are found in early stent thrombosis, is a reasonable alternative and is also covered by the guidelines for the use of these substances in acute coronary syndromes if there are no contraindications.

> Stent thrombosis is associated with significant mortality. They occur equally after implantation of bare-metal and drug-eluting stents, mostly in the early phase after implantation. Characteristic is a high thrombus burden (platelet thrombi), which justifies aggressive antiplatelet therapy as well as thrombectomy. Subsequently, any mechanical inadequacies of the primary intervention should be eliminated and, if necessary, a switch to one of the newer, more metabolically independent ADP antagonists should be made.

2.7 Thromboembolic Complications and Thrombus Management

Thomas Twisselmann

2.7.1 Pathophysiology

Acute coronary syndrome (ACS) is the leading cause of thrombus formation within a coronary vessel. Here, erosion or rupture of an atherosclerotic plaque results in exposure of components of the lipid-rich core in the vessel lumen (Viles-Gonzales et al. 2004). This highly thrombogenic material leads to platelet aggregation and the formation of a "white" thrombus, and additional activation of the coagulation cascade results in the formation of the fibrin-rich "red" thrombus. With complete occlusion of the vascular lumen, myocardial necrosis occurs after about 15–30 min. However, there is often a dynamic situation of partial endogenous thrombolysis and advancing thrombus formation. Analysis of thrombus composition shows that older thrombus components are often present, indicating that the process of thrombus formation can also occur over a longer period of time (Silvain et al. 2011). Here, thrombus age ≥ 1 day has been shown to be an independent predictor of mortality (Kramer et al. 2008), which may correspond to, for example, an increased propensity for peripheral embolization. The TAPAS trial also showed an association of large, erythrocyte-rich thrombi with TIMI-0 or -1 flow before intervention (Svilaas et al. 2008).

Less frequently, thrombus formation occurs during elective coronary interventions, rarely as a result of coronary embolism.

An angiographic classification is provided by the TIMI (Thrombolysis In Myocardial Infarction) grading (◘ Table 2.7), which

assesses the presence of a thrombus in the vessel lumen in six gradations (Gibson et al. 2000).

The essential treatment goal is the immediate restoration of coronary flow. According to the current ESC guidelines (Neumann et al. 2019), primary coronary intervention is the preferred reperfusion strategy (Class I indication). In several comparative studies, PCI has been shown to be superior to lysis therapy (Keeley et al. 2003). Lysis therapy is recommended when PCI is not possible within less than 2 h. Across Europe (based on data from 2004 to 2008), PCI represents the dominant reperfusion procedure in 16 of 30 countries studied (Widimsky et al. 2010), with the proportion varying between 5% and 92%; in Germany, it was 81% in 2007. The main advantage of PCI is that it achieves a significantly higher openness rate: more than 90% TIMI-3 flow compared with 40–60% in thrombolysis patients (Stone et al. 2008). In addition, the risk of serious bleeding, especially cerebral bleeding, is significantly lower.

2.7.2 Prognosis

Peripheral embolization of thrombus material represents a relevant risk factor with regard to the acute course, but also with regard to prognosis (Henriques et al. 2002). Angiographically, peripheral embolization may appear as a distal filling defect, but also the phenomenon of "no-reflow" in the context of acute coronary intervention is probably related to peripheral embolization. In addition, endothelial dysfunction and myocardial edema appear to be involved. In any case, the occurrence is much more frequent in the context of acute coronary syndromes than in elective PCIs.

The TIMI classification, a semiquantitative classification of contrast medium flow and outflow (◘ Table 2.8), originally used in the thrombolysis studies of the 1980s, has proven useful for describing coronary flow.

The myocardial blush grade (MBG) provides a further assessment of myocardial perfusion (◘ Table 2.9). Both parameters are prognostically significant: for example,

◘ Table 2.7	Classification of thrombus load
TIMI thrombus grade	**Definition**
0	No angiographic characteristics of a thrombus
1	Possible thrombus, angiographic characteristics such as reduced contrast density, "haziness", irregular lesion contour (…)
2	Definite thrombus, extent <half of the vessel diameter
3	Definite thrombus, extent >half, but <two times the vessel diameter
4	Definite thrombus, extent >two times the vessel diameter
5	Complete vessel occlusion

According to Gibson et al. (2000)

2

◩ Table 2.8 Classification of vascular perfusion (TIMI classification, Sheehan et al. 1987)

TIMI river degree	Definition
0	Occlusion with missing presentation in the distal part of the vessel
1	Delayed flow with incomplete visualization of the distal vessel segment
2	Visualization of the vessel distal to the stenosis with slower flow of the contrast medium compared to other vessel areas
3	Normal inflow and outflow of the contrast medium

◩ Table 2.9 Myocardial Blush grades (MBG)

MBG	Definition
0	No contrast agent accumulation
1	Minimal contrast agent accumulation
2	Moderate accumulation, but less than in non-infarcted tissue.
3	Comparable contrast agent accumulation as in non-infarcted tissue

(Yip et al. 2001a, b) showed that failure to achieve TIMI-3 flow in the setting of acute PCI was associated with a significant increase in 30-day mortality (TIMI-2 flow: 27.5% versus TIMI-3 flow: 5.3%). MBG correlates with TIMI flow, but more differentially reflects the degree of myocardial perfusion, whereas TIMI flow primarily represents epicardial perfusion. MBG was found to be an independent predictor of mortality. In a study by (Gibson et al. 2000), patients with TIMI-3 flow and Blush grade-3 had an extremely low risk of mortality.

2.7.3 Pharmacological Therapy of Thromboembolic Complications

The primary treatment goals for thromboembolic complications are inhibition of blood clotting and inhibition of platelet aggregation (◩ Tables 2.10 and 2.11).

■ **Platelet Aggregation Inhibitor**

Patients with ACS routinely receive 75–250 mg acetylsalicylic acid (ASA) i.v. and a loading dose of 600 mg clopidogrel. In most cases, these drugs are given directly in the emergency room or the chest pain unit (class I indication in each case).

With prasugrel and ticagrelor, two new substances are available that have advantages over clopidogrel in terms of rapid onset of action and homogeneity of effect (no "resistances"). Class I recommendations are available for both drugs according to the ESC guideline for the indication STEMI and NSTEMI (Neumann et al. 2019). Due to increased bleeding complications in patients undergoing bypass surgery, the administration of prasugrel is recommended only after coronary status is known. Due to increased complication rates, the administration of prasugrel is not recommended in patients older than 75 years, or weighing less than 60 kg, or with a history of TIA or cerebral insult.

Ticagrelor was the first representative of a new substance group of direct and reversible inhibitors of platelet aggregation. For this substance, a mortality reduction in patients with ACS (4.5% vs. 5.9%) was shown in the PLATO study (Wallentin et al. 2009) compared to standard therapy with clopidogrel, see also the detailed recommendations of the ESC for various clinical situations (◩ Fig. 2.51; Valgimigli et al. 2017).

For patients with an indication for oral anticoagulant (OAC) therapy with vitamin K antagonists and receiving coronary intervention, the problem of the duration of "triple"

◻ **Table 2.10** Pharmacological treatment options for thrombus treatment

Drug	Effect	Dose	Complications/Antidote
Acetyl-salicylic acid (ASS)	Irreversibly inhibits cyclooxy-genase 1	250–500 mg i.v.	Caveat: Allergy No antidote
Clopido-grel	Irreversibly inhibits activation of the $P2Y_{12}$ receptor. Prodrug	600 mg loading dose, 75 mg maintenance dose	Interindividual differences in efficacy ("resistance"), no routine testing recommended so far
Prasugrel	Irreversibly inhibits activation of the $P2Y_{12}$ receptor. Prodrug. Faster and more predictable platelet inhibition than clopidogrel	60 mg loading dose, 10 mg maintenance dose	No benefit for patients with previous cerebrovascular event, weight <60 kg and age >75 years. In particular, increase in bleeding rates
Ticagrelor	Reversibly inhibits activation of the $P2Y_{12}$ receptor. Not a prodrug. Faster and more predictable platelet inhibition compared to clopidogrel. Mortality reduction (PLATO study 30)	180 mg loading dose, 2 × 90 mg/day maintenance dose	Due to reversibility, rapid decrease in effect (half-life approx. 12 h). Increase in bleeding rates. Dyspnoea as side effect (up to 15%), bradycardia due to SA block
Heparin	Indirect thrombin inhibitor	5000–10,000 IU i.v./i.c. or weight-adjusted (60–100 IU/kg bw) Target: ACT 250–350 s (under GPIIbIIIa-AA: 200–250 s)	HIT (heparin-induced thrombocytope-nia) risk. Antidote protamine: 1000 IU antagonize 1000 IU heparin, primary onset corresponding to half the administered heparin dose. Then ACT controlled
Bivaliru-din	Direct thrombin inhibitor	Bolus 0.75 mg/kg i.v., continuous infusion 1.75 mg/kg/h	In particular, reduction of the risk of bleeding. Rapid end of effect
Abcix-imab	Irreversible inhibition of the GPIIbIIIa receptor. Monoclo-nal antibody, large molar (approx. 47,000 Da)	0.25 mg/kg i.v. bolus, continuous infusion 0.125 µg/kg/min	In case of severe bleeding, platelet transfusion[a]
Tirofiban	Reversible inhibition of the GPIIbIIIa receptor. Small molecule (495 Da)	0.4 µg/kg bolus, continuous infusion 0.1 µg/kg/min	Dialyzable[a]
Eptifiba-tide	Reversible inhibition of the GPIIbIIIa receptor. Small molecule (832 Da)	Double bolus 180 µg/kg, continuous infusion 2 µg/kg/min	Dialyzable[a]

Ibanez et al. (2017) and Roffi et al. (2015)

[a] For all GPIIbIIIa-AA no fundamental indication in STEMI and NSTEMI: class IIa for abciximab, eptifi-batide: IIb for tirofiban, bail-out for no-reflow or thrombus

2

◘ Table 2.11 Practical procedure: "thrombus management"

Problem	Procedure
1. Is there adequate platelet inhibition and heparinization?	Were ASA and other oral antiplatelet agents given? **ACT** to verify adequate heparin effect Strongly consider the use of GPIIbIIIa antagonists, if necessary also intracoronary
2. Large thrombus load	Perform **thrombus aspiration**, often significantly reduces the thrombus load: – Beginning aspiration from proximal to distal decreases embolization risk (Antonucci et al. 2008) – Direct stenting: reduces risk of embolization (Lip et al. 2010), but may risk underestimation of vessel dimension
3. Large thrombus burden (persisting despite aspiration)	Multiple balloon dilatation, has a "cleaning effect", possibly restores flow
4. Wall thrombus	Stenting to fix the thrombus
5. Peripheral embolization/no reflow	See 1; possibly PCI for fragmentation. Pharmacotherapy see "No Reflow" section
6. Hemodynamic instability	Possibly IABP
7. Prophylaxis	**For PCI**: early use of aspiration catheter Possibly distal protection system in case of very high thrombus load **For bypass intervention**: distal protection system **For rotablation**: low drill head to artery ratio (0.6–0.8), low speed (140,000 rpm). Addition of vasodilators (heparin, verapamil and nitroglycerin) to the irrigation solution

therapy consisting of ASA, clopidogrel (or another $P2Y_{12}$ receptor) and OAC arises. Because of the increased risk of bleeding with "triple" therapy, a new ESC guideline (Valgimigli et al. 2017) provides recommendations for therapy in patients with an indication for OAK (◘ Fig. 2.52). Data on combined therapy are now also available for all NOAKs, so that there is significantly greater safety in the combined use of anticoagulants and antiplatelet therapy. The therapy recommendation must weigh the ischemic risk against the risk of bleeding. An indication for the use of bare-metal stents practically no longer exists.

■ Antithrombotic Therapy

The current ESC guidelines recommend the administration of unfractionated heparin (UFH) (100 U/kg body weight or 60 U/kg body weight when treated with glycoprotein IIbIIIa antagonists (GPIIbIIIa-AA). For therapy monitoring, the ACT (activated clotting time), target: 250–350 or 200–250 s if GPIIbIIIa-AA is used, can be determined. This is particularly recommended for longer procedures (>60 min) or if thrombotic complications occur during an intervention. The use of low-molecular-weight heparins (NMH) is possible and, according to pharmacological considerations, also advantageous compared with unfractionated heparin: according to the current guidelines, however, there is a class IIa recommendation only for enoxaparin. In particular, because of the regular use of unfractionated heparin in emergency medicine, there is a risk of increased bleeding complications when switching between the two types of heparin. With bivalirudin, a direct thrombin inhibitor, an alternative substance is available; in the HORIZONS-AMI study, the therapy of bivalirudin plus "bailout" GPIIbIIIa-AA was superior to that with UFH plus routine use of GPIIbIIIa-AA in terms of cardiac mortality (1.8% vs. 2.9%)

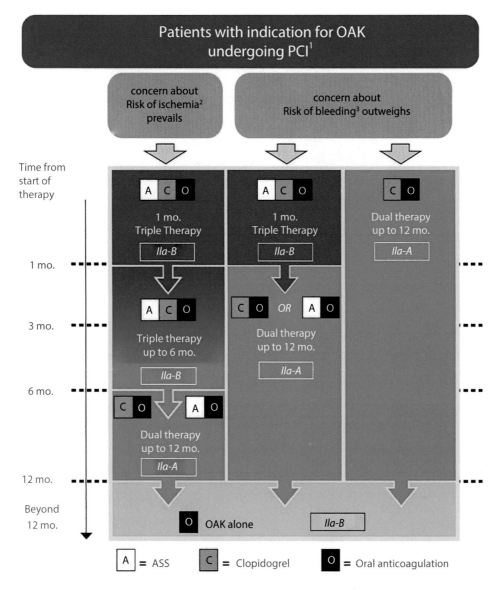

Mo. = month(s)

Color coding refers to the number of concurrent antithrombotic drugs. Triple therapy refers to treatment with DAPT plus oral anticoagulant (OAK). Dual therapy refers to treatment with a single antiplatelet drug (ASA or clopidogrel) plus OAK.
[1]Periprocedural administration of ASA and clopidogrel during PCI is recommended, regardless of treatment strategy.
[2]An acute clinical finding or anatomic/procedural features that may increase the risk of myocardial infarction are considered high risk for ischemia.
[3]The risk of bleeding can be assessed with the HAS-BLED or ABC score.

©ESC2017

▪ **Fig. 2.51** Algorithm for dual antiplatelet therapy (DAPT) in patients with an indication for oral anticoagulation receiving percutaneous coronary intervention (PCI)

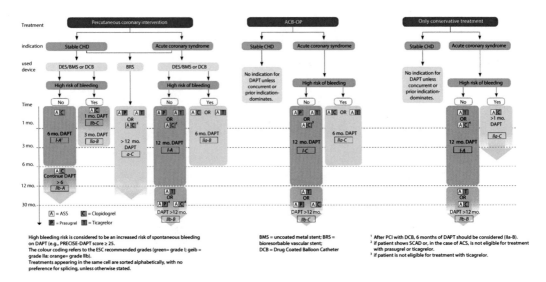

◻ Fig. 2.52 Algorithm for dual antiplatelet therapy (DAPT) in patients with CHD

(Stone et al. 2008). The use of bivalirudin is also useful in patients with heparin-induced thrombocytopenia.

■ **Glycoprotein IIbIIIa Antagonists**

Several studies have demonstrated mortality reduction with the addition of the GPIIbIIIa-AA abciximab in patients with STEMI: in a meta-analysis of over 27,000 patients, 30-day mortality was 2.4% vs. 3.4% with placebo with a sustained benefit even after 6–12 months (De Luca et al. 2005). For currently established therapy with high (600 mg) clopidogrel "loading dose", such as in the BRAVE-3 trial (Mehilli et al. 2009), no difference was shown between conventional therapy and abciximab administration in terms of infarct size in the myocardial spectroscopy before discharge. There is also no advantage for GPIIbIIIa-AA administration with regard to the secondary endpoint (death, myocardial infarction or emergency revascularization) at 30 days. Comparable data exist for the small-molecule GPIIbIIIa-AAs tirofiban and eptifibatide: thus, no basic recommendation can be made for the additional administration of GPIIbIIIa-AA in the acute treatment of STEMI. However, there is a class IIb recommendation for use as a bail-out or in case of thromboembolic complications (Neumann et al. 2019).

◻ Table 2.12 Manual aspiration catheters

Designation	Manufacturer
Diver C.E. Max® Extraction Catheter	Invatec, Roncadelle, Italy
Pronto® Extraction Catheter	Vascular Solutions Inc., Minneapolis, USA
QuickCat® Extraction Catheter	Spectranetics Corp., Colorado Springs, USA
Export® Aspiration Catheter	Medtronic Inc., Santa Rosa, USA
Fetch® Aspiration Catheter	Medrad Inc., Warrendale, USA
Ascap® Aspiration catheter	Merit Medical Inc., South Jordan, USA

2.7.4 Manual Thrombus Aspiration

Manual aspiration systems, e.g. Export® (Medtronic) (overview: ◻ Table 2.12), are relatively simply constructed catheters with two lumen: a smaller one for the guide wire and a larger one for aspiration of the thrombotic material (◻ Fig. 2.53). By connecting a syringe under aspiration, suction is created at the catheter tip. The aspirate can be passed through a filter to document the acquired thrombus material (◻ Fig. 2.54).

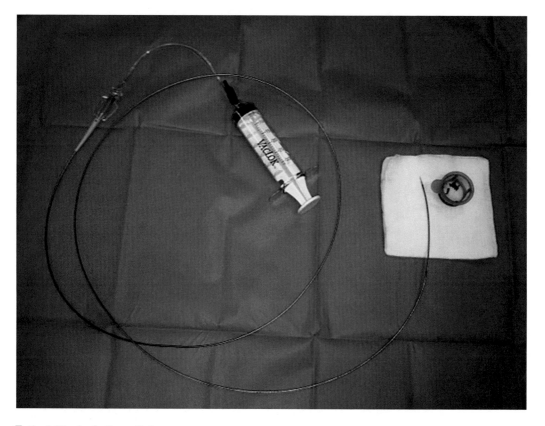

◘ Fig. 2.53 Aspiration catheter

After several small studies had shown improved results with regard to MBG and ST-segment resolution, the large monocentric TAPAS study (Svilaas et al. 2008) additionally demonstrated a reduction in 1-year mortality due to thrombus aspiration with the EXPORT catheter (3.6% vs. 6.7%). It must be mentioned that the study was not designed for this endpoint.

Two large meta-analyses compared different thrombus aspiration systems, showing a mortality benefit for manual thrombus aspiration (2.7% vs. 4.4% for PCI alone) versus a neutral effect for distal protection systems (3.1% vs. 3.4%) and a mortality increase for mechanical aspiration procedures (5.3% vs. 2.8%) (Bavry et al. 2008). In an analysis by Burzotta (Burzotta et al. 2009) of more than 2600 patients, a mortality reduction was found for both thrombus aspiration and the administration of GPIIbIIIa antagonists, combined with indications of a synergistic effect: the best outcome was shown by patients in whom both therapy methods were used. However, the treatment benefit was limited to patients with manual thrombus aspiration.

The main advantage of manual thrombus aspiration catheters is their relatively small size and ease of use. There are few complications associated with the device.

The guidelines only give a class III recommendation for their use in STEMI (Neumann et al. 2019).

The following figures show step-by-step examples of manual thrombus aspiration in an acute STEMI situation in a 70-year-old female patient with subacute posterior myocardial infarction (◘ Fig. 2.55a–e).

2.7.5 Mechanical Thrombus Aspiration

Mechanical aspiration systems are more complex in design: here, for example, either the atherothrombotic material is fragmented and

2

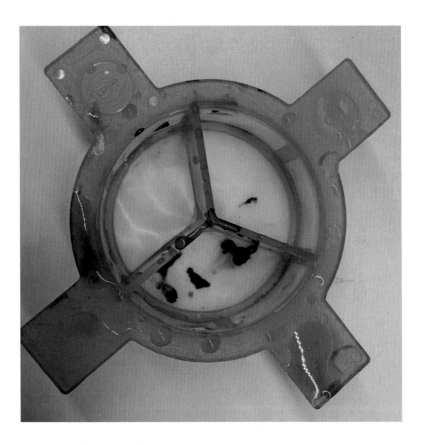

aspirated (X-Sizer®) or a vacuum is created by means of mechanical pumps, according to Bernoulli's principle, through which the thrombotic material can be removed (Angio-Jet®). In smaller studies, both procedures have shown benefits in immediate outcome in STEMI patients, through improvements in parameters such as ST-segment normalization, myocardial blush grade, or TIMI frame count (Gibson et al. 2000). However, the larger AIMI trial of 480 patients showed increased mortality and complication rates in the angio-jet treated group (Ali et al. 2006). In fact, even the extent of infarction as determined by scintigraphy was greater in the thrombus aspiration group. Therefore, routine use of these procedures is not indicated. They may be helpful in the hands of experienced investigators for cases with very high thrombus burden or with already organized thrombi.

2.7.6 Distal Protection

Distal protection systems have either an occluding balloon or a non-occlusive filter system placed distally of the target lesion (**Fig. 2.56**; overview: **Table 2.13**).

The problem is that the protection system must be passed through the lesion, so that embolization is already possible during the passage. Furthermore, embolization is possible next to or through the filter. The balloon occluding system is combined with a manual thrombus aspiration catheter; here, too, a possible peripheral embolization cannot be excluded with certainty. Several studies, as the largest study the DEDICATION study on 626 patients with the filterwire, could not show superiority of the use of distal protection systems in acute STEMI (Bavry et al. 2008). According to the current ESC guideline (Neumann et al. 2019), a recommendation for

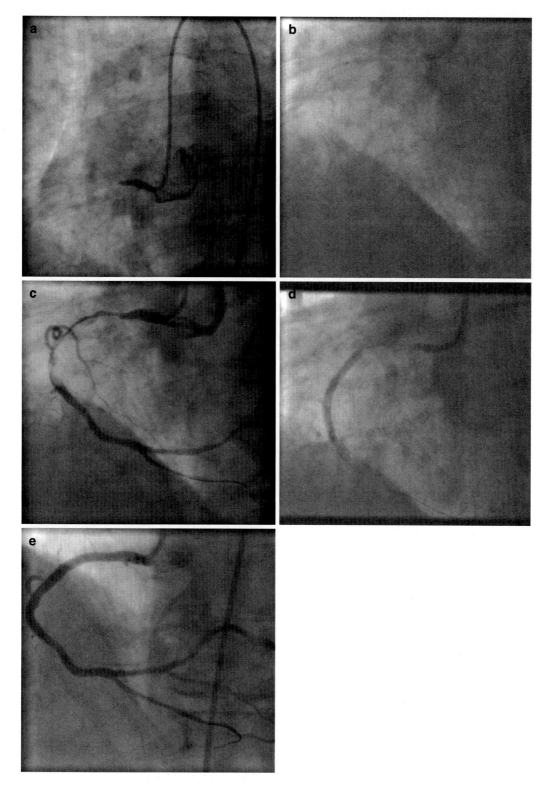

◻ **Fig. 2.55** **a** STEMI due to complete RCA occlusion, **b** Wire passage and advancement of aspiration catheter, **c** Multiple aspirations in the RCA, **d** Stent implantation RCA, **e** Result after thrombus aspiration and stent implantation

Fig. 2.56 Filterwire (Boston Scientific company)

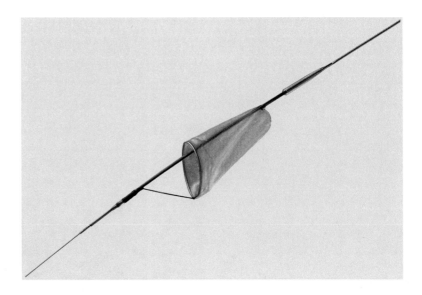

Table 2.13 Distal protection systems

Designation	Manufacturer
Guard Wire Plus®	Medtronic Inc., Santa Rosa, USA
Filter Wire EX.®	Boston Scientific Corp., Natick, USA
SpiderFX®	Ev3 Inc., Plymouth, USA
Emboshield®	Abbot, Abbot Park, USA
Accunet®	Abbot, Abbot Park, USA
Angioguard®	Cordis Corp., Bridgewater, USA

the use of protection systems exists with class IIa exclusively for use in the context of PCI of venous bypasses. Because there are only vague angiographic or clinical predictors of thromboembolic complications in these patients, a general recommendation for the use of distal protection systems applies. Exceptions to this rule, because they are associated in the literature with lower risk of peripheral embolization, may be considered in the case of
(a) Interventions on bypasses less than 3 years old
(b) PCI on ostial lesions or
(c) In-stent stenoses

References

Agirbasli M, Weintraub WS, Chang GL, King SB 3rd, Guyton RA, Thompson TD, Alameddinge F, Ghazzal ZM (2000) Outcome of coronary revascularization in patients on renal dialysis. Am J Cardiol 86:395–399

Agostoni TL, Vermeersch P, Bionde-Zoccai G, van Gaal W, Bhindi R, Brilakis E, Latini RA, Laudisa ML, Pizzocri S, Lanotte S, Brambilla N, Banning A, Bedogni F (2010) Drug eluting stents versus bare metal stents in the treatment of saphenous vein graft disease: a systemic review and meta-analysis. EuroIntervention 6:527–536

Ahmed WH, Shubrooks SJ, Gibson CM, Baim DS, Bittl JA (1994) Complications and long-term outcome after percutaneous coronary angioplasty in chronic hemodialysis patients. Am Heart J 128:152–155

Airoldi F, Colombo A, Morici N et al (2007) Incidence and predictors of drug-eluting stent thrombosis during and after discontinuation of thienopyridine treatment. Circulation 116:745–754

Albertal M, van Langenhove G, Regar E, Kay IP, Foley D, Sianos G, Kozuma K, Beijsterveldt T, Carlier SG, Belardi JA, Boersma E, Sousa JE, de Bruyne B, Serruys PW (2001) Uncomplicated moderate coronary artery dissections after balloon angioplasty: good outcome without stenting. Heart 86: 193–198

Alderman EL, Andrews K, Bost J, Bourassa M, Chaitman BR, Detre K, Faxon DP, Follmann D, Frye RL, Hlatky M, Jones RH, Kelsey SF, Rogers WJ, Rosen AD, Schaff H, Sellers MA, Sopko G, Tyrrell KS, Williams DO (1996) Comparison of coronary bypass surgery with angioplasty in patients with multivessel disease. N Engl J Med 335:217–225

Alfonso F, Almería C, Fernández-Ortíz A, Segovia J, Ferreirós J, Goicolea J, Hernández R, Banuelos C, Gil-Aguado M, Macaya C (1997) Aortic dissection occurring during coronary angioplasty: angiographic and transesophageal echocardiographic findings. Catheter Cardiovasc Diagn 42(4):412–415

Ali A, Cox D, Dib N et al (2006) Rheolytic thrombectomy with percutaneous coronary intervention for infarctsize reduction in acute myocardial infarction: 30 days results from a multicenter randomized study. J Am Coll Cardiol 48(2):244–252

Al-Lamee R, Ielasi A, Latib A, Godino C, Ferraro M, Mussardo M, Arioli F, Carlino M, Montorfano M, Chieffo A, Colombo A (2011) Incidence, predictors, management, immediate and long-term outcomes following grade III coronary perforation. JACC Cardiovasc Interv 4:87–95

Al-Mukhaini M, Panduranga P, Sulaiman K, Riyami AA, Deeb M, Riyami MB (2011) Coronary perforation and covered stents: an update and review. Heart Views 12(2):63–70

Altin RS, Flicker S, Naidech HJ (1989) Pseudoaneurysm and arteriovenous fistula after femoral artery catheterization: association with low femoral punctures. AJR Am J Roentgenol 152(3):629–631

Anderson HV, Vignale SJ, Benedict CR, Willerson JT (1993) Restenosis after coronary angioplasty. J Interv Cardiol 6:187–202

Antonucci D, Valenti R, Migliorini A (2008) Thrombectomy during PCI for acute myocardial infarction: are the randomized controlled trial data relevant to the patients who really need this technique? Catheter Cardiovasc Interv 71:863–869

Appelman YE, Piek JJ, Strikwerda S, Tijssen JG, de Feyter PJ, David GK, Serruys PW, Margolis JR, Koelemay MJ, Montauban van Swijndregt EW, Koolen JJ (1996) Randomised trial of excimer laser angioplasty versus balloon angioplasty for treatment of obstructive coronary artery disease. Lancet 13:79–84

Baim DS (2002) Epinephrine: a new pharmacologic treatment for no-reflow? Catheter Cardiovasc Interv 57(3):310–311

Baim DS, Wahr D, George B et al (2002) Randomized trial of a distal embolic protection device during percutaneous intervention of saphenous vein aorto-coronary bypass grafts. Circulation 105(11):1283–1290

Bapat VN, Venn GE (2003) A rare case of aortocoronary dissection following percutaneous transluminal coronary angioplasty: successful treatment using off-pump coronary artery bypass grafting. Eur J Cardiothorac Surg 24:312–314

Bavry A, Khumbani DJ, Bhatt DL (2008) Role of adjunct thrombectomy and embolic protection devices in acute myocardial infarction: a comprehensive meta-analysis of randomized trials. Eur Heart J 29:2989–3001

Bernat I, Bertrand OF, Rokyta R et al (2011) Efficacy and safety of transient ulnar artery compression to recanalize acute radial artery occlusion after transradial catheterization. Am J Cardiol 107(11):1698–1701

Bhat R, Chakraverty S (2007) Femoral artery thrombosis following percutaneous treatment with thrombin injection of a femoral artery pseudoaneurysm: a case report. Cardiovasc Interv Radiol 30(4):789–792

Black AJR, Namay DL, Niederman AL, Lembo NJ, Roubin GS, Douglas JS, King SB III (1989) Tear or dissection after coronary angioplasty. Morphologic correlates of an ischemic complication. Circulation 79:1035–1042

Blankenship JC, Krucoff MW, Werns SW, Anderson HV, Landau C, White HJ, Green CL, Spokojny AM, Bach RG, Raymond RE, Pinkston J, Rawert M, Talley JD (1999) Comparison of slow oscillating versus fast balloon inflation strategies for coronary angioplasty. Am J Cardiol 83:675–680

Block PC (1990) Restenosis after percutaneous transluminal coronary angioplasty-anatomic and pathophysiological mechanisms. Strategies for prevention. Circulation 81:IV2–IV4

Bonzel T, Erbel R, Hamm CW, Levenson B, Neumann FJ, Rupprecht HJ, Zahn R (2008) Leitlinie Perkutane Koronarinterventionen (PCI). Clin Res Cardiol 97:513–547

Brilakis ES, Best PJ, Elesber AA et al (2005) Incidence, retrieval methods, and outcomes of stent loss during percutaneous coronary intervention: a large single-center experience. Catheter Cardiovasc Interv 66(3):333–340

Brymer JF, Khaja F, Kraft PL (1991) Angioplasty of long or tandem coronary artery lesions using a new longer balloon dilatation catheter: a comparative study. Catheter Cardiovasc Diagn 23:84–88

Burzotta F, de Vita M, Gu YL et al (2009) Clinical impact of thrombectomy in acute ST-elevation myocardial infarction: an individual patient-data pooled analysis of 11 trials. Eur Heart J 30:2193–2203

Carlino M, Al-Lamee R, Ielasi A, Godino C, Latib A, Chieffo A, Colombo A (2011) Treatment of iatrogenic occlusive coronary dissections: a novel approach. EuroIntervention 7:106–111

Chan YC, Morales JP, Reidy JF, Taylor PR (2008) Management of spontaneous and iatrogenic retroperitoneal hemorrhage: conservative management, endovascular intervention or open surgery? Int J Clin Pract 62(10):1604–1613

Choi J, Suh J, Seo HS, Cho YH, Lee NH (2013) A case of sheathless transradial coronary intervention for complex coronary lesions with a standard guiding catheter. Korean Circ J 43:347–350

Colkesen AY, Baltali M, Tercan F (2007) Concurrent dissections of ascending aorta and right coronary artery during primary coronary angioplasty. Emerg Radiol 14(4):249–251

Costa F, Valgimigli M (2018) The optimal duration of dual antiplatelet therapy after coronary stent implantation: to go too far is as bad as to fall short. Cardiovasc Diagn Ther 8(5):630–646

Costopoulos C, Latib A, Naganuma T, Sticchi A, Figini F, Basavarajaiah S, Carlino M, Chieffo A, Montorfano M, Naim C, Kawaguchi M, Giannini F, Colombo A (2013) The role of drug-eluting balloons alone or in combination with drug-eluting stents in the treatment of de novo diffuse coronary disease. JACC 6(11):1153–1159

Cutlip DE, Windecker S, Mehran R et al (2007) Clinical end points in coronary stent trials: a case for standardized definitions. Circulation 115:2344–2351

D'Ayala M, Smith R, Zanieski G, Fahoum B, Tortólani AJ (2008) Acute arterial occlusion after ultrasound-guided thrombin injection of a common femoral artery pseudoaneurysm with a wide, short neck. Ann Vasc Surg 22(3):473–475. (Epub 2008 Mar 25)

Daemen J, Wenaweser P, Tsuchida K et al (2007) Early and late coronary stent thrombosis of sirolimus-eluting and paclitaxel-eluting stents in routine clinical practice: data from a large two institutional cohort study. Lancet 369:667–678

Daniel WC, Pirwitz MJ, Willard JE, Lange RA, Hillis LD, Landau C (1996) Incidence and treatment of elastic recoil occurring in the 15 minutes following successful percutaneous transluminal coronary angioplasty. Am J Cardiol 78:253–259

Danzi GB, Sesana M, Capuano C, Baglini R, Bellosta R, Luzzani L, Carugati C, Sarcina A (2005) Compression repair versus low-dose thrombin injection for the treatment of Iatrogenic femoral pseudoaneurysm: a retrospective case-control study. Ital Heart J 6(5):384–389

Darwazah AK, Aloul J, Abu Shama RA, Eida M, Ismail H (2008) Iatrogenic right coronary artery dissection with retrograde extension to the right coronary sinus. J Card Surg 23:177–179

Darwazah AK, Islim I, Hanbali B, Shama RA, Aloul J (2009) Emergency coronary artery bypass surgery after failed percutaneous coronary intervention. J Cardiovasc Surg 50:795–800

De Feyter PJ, van Suylen R-J, De Jaegere PPT, Topol EJ, Serruys PW (1993) Balloon angioplasty for the treatment of Lesions in saphenous vein bypass grafts. JACC 21:1539–1549

De la Torre-Hernandez IM, Alfonso F, Hernandez F et al (2008) Drug-eluting stent thrombosis: results from the multicenter Spanish registry ESTROFA (Estudio ESpanol sobre TROmbosis de stents FArmacoactivos). J Am Coll Cardiol 51:986–990

De Luca G, Suryapranata H, Stone GW et al (2005) Abciximab as adjunctive therapy to reperfusion in acute ST-segment-elevation myocardial infarction: a meta-analysis of randomized trials. JAMA 293:1759–1765

Deakin CD, Nolan JP, Sunde K, Koster RW (2010) European resuscitation council guidelines for resuscitation 2010. Section 3. Electrical therapies: automated external defibrillators, defibrillation, cardioversion and pacing. Resuscitation 81:1293–1304

Detre K, Holmes DR, Holubkov R, Cowley MJ, Bourassa MG, Faxon DP, Dorros GR, Bentivoglio LG, Kent KM, Myler RK (1990) Incidence and consequences of periprocedural occlusion. The 1985–1986 national heart, lung and blood institute percutaneous transluminal coronary angioplasty registry. Circulation 82:739–750

DiLuzio V, De Remigis F, De Curtis G, Pecce P, Prosperi F, D'Aroma A, Paparoni S, Di Emidio L (1998) Optimal ("Stent-like") acute angiographic results pursuable by traditional PTCA. G Ital Cardiol 28:1083–1093

Dorros G, Cowley MJ, Simpson J, Bentivoglio LG, Block PC, Bourassa M, Detre K, Gosselin AJ, Gruntzig AR, Kelsey SF, Kent KM, Mock MB, Mullin SM, Myler RK, Passamani ER, Stertzer SH, Williams DO (1983) Percutaneous transluminal coronary angioplasty: report of complications from the national heart lung and blood institute PTCA Registry. Circulation 67:723–730

Dunning DW, Kahn JK, Hawkins ET, O'Neill WW (2000) Iatrogenic coronary artery dissections extending into and involving the aortic root. Catheter Cardiovasc Interv 51:387–393

Edgerton JR, Moore DO, Nichols D, Lane BW, Magee MJ, Dewey TM, Mack MJ (2002) Obliteration of femoral artery pseudoaneurysm by thrombin injection. Ann Thorac Surg 74(4):1413–1415

Eeckhout E, Kern MJ (2001) The coronary no-reflow phenomenon: a review of mechanisms and therapies. Eur Heart J 22(9):729–739

Eggebrecht H, Haude M, Birgelen Von C et al (2000) Nonsurgical retrieval of embolized coronary stents. Catheter Cardiovasc Interv 51:432–440

Ellis SG, Vandormael MG, Cowley MJ, DiSciascio G, Deligonul U, Topol EJ, Bulle TM (1990) Coronary morphologic und clinical determinants of procedural outcome with angioplasty for multivessel coronary disease. Circulation 82:1193–1202

Ellis SG, Ajluni S, Arnold A, Popma JJ, Bittl JA, Eigler NL, Cowley MJ, Raymond RE, Safian RD, Whitow PL (1994) Increased coronary perforation in the new device era. Incidence, classification. management and outcome. Circulation 90:2725–2730

Erbel R, Haude M, Höpp HW, Franzen D, Rupprecht HJ, Heublein B, Fischer K, de Jaegere P, Serruys P, Rutsch W, Probst P (1998) Coronary-artery stenting compared with balloon angioplasty for restenosis after initial balloon angioplasty. N Engl J Med 339:1672–1678

Fanggiday J, Stella PR, Guyomi SH, Doevendans PA (2008) Safety and efficacy of drug-eluting balloons in percutaneous treatment of bifurcation lesions: the DEBIUT (drug eluting balloon in bifurcation Utrecht) registry. Catheter Cardiovasc Interv 71:629–635

Farogue HM, Tremmel JA, Raissi Shabari F, Aggarwal M, Fearon WF, Ng MK, Rezaee M, Yeung AC, Lee DP (2005) Risk factors for the development of retroperitoneal hematoma after percutaneous coronary intervention in the era of glycoprotein IIb/IIIa inhibitors and vascular closure devices. J Am Coll Cardiol 45(3):363–368

Ferguson JD, Whatling PJ, Martin V, Walton J, Banning AP (2001) Ultrasound guided percutaneous thrombin injection of iatrogenic femoral artery pseudoaneurysms after coronary angiography and intervention. Heart 85(4):E5

Fischell TA (2008) Pharmaceutical interventions for the management of no-reflow. J Invasive Cardiol 20(7):374–379

Fischell TA, Carter AJ, Foster MT et al (1998) Reversal of "no reflow" during vein graft stenting using high velocity boluses of intracoronary adenosine. Catheter Cardiovasc Diagn 45(4):360–365

Fischman DL, Leon MB, Baim DS, Schatz RA, Savage MP, Penn I, Detre K, Veltri L, Ricci D, Nobuyoshi M (1994) A randomized comparison of coronary stent placement and balloon angioplasty in the treatment of coronary artery disease. N Engl J Med 331: 496–501

Forssmann W (1929) Die Sondierung des rechten Herzens. Klin Wochenschr 8:2085–2087

Foster-Smith K, Garratt KN, Holmes DR Jr (1995) Guidewire transection during rotational coronary atherectomy due to guide catheter dislodgement and wire kinking. Catheter Cardiovasc Diagn 35:224–227

Galbreath C, Salgado ED, Furlan AJ, Hollman J (1986) Central nervous system complications of percutaneous transluminal coronary angioplasty. Stroke 17:616–619

Garrahy PJ, Dean LS, Bulle TM, Anderson JC, Baxley WA, Nath H (1991) The influence of balloon inflation duration on the acute angiographic result of percutaneous transluminal coronary angioplasty. J Interv Cardiol 4:181–187

Garrett PD, Eckart RE, Bauch TD, Thompson CM, Stajduhar KC (2005) Fluoroscopic localization of the femoral head as a landmark for common femoral artery cannulation. Catheter Cardiovasc Interv 65(2):205–207

George BS, Myler RK, Stertzer SH, Clark DA, Cote G, Shaw RE, Fishman-Rosen J, Murphy M (1986) Balloon angioplasty of coronary bifurcation lesions: the kissing balloon technique. Catheter Cardiovasc Diagn 12:124–138

Ghaemian A, Jalalian R (2010) Aortocoronary dissection during diagnostic coronary angiography: treatment with multiple stenting of the coronary artery. Iran Cardiovasc Res J 4:94–96

Gibson CM, Cannon CP, Murphy A et al (2000) Relationship of TIMI myocardial perfusion grade to mortality after administration of thrombolytic drugs. Circulation 101:125–130

Glazier JJ, Varricchione TR, Ryan TJ, Ruocco NA, Jacobs AK, Faxon DP (1989) Outcome in patients with recurrent restenosis after percutaneous transluminal balloon angioplasty. Br Heart J 61:485–488

Godino C, Parodi G, Furuichi S, Latib A, Barbagallo R, Goktekin O, Cera M, Mueller R, Tamburino C, Grube E, Di Mario C, Reimers B, Chieffo A, Antoniucci D, Colombo A, Sangiorgi GM (2010) Long-term follow-up (four years) of unprotected left main coronary artery disease treated with paclitaxel-eluting stents (from the True Registry). EuroIntervention 5:906–916

Goldstein JA, Casserly IP, Katsiyiannis WT, Lasala JM, Taniuchi M (2003) Aortocoronary dissection complicating a percutaneous coronary intervention. J Invasive Cardiol 15:89–92

Goméz-Moreno S, Sabaté M, Jiménez-Quevedo P, Vázquez P, Alfonso F, Angiolillo DJ, Hernàndez-Antolin R, Moreno R, Banuelos C, Escaned J, Macaya C (2006) Iatrogenic dissection of the ascending aorta following heart catheterisation: incidence, management and outcome. EuroIntervention 2(2):197–202

Grassman ED, Leya F, Johnson SA, Lewis BE, Wolfe MW, Strony JT, Adelman B, Bittl JA (1994) Percutaneous transluminal coronary angioplasty for unstable angina: predictors of outcome in a multicenter study. J Thromb Thrombolysis 1:73–78

Grüntzig A, Senning A, Siegenthaler WE (1979) Nonoperative dilatation of coronary-artery stenosis. Percutaneous transluminal coronary angioplasty. N Engl J Med 201:61–68

Hang CL, Wang CP, Yip HK et al (2005) Early administration of intracoronary verapamil improves myocardial perfusion during percutaneous coronary interventions for acute myocardial infarction. Chest 128(4):2593–2598

Hayes PD, Chokkalingam A, Jones R, Bell PR, Fishwick G, Bolia A, Naylor AR (2002) Arterial perforation during infrainguinal lower limb angioplasty does not worsen outcome: results from 1409 patients. J Endovasc Ther 9(4):422–427

Henriques JPS, Zijlstra F, Ottervanger JP et al (2002) Incidence and clinical significance of distal embolization during primary angioplasty for acute myocardial infarction. Eur Heart J 23:1112–1117

Hering D, Piper C, Hohmann C, Schultheiss HP, Horstkotte D (1998) Prospective study of the incidence, pathogenesis and therapy of spontaneous, by coronary angiography diagnosed coronary artery dissection. Z Kardiol 87:961–970

Hofmann I, Wunderlich N, Robertson G, Kieback A, Haller C, Pfeil W, Störk T, Hoffmann G, Bischoff KO, Dorsel T, Görge G, Sievert H (2007) Percutaneous injection of thrombin for the treatment of pseudoaneurysms: the German multicentre registry. EuroIntervention 3(3):321–326

Holmes DR Jr, Holubkov R, Vlietstra RE, Kelsey SF, Reeder GS, Dorros G, Williams DO, Cowley MJ, Faxon DP, Kent KM (1988) Comparison of complications during percutaneous transluminal coronary angioplasty from 1977 to 1981 and from 1985 to 1986: the national heart, lung and blood institute percutaneous transluminal coronary angioplasty registry. J Am Coll Cardiol 12:1149–1155

Hruby W, Mosser H, Urban M, Tuchmann A, Stellamor K (1989) Noninvasive diagnosis of post-puncture vascular complications of the femoral artery: i.v. DSA and duplex sonography. Radiologe 29(9):451–453

Huber MS, Mooney JF, Madison J, Mooney MR (1991) Use of a morphologic classification to predict clinical outcome after dissection from coronary angioplasty. Am J Cardiol 68:467–471

Iakovou I, Schmidt T, Bonizzoni E et al (2005) Incidence, predictors, and outcome of thrombosis after successful implantation of drug-eluting stents. JAMA 293:2126–2130

Ibanez B, James S, Agewall S et al (2017) ESC guidelines for the management of acute myocardial infarction in patients presenting with ST-segment elevation. The task force for the management of acute myocardial infarction in patients presenting with ST-segment elevation oft the European Society of Cardiology (ESC). EHJ 39:119–177

Judkins MP (1967) Selective coronary arteriography: a percutaneous transfemoral technique. Radiology 89:815–824

Kacila M, Vranic H, Hadzimehmedagic A, Sehovic S, Granov N (2011) The frequency of complications of pseudoaneurysms after cardiac interventional diagnostic and therapeutic interventions. Med Arh 65(2):78–81

Kahlert P, Al-Rashid F, Weber M, Wendt D, Heine T, Kottenberg E, Thielmann M, Kühl H, Peters J, Jakob HG, Sack S, Erbel R, Eggebrecht H (2009) Vascular access site complications after percutaneous transfemoral aortic valve implantation. Herz 34(5):398–408

Kaltenbach M, Kober G, Scherer D, Vallbracht C (1985) Recurrence rate after successful coronary angioplasty. Eur Heart J 6:276–281

Kaplan BM, Benzuly KH, Kinn JW et al (1996) Treatment of no-reflow in degenerated saphenous vein graft interventions: comparison of intracoronary verapamil and nitroglycerin. Catheter Cardiovasc Diagn 39(2):113–118

Kawaguchi K, Kondo T, Shumiya T, Uchikawa T, Suzuki T, Awaji Y, Mochizuki M (2002) Reduction of early elastic recoil by cutting balloon angioplasty as compared to conventional balloon angioplasty. J Invasive Cardiol 14:515–519

Keeley EC, Boura JA, Grines CL (2003) Primary angioplasty versus intravenous thrombolytic therapy for acute myocardial infarction: a quantitative review of 23 randomized trials. Lancet 361(9351):13–20

Kelm M, Perings SM, Jax T, Lauer T, Schoebel FC, Heintzen MP, Perings C, Strauer BE (2002) Incidence and clinical outcome of iatrogenic femoral arteriovenous fistulas: implications for risk stratification and treatment. J Am Coll Cardiol 40(2):291–297

Kent KC, McArdle CR, Kennedy B, Baim DS, Anninos E, Skillman JJ (1993a) A prospective study of the clinical outcome of femoral pseudoaneurysms and arteriovenous fistulas induced by arterial puncture. J Vasc Surg 17(1):125–131, discussion 131–133

Kent KC, McArdle CR, Kennedy B, Baim DS, Anninos E, Skillman JJ (1993b) Accuracy of clinical examination in the evaluation of femoral false aneurysm and arteriovenous fistula. Cardiovasc Surg 1(5):504–507

Kereiakis DJ, Smits PC, Kedhi E et al (2011) Predictors of death or myocardial infarction, ischaemic-driven revascularisation, and major adverse cardiovascular events following everolimus-eluting or paclitaxel-eluting stent deployment: pooled analysis from the SPIRIT II, III, IV and COMPARE trials. EuroIntervention 7(1):74–83

King SB 3rd, Yeung AC (2007) Interventional cardiology. McGraw Hill, New York

Koch KC, vom Dahl J, Kleinhans E et al (1999) Influence of a platelet GPIIb/IIIa receptor antagonist on myocardial hypoperfusion during rotational atherectomy as assessed by myocardial Tc-99m sestamibi scintigraphy. J Am Coll Cardiol 33(4):998–1004

Köckeritz U, Reynen K, Knaut M, Strasser RH (2004) Results of angioplasty (with or without stent) at the site of a narrowed coronary anastomosis of the left internal mammary artery graft or via the internal mammary artery. Am J Cardiol 93:1531–1533

Krakau I (1999) Das Herzkatheterbuch. Diagnostische und interventionelle Kathetertechniken. Thieme, Stuttgart

Kramer MCA, van der Wal AC, Koch KT et al (2008) Presence of older thrombus is an independent predictor of long-term mortality in patients with ST-elevation myocardial infarction treated with thrombus aspiration during primary percutaneous coronary intervention. Circulation 118:1810–1816

Kron J, Sutherland D, Rosch J, Morton MJ, McAnulty JH (1985) Arteriovenous fistula: a rare complication of arterial puncture for cardiac catheterization. Am J Cardiol 55(11):1445–1446

Kuntz RE, Gibson CM, Nobuyoshi M, Baim DS (1993) Generalized model of restenosis after conventional balloon angioplasty, stenting and directional atherectomy. J Am Coll Cardiol 21:15–25

Lafont A, Guzman LA, Whitlow PL, Goormastic M, Cornhill JF, Chisolm GM (1995) Restenosis after experimental angioplasty. Intimal, medial and adventitial changes associated with constrictive remodeling. Circ Res 76:996–1002

Lagerqvist B et al (2014) Outcomes 1 year after thrombus aspiration for myocardial infarction. N Engl J Med 371(12):1111–1120

Lambert B, Bonan R, Cote G, Crepeau J, de Guise P, Lesperance J, David PR, Waters DD (1988) Multiple coronary angioplasty: a model to discriminate systemic and procedural factors related to restenosis. J Am Coll Cardiol 12:310–314

Levenson B, Albrecht A, Göhring S, Haerer W, Reifart N, Ringwald G, Schräder R, Troger B (2011) 6. Bericht des Bundesverbandes Niedergelassener Kardiologen zur Qualitätssicherung in der diagnostischen und therapeutischen Invasivkardiologie 2006–2009. Herz 36:41–49

Lewandowski P, Maciejewski P, Wąsek W, Pasierski T, Budaj A (2011) Efficacy and safety of closing post-catheterisation pseudoaneurysms with ultrasound-guided thrombin injections using two approaches: bolus versus slow injection. A prospective randomised trial. Kardiol Pol 69(9):898–905

Li L, Cao Y (2011) Extensive dissection to the coronary sinus of valsalva during percutaneous intervention in right coronary artery—a case report and literature review. Cardiology 5:41–44

Li Q, He Y, Jiang R, Huang D (2013) Using sheathless standard guiding catheters for transradial percutaneous coronary intervention to treat bifurcation lesions. Exp Clin Cardiol 18(2):73–76

Lincoff AM, Popma JJ, Ellis SG, Hacker JA, Topol EJ (1992) Abrupt vessel closure complicating coronary angioplasty: clinical, angiographic and therapeutic profile. J Am Coll Cardiol 19:926–935

Lip GYH, Huber K, Andreotti F et al (2010) Antithrombotic management of atrial fibrillation patients presenting with acute coronary syndrome and/or undergoing coronary stenting: executive summary—a Consensus document of the European Society of Cardiology Working Group on Thrombosis, endorsed by the European Heart Rhythm Association (EHRA) and the European Association of Percutaneous Cardiovascular Interventions. Eur Heart J 31(11):1311–1318

Little T, Milner MR, Lee K, Constantine J, Pichard AD, Lindsay J Jr (1993) Late outcome and quality of life following percutaneous transluminal coronary angioplasty in octogenarians. Catheter Cardiovasc Diagn 29:261–266

Lodge JP, Hal R (1993) Retroperitoneal haemorrhage: a dangerous complication of common femoral arterial puncture. Eur J Vasc Surg 7(3):355–357

Lönn L, Olmarker A, Geterud K, Klingenstierna H, Delle M, Grip L, Risberg B (2002) Treatment of femoral pseudoaneurysms. Percutaneous US-guided thrombin injection versus US-guided compression. Acta Radiol 43(4):396–400

Lopez-Minguez JR, Climent V, Yen-Ho S, Gonzalez-Fernandez R, Nogales-Asensio JM, Sanchez-Quintana D (2006) Structural features of sinus of valsalva and the proximal portion of the coronary arteries: their relevance to retrograde aortocoronary dissection. Rev Esp Cardiol 59:696–702

Luedde M, Krumsdorf U, Zehelein J, Ivandic B, Dengler T, Katus HA, Tiefenbacher C (2007) Treatment of iatrogenic femoral pseudoaneurysm by ultrasound-guided compression therapy and thrombin injection. Angiology 58(4):435–439

Luo H, Nishioka T, Eigler NL, Forrester JS, Fishbein JS, Fishbein MC, Berglund H, Siegel RJ (1996) Coronary artery restenosis after balloon angioplasty in humans is associated with circumferential coronary constriction. Arterioscler Thromb Vasc Biol 16:1393–1398

Lupi A, Navarese EP, Lazzero M, Sansa M, De Servi S, Serra A, Bongo AS, Buffon A (2010) Drug-Eluting stents versus bare metal stents in saphenous vein graft disease. Circ J 75:280–289

Madaric J, Mistrik A, Vulev I, Liska B, Vozar M, Lederer P, Gocar M, Kozlovska T, Fridrich V, De Bruyne B, Bartunek J (2009) The recurrence of iatrogenic femoral artery pseudoaneurysm after occlusion by ultrasound guided percutaneous thrombin injection. EuroIntervention 5(4):443–447

Maiello L, La Marchesina U, Presbitero P, Faletra F (2003) Iatrogenic aortic dissection during coronary intervention. Ital Heart J 4:419–422

Maier W, Mini O, Antoni J, Wischnewsky MB, Meier B (2001) ABC-stenosis morphology classification and outcome of coronary angioplasty. Reassessment with computing techniques. Circulation 103:1225–1231

Majesky MW (1994) Neointima formation after acute vascular injury. Role of counteradhesive extracellular matrix proteins. Tex Heart Inst J 21:78–85

Maluenda G, Mitulescu L, Ben-Dor I, Gaglia MA Jr, Weissman G, Torguson R, Satler LF, Pichard AD, Bernardo NL, Waksman R (2011) Retroperitoneal hemorrhage after percutaneous coronary intervention in the current practice era: clinical outcomes and prognostic value of abdominal/pelvic computed tomography. Catheter Cardiovasc Interv. https://doi.org/10.1002/ccd.23200. Epub ahead of print

Marsan RE, McDonald V, Ramamurthy S (1990) Iatrogenic femoral arteriovenous fistula. Cardiovasc Interv Radiol 13(5):314–316

Martin-Reyes R, Jimenez-Valero S, Moreno R (2010) Effectiveness of cutting balloon angioplasty for a calcified coronary lesion. Evaluation by optical coherence tomography and intravascular ultrasound. Rev Port Cardiol 29:1889–1890

Masaki Y, Sumiyoshi M, Suwa S, Ohta H, Matsunaga E, Tamura H, Takaya N, Mineda Y, Kojima S, Nakata Y (2005) Localised dissection of the sinus of valsalva without coronary artery involvement during percutaneous coronary intervention. Int Heart J 46:323–326

Mathias DW, Mooney JF, Lange HW, Goldenberg IF, Gobel FL, Mooney MR (1991) Frequency of success and complications of coronary angioplasty of a stenosis at the ostium of a branch vessel. Am J Cardiol 67:491–495

Mauri L, Hsieh WH, Massaro JM et al (2007) Stent thrombosis in randomized clinical trials of drug-eluting stents. N Engl J Med 356(10):1020–1029

Medina A, Suarez de Lezo J, Pan M (2006) A new classification of coronary bifurcation lesions. Rev Esp Cardiol 59:183

Mehilli J, Kastrati A, Schulz S et al (2009) Abciximab in patients with acute ST-segment-elevation myocardial infarction undergoing primary percutaneous coronary intervention after clopidogrel loading: a randomized double-blind trial. Circulation 119:1933–1940

Meller J, Friedman S, Dack S, Herman MV (1976) Coronary artery dissection—a complication of cardiac catheterization sequelae: case report and review of the literature. Catheter Cardiovasc Diagn 2(3):301–308

Mintz GS, Popma JJ, Hong MK, Pichard AD, Kent KM, Satler LF, Leon MB (1996a) Intravascular ultrasound to discern device-specific effects and mechanisms of restenosis. Am J Cardiol 78:18–22

Mintz GS, Popma JJ, Pichard AD, Kent KM, Satler LF, Wong SC, Hong MK, Kovach JA, Leon MB (1996b) Arterial remodeling after coronary angioplasty. A serial intravascular ultrasound study. Circulation 94:35–43

Muhs BE, Galloway AC, Lombino M, Silberstein M, Grossi EA, Colvin SB, Lamparello P, Jacobowitz

G, Adelman MA, Rockman C, Gagne PJ (2005) Arterial injuries from femoral artery cannulation with port access cardiac surgery. Vasc Endovasc Surg 39(2):153–158

Nanto S, Kodama K, Mishima M, Komamura K, Asada S, Inoue M (1990) Percutaneous transluminal coronary angioplasty using kissing balloon technique in the left main trunk. Heart Vessel 5:107–112

Neise M, Ranke C, Laschewski F, Trappe HJ (1998) Pseudoaneurysm with associated arteriovenous fistula after transfemoral puncture. Med Klin (Munich) 93(2):107–110

Neumann FJ, Sousa-Uva M, Ahlsson A et al (2019) 2018 ESC/EACTS guidelines on myocardial revascularization. The task force on myocardial revascularization of the European Society of Cardiology (ESC) and the European association of Cardio-Thoracic Surgery (EACTS). Developed with the special contribution of the European association of Percutaneous Cardiovascular Interventions (EAPCI). EHJ 40: 87–165

Niccoli G, Burzotta F, Galiuto L, Crea F (2009) Myocardial no-reflow in humans. J Am Coll Cardiol 54:281–292

Nichols AB, Smith R, Berke AD, Shlofmitz RA, Powers ER (1989) Importance of balloon size in coronary angioplasty. J Am Coll Cardiol 13:1094–1100

Nordon IM, Hinchliffe RJ, Loftus IM, Thompson MM (2011) Pathophysiology and epidemiology of abdominal aortic aneurysms. Nat Rev Cardiol 8(2):92–102

Ochi M, Yamauchi S, Yajima T, Kutsukata N, Bessho R, Tanaka S (1996) Aortic dissection extending from the left coronary artery during percutaneous coronary angioplasty. Ann Thorac Surg 62:1180–1182

Ohman EM, Marquis MD, Ricci DR, Brown RIG, Knudtson ML, Kereiakes CJ, Samaha JK, Margolis JR, Niederman AL, Dean LS, Turbel PA, Sketch MH, Wildermann NM, Lee KL, Califf RM (1994) A randomized comparison of the effects of gradual prolonged versus standard primary balloon inflation of early and late outcome. results of a multicenter clinical trial. Circulation 89:1118–1125

Onal B, Kosar S, Gumus T, Ilgit ET, Akpek S (2004) Postcatheterization femoral arteriovenous fistulas: endovascular treatment with stent-grafts. Cardiovasc Interv Radiol 27(5):453–458. (Epub 2004 Jul 30)

Ozaki Y, Lemos PA, Yamaguchi T, Suzuki T, Nakamura M, Ismail TF, Kitayama M, Nishikawa H, Kato O, Serruys PW (2010) A quantitative coronary angiography-matches comparison between a prospective randomized multicentre cutting balloon angioplasty and bare metal stent trial (REDUCE III) and the Rapamycin-Eluting Stent Evaluation at Rotterdam Cardiology Hospital (RESEARCH) study. EuroIntervention 6:400–406

Pan M, Medina A, Suarez de Lezo J, Romero M, Segura J, Martin P, Suarez de Lezo J, Hernandez E, Mazuelos F, Moreno A, Pavlovic D, Ojeda S, Toledano F, Leon C (2011) Coronary bifurcation lesions treated with simple approach (from the cordoba and las Palmas (CORPAL) Kiss trial). Am J Cardiol 107:1460–1465

Park SJ, Kim KH, Oh IY, Shin DH, Park KI, Seo MK, Chung JW, Park KW, Lee HY, Kang HJ, Koo BK, Youn AJ, Kim HS (2010) Comparison of plain balloon and cutting balloon angioplasty for the treatment of restenosis with drug-eluting stents vs bare metal stents. Circ J 74:1837–1845

Perez-Castellano N, Garcia-Fernandez MA, Garcia EJ, Delcan JL (1998) Dissection of the aortic sinus of valsalva complicating coronary catheterization: cause, mechanism, evolution and management. Catheter Cardiovasc Diagn 43:273–279

Perings SM, Kelm M, Lauer T, Strauer BE (2002) Duplex ultrasound determination of shunt volume in iatrogenic arteriovenous fistulas after heart catheterization. Z Kardiol 91(6):481–486

Pijls NHJ, Klauss V, Siebert U, Powers E, Takazawa K, Fearon WF, Escaned J, Tsurumi Y, Akasaka T, Samady H, De Bruyne B (2002) Coronary pressure measurement after stenting predicts adverse events at follow-up. Circulation 105:126–130

Pinkerton CA, Slack JD (1985) Complex coronary angioplasty: a technique for dilatation of bifurcation stenoses. Angiology 36:543–548

Platko WP, Hollman J, Whitlow PL, Franco I (1989) Percutaneous transluminal angioplasty of saphenous vein graft stenosis: long-term follow-up. JACC 14:1645–1650

Platts MM, Ridgway BA (1965) Arterial puncture dangerous? Br Med J 1(5436):724–725

Porto I, Mitchell AR, Selvanayagam JB, Neubauer S, Banning AP (2005) Percutaneous treatment of simultaneous aortic dissection and pericardial tamponade during coronayr intervention. Int J Cardiol 105(1):104–107

Prasad A, Compton PA, Prasad A, Roesle M, Makke L, Rogers S, Banerjee S, Brilakis ES (2008) Incidence and treatment of arterial access dissections occurring during cardiac catheterization. J Interv Cardiol 21(1):61–66

Preisack MB, Elsenberger R, Athanasiadis A, Karsch KR (1998) The influence of coronary artery dissection on long-term outcome after percutaneous transluminal coronary angioplasty. Z Kardiol 87: 41–50

Quan VH, Stone JR, Couper GS, Rogers C (2005) Coronary artery perforation by cutting balloon resulting in dissecting subepicardial hematoma an avulsion of the vasculature. Catheter Cardiovasc Interv 64:163–168

Quigley PJ, Erwin J, Maurer BJ, Walsh MJ, Gearty GF (1986) Percutaneous transluminal coronary angioplasty in unstable angina: comparison with stable angina. Br Heart J 55:227–230

Rapoport S, Sniderman KW, Morse SS, Proto MH, Ross GR (1985) Pseudoaneurysm: a complication of faulty technique in femoral arterial puncture. Radiology 154(2):529–530

Reeves F, Bonan R, Crepeau J, de Guise P, Gosselin G, Campeau L, Leperance J (1991) Long-term angiographic follow-up after angioplasty of venous coronary bypass. Am Heart J 122:620–627

Rensing BJ, Hermans WR, Beatt KJ, Laarman GJ, Suryapranata H, van den Brand M, de Feyter PJ, Serruys PW (1990) Quantitative angiographic assessment of elastic recoil after percutaneous transluminal coronary angioplasty. Am J Cardiol 66:1039–1044

Roffi M, Patrono C, Collet JP et al (2015) 2015 ESC Guidelines for the management of acute coronary syndromes in patients presenting without persistent ST-segment elevation. The task force for the management of acute coronary syndromes in patients presenting without persistent ST-segment elevation of the European Society of Cardiology (ESC). EHJ 37:267–315

Roubin GS, Douglas JS, King SB 3rd, Lin S, Hutchison N, Thomas RG, Gruentzig AR (1988) Influence of balloon size on initial success, acute complications and restenosis after percutaneous transluminal coronary angioplasty. A prospective randomized study. Circulation 78:557–565

Rozenman Y, Gilon D, Welber S, Sapoznikov D, Gotsman MS (1993) Clinical and angiographic predictors of immediate recoil after successful coronary angioplasty and relation to late restenosis. Am J Cardiol 72:1020–1025

Ruebben A, Tettoni S, Muratore P, Rossato D, Savio D, Rabbia C (1998) Arteriovenous fistulas induced by femoral arterial catheterization: percutaneous treatment. Radiology 209(3):729–734

Sadiq S, Ibrahim W (2001) Thromboembolism complicating thrombin injection of femoral artery pseudoaneurysm: management with intraarterial thrombolysis. J Vasc Interv Radiol 12(5):633–636

Savage MP, Douglas JSJR, Fischman DL, Pepine CJ, King SB 3rd, Werner JA, Bailey SR, Overlie PA, Fenton SH, Brinker JA, Leon MB, Goldberg S (1997) Stent placement compared with balloon angioplasty for obstructed coronary bypass grafts. N Engl J Med 337:740–747

Scheller B, Hehrlein C, Bocksch W, Rutsch W, Haghi D, Dietz U, Böhm M, Speck U (2006) Treatment of in-stent-restenosis with a paclitaxel-coated balloon catheter. N Engl J Med 355:2113–2124

Scheller B, Hehrlein C, Bocksch W, Rutsch W, Haghi D, Dietz U, Böhm M, Speck U (2008) Two year follow-up after treatment of coronary in-stent-restenosis with the paclitaxel coated balloon catheter. Clin Res Cardiol 97:773–781

Seldinger SI (1953) Catheter replacement of the needle in percutaneous arteriography: a new technique. Acta Radiol 39:368–376

Serruys PW, Luijten HE, Beatt KJ, Geuskens R, de Feyter PJ, van den Brand M, Reiber JHC, Ten Katen HJ, van Es GA, Hugenholtz PG (1988) Incidence of restenosis after successful coronary angioplasty: a time related phenomenon. Circulation 77:361–371

Serruys PW, Foley DP, King SB 3rd (1993) Restenosis revisited: insights provided by quantitative coronary angiography. Am Heart J 126(5):1243–1267

Serruys PW, Foley DP, Suttorp M-J, Rensing BJWM, Suryapranata H, Materne P, van den Bos A, Benit E, Anzini A, Rutsch W, Legrand V, Dawkins K, Cobaugh M, Bressers M, Backx B, Wijns W, Colombo A (2002) A randomized comparison of the value of additional stenting after optimal balloon angioplasty for long coronary lesions. Final results of the additional value of NIR Stents for treatment of long coronary lesions (ADVANCE) study. J Am Coll Cardiol 39:393–399

Seshadri N, Whitlow PL, Acharya N, Houghtaling P, Blackstone EH, Ellis SG (2002) Emergency coronary artery bypass surgery in the contemporary percutaneous coronary intervention era. Circulation 106:2346–2350

Sheehan FH, Braunwald E, Canner P et al (1987) The effect of intravenous thrombolytic therapy on left ventricular function: a report on tissue-type plasminogen activator and streptokinase from the Thrombolysis In Myocardial Infarction (TIMI Phase 1) trial. Circulation 75:817–829

Sheiman RG, Mastromatteo M (2003) Iatrogenic femoral pseudoaneurysms that are unresponsive to percutaneous thrombin injection: potential causes. AJR Am J Roentgenol 181(5):1301–1304

Shimony A, Joseph L, Mottillo S, Eisenberg MJ (2011) Coronary artery perforation during percutaneous coronary intervention: a systematic review and meta-analysis. Can J Cardiol 27(6):843–850

Shirakabe A, Takano H, Nakamura S, Kikuchi A, Sasaki A, Yamamoto E, Kawashima S, Takagi G, Fujita N, Aoki S, Asai K, Yoshikawa M, Kato K, Yamamoto T, Takayama M, Takano T (2007) Coronary perforation during percutaneous coronary intervention: lessons from our experience. Int Heart J 48(1):1–9

Sidawy AN, Neville RF, Adib H, Curry KM (1993) Femoral arteriovenous fistula following cardiac catheterization: an anatomic explanation. Cardiovasc Surg 1(2):134–137

Sigwart U, Puel J, Mirkovitch V, Joffre F, Kappenberger L (1987) Intravascular Stents to prevent occlusion and re-stenosis after transluminal angioplasty. N Engl J Med 316:701–706

Silvain J, Collet JP, Nagaswami C et al (2011) Composition of coronary thrombus in acute myocardial infarction. J Am Coll Cardiol 57:1359–1367

Sones FM, Shirey EK, Proudfit WL, Westcott RN (1959) Cinecoronary arteriography. Circulation 20:773

Srinivas VS, Brooks MM, Detre KM, King SB III, Jacobs AK, Johnston J, Williams DO (2002) Contemporary percutaneous coronary intervention versus balloon angioplasty for multivessel coronary artery disease. Circulation 106:1627–1633

Staudacher RA, Hess KR, Harris SL, Abu-Khalil J, Heibig J (1991) Percutaneous transluminal coronary angioplasty utilizing prolonged balloon inflations: initial results and six-month follow-up. Catheter Cardiovasc Diagn 23:239–244

Stawicki SP, Hoey BA (2007) Lower extremity arterial thrombosis following sonographically guided thrombin injection of a femoral pseudoaneurysm. J Clin Ultrasound 35(2):88–93

Steffenino G, Meier B, Finci L, Velebit V, von Segesser L, Faidutti B, Rutishauser W (1988) Acute complications of elective coronary angioplasty: a review of 500 consecutive procedures. Br Heart J 59:151–158

Stein B, Weintraub WS, Gebhart SP, Cohen-Bernstein CL, Grosswald R, Liberman HA, Douglas JS Jr, Morris DC, King SB 3rd (1995) Influence of diabetes mellitus on early and late outcome after percutaneous transluminal coronary angioplasty. Circulation 91:979–989

Stellin G, Ramondo A, Bortolotti U (1987) Guidewire fracture: an unusual complication of percutaneous transluminal coronary angioplasty. Int J Cardiol 17:339–342

Stone GW, Witzenbichler B, Guagliumi G et al (2008) Bivalirudin during primary PCI in acute myocardial infarction. N Engl J Med 358:2218–2230

Svilaas T, Vlaar PJ, van der Horst IC et al (2008) Thrombus aspiration during primary percutaneous coronary intervention. N Engl J Med 358:557–567

Takahashi Y, Tsutsumi Y, Monta O, Kohshi K, Skamoto T, Ohashi H (2010) Closure of the left main trunk of the coronary artery and total arch replacement in acute type a dissection during coronary angiography. Ann Thorac Surg 89:618–621

Talley JD, Weintraub WS, Roubin GS, Douglas JS, Anderson HV, Jones EL, Morris DC, Liberman HA, Craver JM, Guyton RA, King SB III (1990) Failed elective percutaneous transluminal coronary angioplasty requiring coronary artery bypass surgery. In hospital and late clinical outcome at 5 years. Circulation 82:1203–1213

Tamura T, Kimura T, Morimoto T, Nakagawa Y, Furukawa Y, Kadota K, Tatami R, Kawai K, Sone T, Myazaki S, Mitsudo K (2011) Three-year-outcome of sirolimus-eluting stent implantation in coronary bifurcation lesions: the provisional side branch stenting approach versus the elective two-stent approach. EuroIntervention 7:588–596

Tan KH, Sulke N, Taub N, Sowton E (1995a) Clinical and lesion morphologic determinants of coronary angioplasty success and complications: current experience. J Am Coll Cardiol 25:855–865

Tan KH, Sulke N, Taub N, Sowton E (1995b) Percutaneous transluminal coronary angioplasty of aorta ostial, non-aorta ostial, and branch ostial stenoses: acute and long-term outcome. Eur Heart J 16:631–639

Tanasie C, Chandonnet M, Chin A, Kokis A, Ly H, Perrault LP, Chartrand-Levebvre C (2011) Catheter-induced aortic dissection after invasive coronary angiography: evaluation with MDCT. Am J Roentgenol 197(6):1335–1340

Ten Berg JM, Gin MT, Ernst SM, Kelder JC, Suttorp MJ, Mast EG, Bal E, Plokker HW (1996) Ten-year follow-up of percutaneous transluminal coronary angioplasty for proximal left anterior descending coronary artery stenosis in 351 patients. J Am Coll Cardiol 28:82–88

Thalhammer C, Kirchherr AS, Uhlich F, Waigand J, Gross CM (2000) Postcatheterization pseudoaneurysms and arteriovenous fistulas: repair with percutaneous implantation of endovascular covered stents. Radiology 214(1):127–131

Thiele H, Schindler K, Friedberger J et al (2008) Intracoronary compared with intravenous Abciximab application in patients with ST-elevation myocardial infarction undergoing primary percutaneous coronary intervention: the randomized Leipzig immediate percutaneous coronary intervention abciximab iv. versus ic. in ST-elevation myocardial infarction trial. Circulation 118:49–57

Tillmann BN (2010) Atlas der Anatomie. Springer Medizin Verlag, Heidelberg

Tiroch KA, Arora N, Matheny ME, Liu C, Lee TC, Resnic FS (2008) Risk predictors of retroperitoneal hemorrhage following percutaneous coronary intervention. Am J Cardiol 102(11):1473–1476

Tochii M, Ando M, Takagi Y, Kaneko K, Ishida M, Akita K, Higuchi Y (2010) Iatrogenic type a aortic dissection after catheter intervention for the left subclavian artery. Ann Thorac Cardiovasc Surg 16(6):451–453

Topol EJ, Ellis SG, Fishman J, Leimgruber P, Myler RK, Stertzer SH, O'Neill WW, Douglas JS, Roubin GS, King SB 3rd (1987) Multicenter study of percutaneous transluminal angioplasty for right coronary artery ostial stenosis. J Am Coll Cardiol 9:1214–1218

Tsang TS, Freeman WK, Barnes ME, Reeder GS, Packer DL, Seward JB (1998) Rescue echocardiographically guided pericardiocentesis for cardiac perforation complicating catheter-based procedures. The mayo clinic experience. J Am Coll Cardiol 32:1345–1350

Ueda M, Becker AE, Fujimoto T, Tsukada T (1991) The early phenomena of restenosis following percutaneous transluminal coronary angioplasty. Eur Heart J 12:937–945

Unverdorben M, Vallbracht C, Cremers B, Heuer H, Hengstenberg C, Maikowski C, Werner GS, Antoni D, Kleber FX, Bocksch W, Leschke M, Ackermann H, Boxberger M, Speck U, Degenhardt R, Scheller B (2009) Paclitaxel-coated balloon catheter versus paclitaxel-coated stent for the treatment of coronary in-stent restenosis. Circulation 119:2986–2994

Valgimigli M et al (2017) 2017 ESC focused update on dual antiplatelet therapy in coronary artery disease developed in collaboration with EACTS: the task force for dual antiplatelet therapy in coronary artery disease of the European Society of Cardiology (ESC) and of the European Association for Cardio-Thoracic Surgery (EACTS). ESC scientific document group; ESC Committee for Practice Guidelines (CPG); ESC National Cardiac Societies. Eur Heart J 39(3):213–260

Van Leeuwen K, Blans W, Pijls NHJ, van der Werf T (1989) Kissing balloon angioplasty of a circumflex artery bifurcation lesion. A new approach utilizing two balloon-on-wire probes and a single guiding catheter. Chest 95:1144–1145

Van Werkum JW, Heestermans AA, Zomer AC et al (2009) Predictors of coronary stent thrombosis: the Dutch Stent Thrombosis Registry. J Am Coll Cardiol 53:1399–1409

Viles-Gonzales JF, Fuster V, Badimon JJ (2004) Atherothrombosis: a widespread disease with unpredictable and life-threatening consequences. Eur Heart J 25:1197–1207

Violaris AG, Melkert R, Serruys PW (1995) Long-term luminal renarrowing after successful elective coronary angioplasty of total occlusions. A quantitative angiographic analysis. Circulation 91:2140–2150

Wallentin L, Becker RC, Budaj A et al (2009) Ticagrelor vs. clopidogrel in patients with acute coronary syndrome. N Engl J Med 361:1045–1057

Weintraub WS, Jones EL, Graver JM, Guyton RA (1994) Frequency of repeat coronary bypass or coronary angioplasty after coronary artery bypass surgery using saphenous venous grafts. JACC 73:103–112

Widimsky P, Wijns W, Fajadet J et al (2010) Reperfusion therapy for ST elevation acute myocardial infarction in Europe: description of the current situation in 30 countries. Eur Heart J 31:943–957

Williams DO, Holubkov R, Yeh W, Bourassa MG, Al-Bassam M, Block PC, Coady P, Cohen H, Cowley M, Dorros G, Faxon D, Holmes DR, Jacobs A, Kelsey SF, King SB 3rd, Myler R, Slater J, Stanek V, Vlachos A, Detre KM (2000) Percutaneous coronary intervention in the current era compared with 1985–1986. Circulation 102:2945–2951

Wyman RM, Safian RD, Portway V, Skillman JJ, McKay RG, Baim DS (1988) Current complications of diagnostic and therapeutic cardiac catheterization. J Am Coll Cardiol 12:1400–1406

Wyss CA, Steffel J, Lüscher TF (2008) Isolated acute iatrogenic aortic dissection during percutaneous coronary intervention without involvement oft he coronary arteries. J Invasive Cardiol 20(7):380–382

Yao Q, Cong H, Wu S, Sun S, Dong Q, Chen D, Li P (2008) Ultrasound-guided thrombin injection: an alternative treatment for femoral artery pseudoaneurysm with better efficiency and safety. J Huazhong Univ Sci Technol Med Sci 28(3):373–374

Yarlioglues M, Tasdemir K, Kaya MG, Kalay N (2011) Aortic and coronary artery dissection during percutaneous coronary intervention: a case report and review article. Clin Cardiol 34(5): 283–286

Yip H, Chen MC, Wu CJ, Yeh KH, Fu M, Hang CL, Fang CY, Hsieh KY (2001a) Primary angioplasty in acute inferior myocardial infarction with anomalous-origin right coronary arteries as infarct-related arteries: focus on anatomic and clinical features, outcomes, selection of guiding catheters and management. J Invasive Cardiol 13:290–297

Yip H, Wu CJ, Yeh KH, Hang CL, Fang CY, Hsieh KY, Fu M (2001b) Unusual complication of retrograde dissection to the coronary sinus of valsalva during percutaneous revascularization: a single-center experience and literature review. Chest 119: 493–501

Youn JY, Yoon J, Han SW, Lee JW, Sung JK, Ahn SG, Kim JY, Yoo BS, Lee SH, Choe KH (2011) Feasibility of transradial coronary intervention using a sheathless guiding catheter in patients with small radial artery. Circ J 41:143–148

Zankl AR et al (2010) Radial artery thrombosis following transradial coronary angiography: incidence and rationale for treatment of symptomatic patients with low-molecular-weight heparins. Clin Res Cardiol 99(12):841–847

Zhou T, Liu ZJ, Zhou SH, Shen XQ, Liu QM, Fang ZF, Hu XQ, Li J, Lü XL (2007) Treatment of post-catheterization femoral arteriovenous fistulas with simple prolonged bandaging. Chin Med J (Engl) 120(11):952–955

Periprocedural Complications

Erhard Kaiser, Jan Pollmann, Carsten Skurk, and Martin Müller

Contents

E. Kaiser (ed.), *Complication Management In The Cardiac Catheter Laboratory*, https://doi.org/10.1007/978-3-662-66093-5_3

3.1 Contrast Media Induced Allergy

Erhard Kaiser

3.1.1 Clinical Presentation

The diagnostic and therapeutic possibilities in the cardiac catheterization laboratory result from the application of iodine-containing X-ray contrast media and visualization by means of X-rays. If one considers the applied X-ray contrast media as a kind of drug, it is easy to understand that in addition to the desired effect, undesirable effects can also occur, such as:

- Skin itching
- Urticaria
- Increased sweating
- Tachycardia
- Dyspnea
- Bronchospasm
- Hypotension
- Allergic shock

In direct comparison with other drugs that carry a high risk of anaphylaxis, such as diclofenac, paracetamol, ampicillin or cephalosporins, the risk of anaphylaxis to contrast media can be classified as intermediate (International Collaborative Study of Severe Anaphylaxis 2003). Patient reactions to iodinated contrast media are not uncommon in daily cardiac catheterization laboratory routine, but very severe allergic reactions, including anaphylactic shock, are. The incidence for contrast-induced complications in the cardiac catheterization laboratory is 0.23% with a lethal outcome in one in 55,000 patients (Goss et al. 1995). Allergic reactions to ionic contrast media are found more frequently than to nonionic contrast media (Gertz et al. 1992). Relevant hypotension, with a systolic blood pressure drop to 65 mmHg after contrast administration, or relevant bradycardia below 40/min occur with equal frequency after application of ionic or non-ionic contrast media. However, the frequency of ventricular tachycardia and ventricular fibrillation after contrast injection is significantly lower after

application of non-ionic contrast (Lembo et al. 1991). The administration of an intravenous test dose of the contrast agent to be used has been shown to be ineffective and inconclusive and therefore cannot be recommended for clinical routine (Yamaguchi et al. 1991). However, it can be generally assumed that patients who already have a known allergy to other substances are at twice the risk of also reacting to the X-ray contrast media to be administered (Enright et al. 1989). Increased caution is therefore required in these patients.

3.1.2 Prophylaxis of Contrast Agent Incidents

In the context of the general anamnesis, the patient should be asked in particular about allergic dispositions. If the patient has an allergic disposition, it is advisable to administer intravenous prophylaxis before the start of the examination. This should generally be kept ready for injection in the cardiac catheterization laboratory for rapid administration. In addition to the administration of intravenous corticosteroids, the administration of H1-blockers (e.g. Clemastine) and H2-blockers (e.g. Cimetidine) has proven to be particularly useful (Ring et al. 1985).

> **Anaphylaxis Prophylaxis Before Contrast Media Administration in the Cardiac Catheter Laboratory**
> - H1 blockers, e.g. Clemastine 2–4 mg i.v.
> - H2 blocker, e.g. Simetidine 50 mg i.v.
> - Corticosteroids, e.g. Solu Decortin 50–150 mg i.v.
> - Isotonic saline slowly i.v.

3.1.3 Management of Severe Contrast Reaction

If a rare and fulminant allergic reaction to the X-ray contrast media occurs during the cardiac catheterization and the patient goes into anaphylactic shock, it is necessary to quickly supply volume via a large-lumen venous access and give Suprarenin as a bolus and continuous infusion via syringe pump. Further administration of contrast must be avoided. Further circulatory stabilization therapy depends on the individual requirements under resuscitation standby.

Drug Therapy of Anaphylactic Shock
- H1 blocker, e.g. Clemastine 4 mg i.v.
- H2 blocker, e.g. Cimetidine 150 mg i.v.
- Corticosteroids, e.g. Solu Decortin 250–1000 mg i.v.
- Isotonic saline solution rapidly i.v.
- Suprarenin 1:10,000 repetitive i.v.
- Suprarenin continuous infusion

3.1.4 Examination in Latent and Evident Hyperthyroidism

Thyroid metabolism is of particular importance in patient screening prior to cardiac catheterization because iodine-containing contrast media is used to visualize the coronaries. In the presence of increased thyroid hormone production and secretion, for example in the presence of thyroid autonomy, further administration of iodine can lead to the development of a dangerous thyrotoxic crisis. This situation can be avoided by adequate patient preparation and strict indication. Thus, there is an absolute contraindication for elective examinations or elective interventions in the presence of evident hyperthyroidism. The intervention must be planned and the hyperthyroidism must be treated beforehand. In contrast, there is no absolute contraindication for acute situations, for example in patients with acute coronary syndrome or ST-segment elevation myocardial infarction, because the patient's life is usually at risk. In the presence of latent hyperthyroidism, there is a relative contraindication for both elective examinations and elective interventions. In these two cases, the patient must be pretreated with perchlorate at least on the day before the examination, preferably even earlier.

Perchlorate (Irenat® drops) competitively inhibits the uptake of iodine into the thyroid gland, which is then not available for hormone production. Routine pretreatment of patients with euthyroid metabolic state with perchlorate or thiamazole before contrast agent application in the cardiac catheterization laboratory is not appropriate (Hintze et al. 1999), but it is in patients with thyroid autonomy and peripheral euthyroid metabolic state (Nolte et al. 1996).

Thiamazole is a prodrug and is metabolized to the active metabolite methimazole. As such, it acts as an iodization inhibitor and inhibits the oxidation of iodide to iodine. In addition, thiamazole prevents the incorporation of iodine into thyroglobulin and the conversion of T3–T4 (◘ Fig. 3.1 and ◘ Table 3.1).

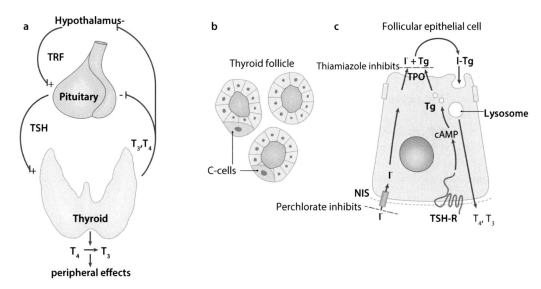

☐ Fig. 3.1 Regulation of thyroid hormone production. **a** Control of the thyroid gland by hypothalamus and pituitary gland. **b** Thyroid follicle. **c** Cell biology of follicular epithelial cells *NIS* sodium-iodine symporter, *I* iodine, *Tg* thyroglobulin, *TPO* thyroid peroxidase, *TSH-R* TSH receptor, *TRF* thyrotropin (= TSH) releasing factor, *TSH* thyroid-stimulating hormone, *I-Tg* iodinated thyroglobulin

☐ Table 3.1 Drug preparation and follow-up treatment of patients with latent/evident hyperthyroidism

Hyper-thyroid-ism	Medication 2 days before to 1 week after examination
Latent	Perchlorate (Irenat® drops) 3 × 15 drops daily (equivalent to 300 mg each)
Evident	Perchlorate (Irenat® drops) 3 × 15 drops daily (equivalent to 300 mg each) Thiamazole/Carbimazole 2 × 20 mg daily 2 days before examination until 3 weeks after examination

❯ The aim of the medicinal pre-treatment prior to contrast agent application is thus on the one hand to inhibit iodine uptake in the thyroid gland and on the other hand to inhibit hormone synthesis within the thyroid gland.

Treatment of life-threatening thyrotoxic crisis consists of primary effective drug blockade of the thyroid gland and inhibition of intrathyroidal hormone synthesis by intravenous administration of thyrostatic drugs. In addition, possible malignant hyperthermia must be treated and frequency controlled by administration of beta-blockers. Further circulatory stabilizing measures may be necessary. After stabilization of the patient, surgical thyroidectomy is the method of choice.

3.2 Contrast-Induced Nephropathy

Jan Pollmann

3.2.1 Definition and Incidence

According to the guidelines of the European Society of Urogenital Radiology (ESUR) (▶ www.esur.org/Contrast-media.51.0. html), contrast induced nephropathy (CIN) is defined by an increase in serum creatinine of >0.5 mg/dl or >25% of baseline, or a decrease in glomerular filtration rate of >25% within 48–72 h after exposure to iodinated contrast media. Severe renal dysfunction is present with an absolute increase in serum creatinine

>1 mg/dL or >50% of baseline. Other causes of renal dysfunction must be excluded.

Depending on the definition, contrast induced nephropathy occurs in the following frequencies:
- About 2% of the general population.
- Approximately 5–10% in patients with mild to moderate reduced renal function (Katzberg and Newhouse 2010).
- 10–40% in patients with diabetes mellitus and mild to moderately reduced renal function.
- 50% or more in patients with advanced renal failure (Thomsen et al. 2008).

The morbidity and mortality of patients with contrast induced nephropathy is influenced by a number of additional factors and is more pronounced the more comorbidities exist (Gruberg et al. 2000). For example, preexisting renal insufficiency, impaired left ventricular function, age, and the amount of contrast applied increase the incidence. In a meta-analysis, no renal failure requiring dialysis was observed with a contrast media quantity of less than 100 ml (McCullough et al. 2006). In high-risk patients, however, even very small amounts of contrast media can trigger nephropathies (Kane et al. 2008).

A basic distinction is made between primary and additional risk factors.

Primary risk factors for contrast induced nephropathy:
- Amount and type of contrast agent administered
- Pre-existing chronic renal insufficiency, serum creatinine >1.5 mg/dl
- Impaired left ventricular function (LVEF)
- Arterial hypotension
- Nephrotoxic substances

Additional risk factors for contrast induced nephropathy:
- Reduced nephron reserve
- Higher age
- Diabetes mellitus
- Proteinuria, especially paraproteinuria
- Diuretic therapy (especially high doses)
- Dehydration (hematocrit increase)
- Anemia (enhancement of renal medullary hypoxia)
- Kidney transplant

Various models are available for risk stratification prior to cardiac catheterization (❏ Table 3.2). In addition, once the risk score has been determined, the corresponding risk of needing dialysis can also be calculated (❏ Table 3.3).

❏ **Table 3.2** Risk stratification for the development of a CIN according to Mehran and Nikolsky (Mehran et al. 2004)

Risk factors	Score
Arterial hypotension (systolic RR <100 mmHg)	5
Intra-aortic balloon pump (JABP)	5
Heart failure NYHA stage III or IV (CHF)	5
Age >75 years	4
Contrast agent	1/100 cm^3
Serum creatinine >1.5 mg/dl	4
GFR mL/min/1.73 m^2	
40–60	2
20–40	4
<20	6
Diabetes mellitus or anemia	3

❏ **Table 3.3** Contrast induced nephropathy, score and dialysis risk according to Mehran and Nikolsky (Mehran et al. 2004)

Score	CIN risk (%)	Dialysis risk (%)
0–5	7.5	0.04
6–10	14	0.12
11–16	26.1	1.09
>16	57.3	12.6

3.2.2 Pathogenesis

Contrast induced nephropathy is mainly due to the following factors:
- Medullary hypoxia
- Direct cytotoxicity of the contrast agent
- Increase in viscosity in the tubule

After contrast administration, a brief increase in renal perfusion is followed by a decrease in renal blood flow. This leads to a decrease in filtration pressure and an increase in intratubular pressure. A constriction of the afferent arteriole in conjunction with a mesangial contraction is possible. In addition, erythrocyte aggregation, vasoactive stimuli (endotheline, adenosine), and also redistribution of renal blood flow to deeper nephrons play a role in addition to increasing blood viscosity. Eventually, cytotoxic renal medullary injury occurs. Critical lowering of medullary partial pressure of oxygen also reduces GFR (Persson and Tepel 2006).

Non-steroidal anti-inflammatory drugs and aminoglycosides increase medullary hypoxia. In addition, apoptosis induction and release of radicals may occur.

In the tubule there is increased precipitation of the so-called Tamm-Horsefall protein as well as reabsorption disorders with proteinuria and increased uric acid and oxate excretion.

3.2.3 Prophylaxis and Therapy

Contrast media: Non-ionic, isoosmolar contrast media (e.g. iodixanol) should be used. These have a significantly lower nephrotoxicity than conventional contrast media (e.g. iohexol) (Sandler 2003).

Hydration: In principle, sufficient hydration must be ensured before exposure to contrast media. In case of normal renal function, a sufficient oral drinking quantity is sufficient. In contrast, if serum creatinine levels are elevated >1.5 mg/dL or creatinine clearance is reduced <60 mL/min, parenteral administration of Saline 0.9% at 1 ml/kg/h for at least 6 h before to 6 h after contrast administration is recommended (Schonenberger et al. 2010). Diuretics should be discontinued if possible.

Sodium bicarbonate: The use of Sodium Bicarbonate for the prevention of contrast nephropathy is discussed contradictorily in the literature. So far, there is no clear evidence for an advantage of sodium bicarbonate administration over infusion of physiological saline.

N-acetylcysteine: Despite antioxidant properties, no study has yet been able to demonstrate a clear reduction in the toxic effects of the contrast agent (Berwanger 2010).

Statins: Studies show a reduced incidence of contrast nephropathy in patients treated with statins. The glomerular filtration rate was also higher than in patients without statin therapy.

Hemodialysis: According to recent studies, dialysis treatment cannot reliably prevent contrast induced nephropathy. Thus, this procedure does not play a role as a preventive measure.

Metformin: Metformin may be continued if renal function is normal; however, it has become a common practice to pause metformin per se before cardiac catheterization. Metformin should not be given 48 h before to 48 h after contrast administration if the GFR is 30–60 ml/min/1.73 m^2.

> To avoid contrast induced nephropathy, consider the type of contrast agent, the amount administered, adequate hydration, and avoidance of concomitant administration of potentially nephrotoxic substances. Prophylaxis with dopamine, fenoldopam, iloprost, statins, or mannitol have no effect and do not avoid contrast induced nephropathy. N-acetylcysteine and theophylline at least do no harm and have some renoprotective effects. Diuretics, however, increase the occurrence of contrast nephropathy.

3.3 Hemodynamic Instability and Circulatory Management

Carsten Skurk

Hemodynamic instabilities can occur in the cardiac catheterization laboratory during elective examinations and elective interventions, but especially in the course of an acute intervention, for example in acute coronary syndromes. In the following, the circumstances and conditions to be taken into account will be discussed and solutions for patient stabilization will be presented. One focus is on the therapy of cardiogenic shock.

3.3.1 Monitoring in the Cardiac Catheterization Laboratory

Both during elective examinations and interventions and in the event of an acute intervention, patients must receive monitoring of circulatory and vital parameters in the cardiac catheterization laboratory. This is done in a standardized manner and can be adapted and extended according to individual needs and depending on the procedure performed and procedure duration.

By default, at least:
- Cardiovascular monitoring (invasive blood pressure measurement, continuous heart rate and ECG)
- ACT determination, if applicable

Extended monitoring may be required depending on the procedure performed or the clinical condition of the patient:
- Respiratory monitoring (pulse oximetry, respiratory rate, respiratory pattern, respiratory monitoring if necessary)
- Temperature measurement
- Blood gas analyses (venous and arterial)
- Pressure measurement by means of pulmonary artery catheter
- Cardiac output measurement
- LV function assessment with transesophageal echocardiography (TEE)
- Cardiac valve assessment by means of TEE

The patient's cabling necessary for monitoring should be positioned so that the view of the intervention area is not obstructed. This applies equally to adhesive pads from the defibrillator, but also, in the case of interventions for structural heart disease, to the intraprocedural position of the TEE probe. In principle, monitoring in the cardiac catheterization laboratory is mandatory and supports the operator in his interventions on the patient.

3.3.2 Bradycardic Arrhythmias

AV block and sinus bradycardia are the most common. These can occur with occlusion of the proximal RCA, but also of the RCX in left-supply type, or exit of the sinus node artery from the RCX.

Therapy: Initial 0.5–1 mg atropine i.v., alternatively orciprenaline i.v. 1–3 μg/min, theophylline i.v. If the bradycardia persists, a rapid temporary VVI pacemaker should be placed via the femoral vein (7F sheath) or transjugularly. Bradycardic arrhythmias are often transient in nature and often temporary pacemakers can be removed. It is crucial that arrhythmias are detected and that patients are adequately monitored postprocedurally, for example on an intermediate care unit or at least on telemetry.

3.3.3 Tachycardic Arrhythmias

■ **Ventricular Tachycardia**

Non-sustained ventricular tachycardia that is not hemodynamically relevant does not require primary treatment. If rapid revascularization can be ensured, the ischemically triggered ventricular arrhythmias are also reduced. Otherwise, in addition to an optimal electrolyte situation (sodium, potassium, calcium, magnesium), the O_2 supply is decisive. In the past, glucose supplementation has not produced any clear benefit. In case of frequent ventricular tachycardia or electrical storm, early administration of amiodarone (initially 150–300 mg slowly i.v., better as a short infusion) is recommended. Persistent ventricular tachycardia must be immediately cardioverted electrically with the lowest possible energy (100 J biphasic).

Ventricular flutter or fibrillation must be defibrillated immediately and Amiodarone given i.v. Start with 150 J biphasic, increase to 200 J. Rapid revascularization must absolutely be pursued predominantly.

3.3.4 Cardiogenic Shock: Causes, Diagnosis and Therapy

Cardiogenic shock (CS) is a complex clinical picture caused by primary cardiac pump failure with hemodynamic instability and reduced end-organ perfusion as well as pulmonary and venous congestion. Approximately 10% of ST Elevation Myocardial Infarction (STEMI) patients develop cardiogenic shock (Rathod et al. 2018). Mortality is approximately 45–70% despite advances in therapy (Rathod et al. 2018). The initial catecholamine-induced centralization of the circulation is modified by paracrine and hormonal signaling pathways of the neurovascular and innate immune systems (shock spiral). The compensatory increased release of endogenous catecholamines causes a perfusion imbalance, arrhythmia, water and salt retention, and an increase in preload and afterload. A later developing inflammatory response syndrome (SIRS) leads to cardiodepression, vasodilation, capillary leakage and microvascular dysfunction via TNFα and IL-6 (◘ Fig. 3.2). Cardiogenic shock is a spectrum from mild hypoperfusion to marked irreversible shock.

Established criteria for making the diagnosis of cardiogenic shock are (Thiele et al. 2012, 2017b):

(a) Systolic blood pressure <90 mmHg for >30 min or need for therapy with vasopressors to maintain systolic blood pressure >90 mmHg.

(b) Pulmonary congestion or elevated left ventricular filling pressures.

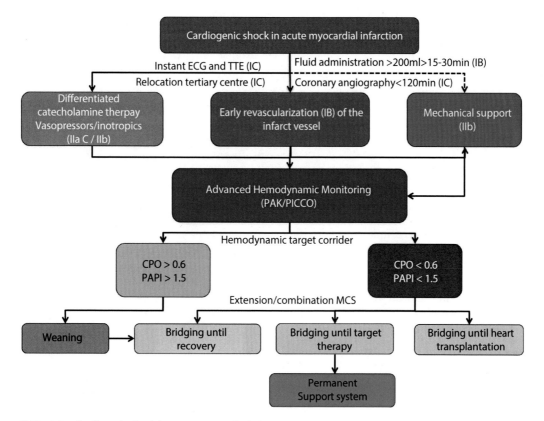

◘ Fig. 3.2 Cardiogenic shock in acute myocardial infarction

(c) Signs of decreased organ perfusion with at least one of the following:
  - Altered mental status; agitation
  - Pale, cool, sweaty skin with reticular markings
  - Oliguria (<20 ml/h)
  - Elevated serum lactate (>2 mmol/l)

Diagnosis may be made on the basis of these clinical criteria, although extended hemodynamic monitoring is also recommended (Hochman et al. 1999):
  - Cardiac Index <1.8 l/min/m^2 without and <2.2 l/min/m^2 with vasopressor therapy
  - PCPW >15 mmHg

■ **Causes of Cardiogenic Shock**

Acute myocardial infarction with ventricular dysfunction is the most common cause, accounting for approximately 80% of all cardiogenic shocks (Harjola et al. 2015). This is a classic left heart failure in the majority of cases, but complications of the infarct such as free wall perforation, ventricular septal defect, acute mitral regurgitation and right heart involvement can also be causative (Hochman et al. 2000). Patients with chronic heart failure present with acute decompensation in approximately 20% (Kar et al. 2011). Other causes are rare:
  - Myogen:
    - Tako-Tsubo cardiomyopathy, pregnancy cardiomyopathy, hypertrophic obstructive cardiomyopathy, restrictive cardiomyopathy, myocarditis.
    - Pharmaco-cardiotoxicity/Intoxications: Cytostatics (especially anthracyclines), overdose/combination calcium antagonists, beta-blockers, antiarrhythmics, digitalis, antidepressants, neuroleptics, drugs.
  - Mechanical:
    - Valvular disease (stenosis, insufficiency), intracavitary/extracardiac flow obstruction such as myxoma or other (cardiac) tumors, pulmonary embolism, pericardial tamponade, aortic dissection, traumatic cardiac injury.
  - Rhythmogenic:
    - Tachycardic arrhythmias, supraventricular/ventricular tachycardia, bradycardic arrhythmias.

■ **Diagnostics and Therapy of Cardiogenic Shock**

Rapid diagnosis is of paramount importance, as any delay in diagnosis increases the risk of mortality. The diagnosis of infarct-related cardiogenic shock can be made from the clinical signs and on the basis of the ECG and bedside echocardiography. Further hemodynamic measurements are not initially required for this purpose.

Basic monitoring in the ICU includes the following components:
  - Cardiovascular monitoring with invasive blood pressure measurement, continuous heart rate and ECG derivation, including recurrent 12-lead ECG registrations and performance of transthoracic echocardiography.
  - Respiratory monitoring by means of pulse oximetry.
  - Basic laboratory analyses incl. Arterial blood gas analysis (BGA).
  - Chest X-ray.
  - Body temperature measurement.
  - Import and export balancing (urine catheter).

Initially, volume administration (500–1000 ml crystalline solution, caution: contraindication pulmonary oedema) may be necessary to increase preload in case of pre-existing relative/absolute volume deficiency. If stabilization is not achieved, the use of catecholamines is recommended (◘ Fig. 3.2). In respiratory insufficiency, noninvasive ventilation or intubation and mechanical ventilation should be sought. All these measures should not delay revascularization.

Current treatment recommendations are often empirical, as randomized trials are often lacking in this patient population. Recently, standardized and team-based treatment strategies in specialized centers have been favored due to the complexity of treatment (Tehrani et al. 2019). This approach may be associated with significantly lower mortality (Basir et al. 2018; Tehrani et al. 2019; Rab et al. 2018; van Diepen et al. 2017). With early recognition of the clinical picture, several hemodynamic targets can be met and progression to cardiogenic shock and multiorgan failure can be prevented. These targets are as follows:

- Support of the systemic circulation.
- Unloading of the left and/or right ventricle.
- Improvement of myocardial perfusion.
- Reduction of systemic venous congestion.

Because of the importance of acute myocardial infarction for the development of cardiogenic shock, the randomized trials were conducted in this patient population; the other therapeutic strategies also apply to acute decompensated heart failure (ADHF), although the data on this are much poorer.

■ **Intervention**

Immediate revascularization is the most important therapeutic measure in cardiogenic shock due to myocardial infarction (NNT = 8 patients) (Hochman et al. 1999, 2006). Stabilization of patients in the ICU with delay of intervention, however intended, should be avoided under all circumstances (Jeger et al. 2006; Zeymer et al. 2004). Current guidelines recommend early revascularization by PCI or aorto-coronary bypass surgery according to coronary morphology (I B recommendation) (Neumann et al. 2019). A subanalysis of the SHOCK trial showed similar results in terms of survival between patients treated with bypass surgery or PCI (Hochman et al. 1999). In this non-randomized comparison, the operative group contained significantly more patients with diabetes, three-vessel coronary disease, and left main involvement. Despite equal mortality, bypass surgery is rarely performed in the acute setting (<5% of cases). Current recommendations clearly favor intervention due to the time factor; only in cases of unfavorable anatomy or lack of successful intervention should emergency bypass surgery be performed (I B recommendation) (Neumann et al. 2019).

According to the results of the largest randomized study in cardiogenic shock, only the culprit lesion should be treated initially. Multivessel PCI in cardiogenic shock resulted in increased mortality and a higher incidence of acute renal failure (Thiele et al. 2017a) and is therefore no longer recommended in the current guidelines (Ibanez et al. 2018a, b). Radial access should also be preferred in cardiogenic shock (Pancholy et al. 2015). Only for patients who cannot be treated in a PCI center within 120 min should lysis be considered (IIa C recommendation) (Ibanez et al. 2018a, b).

■ **Concomitant Antithrombotic Therapy**

Gastrointestinal absorption of drugs is impaired after acute myocardial infarction and especially due to lack of gastrointestinal perfusion in cardiogenic shock (Orban et al. 2014). The influence of additional drugs affecting the absorption of antiplatelet agents or enzymes of degradation might have a further impact on the risk of bleeding or the anti-platelet efficacy of the drugs. However, data on this are lacking from patients with cardiogenic shock. Observational studies on the use of GpIIb/IIIa inhibitors with small case numbers showed a mortality benefit after stent implantation (Antoniucci et al. 2002). However, a small randomized trial showed no benefit of routine application in the presence of increased bleeding risk (Chan et al. 2002). Guideline-compliant therapy with dual platelet inhibition and, if administration is not possible, liberal use of GpIIb/IIIa antagonists or parenteral anti-platelet agents such as cangrelor should be used. The administration of crushed ticagrelor by gavage is also an alternative (Parodi et al. 2015). Due to the frequent occurrence of acute renal or liver failure, the administration of unfractionated heparin should be favoured over that of low-molecular-weight heparin or fondaparinux.

■ **Vasopressors and Inotropics**

In addition to rapid revascularization, drug therapy with positive inotropic substances or vasopressors (SIRS component) is essential in cardiogenic shock, especially in the absence of the option of implantation of a mechanical cardiac support. Despite their wide use, very few outcome data are available on the selection and use of catecholamines (recommendation grade IIb, C) (Ibanez et al. 2018a, b). An overview of the hemodynamic effects and dosages of vasopressors and inotropics is presented in ◻ Table 3.4.

3

◻ Table 3.4 Mechanism of action and hemodynamic effects of drugs frequently used in CS

Drug	Infusion dose	Mode of action				Hemodynamic effects				Special features
		α_1	β_1	β_2	D	CO	SVR	PVR	MABP	
Vasopressor/inotrope										
Dopamine	0.5–2 µg/kg/min	–	+	–	+		–	–	–	Tachycardia, decreased intestinal perfusion, no nephroprotective effect, SOAP data
	5–10 µg/kg/min	+	+++	+	++	↑↑	↑	–	↑	
	10–20 µg/kg/min	+++	++	–	++	↑	↑↑	↑	↑	
Norepineph-rine	0.05–0.4 µg/kg/min	++++	++	+	–	↑	↑↑	↑	↑↑	High doses can lead to necrosis of the acras
Epinephrine	0.01–0.5 µg/kg/min	++++	++++	+++	–	↑↑	↑↑	↑↑	↑↑	Tachycardia, VT/VF, increase in myocardial oxygen consumption and lactate
Dobutamine	2.5–20 µg/kg/min	+	++++	++	–	↑↑	↓	↓	–/↓	Tachycardia, increase in myocardial oxygen consumption
Vasopressin	0.02–0.04 rpm	Stimulates V_1 receptors in vascular smooth muscle					↑↑	–	↑↑	No data in cardiogenic shock

Inodilator			
Milrinone	0.125–0.75 µg/ kg/min	PDE-3 inhibitor, inhibition of c-AMP degradation	Increase of CO, decrease of SVR	Administration together with dobutamine recommended, no bolus administration recommended (hypotension), caution: cardiac arrhythmias, intrapulmonary shunts
Enoximone	2–10 µg/kg/min	PDE-3 inhibitor, inhibition of c-AMP degradation	Increase of CO, decrease of SVR	Administration together with dobutamine recommended, no bolus administration (hypotension). Caution: cardiac arrhythmias, intrapulmonary shunts
Levosimen-dan	Bolus: 12–24 µg/kg over 10 min 0.05–0.2 µg/kg/ min	Myofilament Ca^{2+} Sensitizer, increase in inotropy, decrease SVR by activation of K^+ channels	Increase of CO, decrease of SVR	Caution with bolus administration (hypotension), little arrhythmia tendency, no increase in cardiac O_2 consumption, long-lasting effect

In the SOAP-II trial, dopamine showed a greater arrhythmic potential compared with norepinephrine in a prespecified CS group, as well as higher mortality (De Backer et al. 2010). Furthermore, higher lactate levels and heart rate with more frequent incidence of refractory shock were detectable with epinephrine therapy in post-PCI patients in CS due to acute myocardial infarction in a randomized trial (Levy et al. 2018). These data confirm the theoretical benefits of norepinephrine. Because of its peripherally constricting effect, norepinephrine combines well with dobutamine. Dobutamine has a positive myocardial inotropic effect and leads to afterload reduction as a result of peripheral vasodilation. The eventual drop in blood pressure or lack of increase in blood pressure can be counteracted by a vasopressor. Differentiated catecholamine therapy consists of dobutamine (Cardiac Index [CI] titration) and norepinephrine (peripheral vascular resistance [SVR] adjustment) after hemodynamic measurement. In summary, few study data are available on the use of catecholamines. The specific use of the drugs should be pragmatic according to the causes of shock (🔲 Table 3.4). Because of the side-effect profile, the lowest possible dose and duration of therapy should be aimed for.

- ■ **Cardiac Mechanical Support**

Percutaneous implantable mechanical support systems (MCS) can be used for short-term maintenance of cardiac output. The use of such systems in cardiogenic shock is increasing (Stretch et al. 2014) and depends on local availability. As the use of the systems requires a lot of personnel and training, it is recommended that patients are treated in specialized centers (Basir et al. 2018; Tehrani et al. 2019).

The objectives of using a mechanical support system can be defined as follows:
- ▬ The system should provide sufficient haemodynamic support,
- ▬ Be able to be implanted quickly and without complications and be easy to operate,
- ▬ The operation should have few complications.

Depending on the indication, different systems are used, some of which differ greatly in the criteria mentioned above. The timing of implantation, duration of support and weaning are currently based on empirical criteria due to a lack of data and should be performed according to local availability and familiarity with the system as well as adapted to the needs of the patient (age, comorbidities, neurological function, chances of survival and quality of life) (class IIb C indication). Again, the time factor in acute myocardial infarction is crucial (Flaherty et al. 2017; Kapur and Davila 2017). In principle, there should be a clear therapeutic goal for the initiation of MCS therapy, either temporary stabilization of the patient ("bridge to recovery"), support until definitive therapeutic care ("bridge to destination therapy"), or support until transplantation ("bridge to transplant").

The following systems are in use in clinical practice:

Intraaortic counterpulsation—IABP: The system augments the cardiac action. An increase in diastolic pressure (filling in diastole) causes an increase in diastolic coronary perfusion. Decreasing left ventricular afterload (slackening in systole) causes a small increase in cardiac index without increasing myocardial oxygen consumption. In the IABP-SHOCK-II trial, no effect of IABP on outcome or various surrogate parameters was obtained in patients with CS due to ACS compared with a drug-treated cohort (Thiele et al. 2012). The reason for this is the lack of hemodynamic support of the device. Therefore, this therapy is generally no longer recommended in this patient population (Class III recommendation). Use may occur in patients with acute, severe, decompensated mitral regurgitation or with a ventricular septal effect in centers without other MCS (Class IIa C recommendation) (Ibanez et al. 2018a, b; Neumann et al. 2019).

Axial rotary pumps—Impella 2.5/CP/5.0: The system consists of a miniaturized axial pump on a pigtail catheter advanced into the ventricle via, for example, the femoral artery (12–14F), which transports blood from the left ventricle into the ascending aorta (🔲 Figs. 3.3 and 3.4). The system can gener-

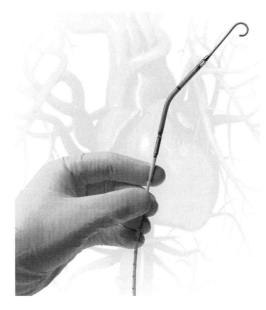

Fig. 3.3 Impella, axial rotary pump

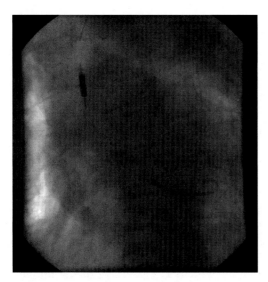

Fig. 3.4 Impella, axial rotary pump in situ

ate cardiac output from 2.5 l/min (Impella® 2.5) up to 4.0 l/min (Impella® CP) or 5 L/min (Impella 5.0) (Thiele et al. 2015). The Impella® actively unloads ("unloads") the left ventricle (Esposito et al. 2018), reducing wall stress, work of beating, and myocardial oxygen consumption while improving perfusion (Kapur et al. 2013; O'Neill et al. 2014, 2017). Unloading has a cardioprotective effect (Esposito et al. 2018). Due to its mechanism of action, the system is used in left heart failure. The systems are approved for temporary therapy in cardiogenic shock for <4 days (Impella 2.5 and CP) and for <6 days (Impella 5.0 and LD); however, longer therapies have been described. Contraindications for use include mechanical aortic valve replacement, intracardiac thrombus, severe aortic stenosis (KOF 0.6 cm^2), severe aortic regurgitation, severe right heart failure, cardiorespiratory failure, ASD/VSD, cardiac tamponade, and severe peripheral arterial occlusive disease (PAOD).

Three smaller randomized trials and one meta-analysis demonstrated better hemodynamic support compared to IABP. These studies were underpowered for evidence of a mortality benefit (Ouweneel et al. 2017; Seyfarth et al. 2008; Thiele et al. 2017b). The current largest registry of Impella use in CS after ACS failed to demonstrate an effect on 30-day mortality (Schrage et al. 2019). The randomized DanGER-SCHOCK trial (NCT01633502) will provide clarity on its clinical use in CS.

Axial rotation pump—Impella RP: The Impella RP is an axial rotation pump implanted through the femoral vein (22F) that delivers blood from the inferior vena cava to the pulmonary artery. This relieves the right ventricle and increases LV preload. The system is used for right heart failure. It was approved for use <14 days for patients with a body surface area of >1.5 m^2. Contraindications include changes in the pulmonary artery that preclude implantation, significant tricuspid or pulmonary insufficiency or stenosis, and thrombus formation in the right atrium or vena cava.

Extracorporeal centrifugal pumps with oxygenator (VA-ECMO): This system delivers blood from the right atrium via an external oxygenator into the descending aorta against the physiological direction of blood flow. This can treat concomitant pulmonary failure (O$_2$-enrichment, CO$_2$-elimination) (Fig. 3.5). Hemodynamic support is 5–7 L/min. The system is implanted in global cardiac failure (iCPR) or concomitant right heart involvement (posterior wall infarction) and

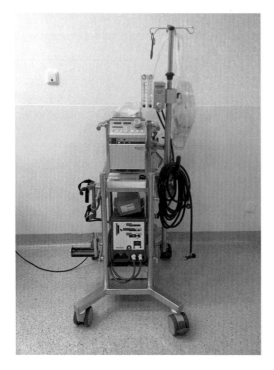

◘ Fig. 3.5 Portable heart-lung machine

can replace complete cardiac and pulmonary function. The disadvantage is the increase in preload of the left ventricle with increased wall stress and increased oxygen consumption and the higher invasiveness of the procedure (femoral 18–23F sheaths). The afterload increase with distension of the LV and consecutive increase in pulmonary pressures can be compensated by different venting techniques such as extension to VAV-ECMO with return of part of the arterial limb via the jugular vein or combination with an Impella. These techniques can also prevent Harlequin syndrome, which occurs when spontaneous cardiac action resumes and deoxygenated blood is ejected from the LV against the ECMO blood flow with consecutive myocardial and cerebral damage. Indications for VA-ECMO therapy include cardiogenic shock due to global cardiac failure or associated ARDS or right heart failure. Contraindications for use include patients who are not suitable for anticoagulation, have aortic dissection or high-grade aortic regurgitation, or suffer from severe PAOD that makes cannulation impossible.

Randomized data on the use of the system do not exist, registry data show poor long-term prognosis (de Waha et al. 2016). The place of therapy in CS due to ACS is currently being investigated in the ECLS-SCHOCK trial (NCT03637205).

Combination of devices: Based purely on pathophysiological considerations, a combination of different devices may be useful. Combinations of left and right ventricular Impella have been described (Kuchibhotla et al. 2017). The combination of left ventricular Impella and VA-ECMO to relieve the left ventricle and prophylaxis of Harlequin syndrome showed good results in registries (Pappalardo et al. 2017).

■ **Advanced Hemodynamic Monitoring**

Although several scoring systems have been proposed to estimate outcome in cardiogenic shock, none is universally accepted. Invasive arterial blood pressure measurement due to hemodynamic instability and to titrate commonly used vasoactive drugs, as well as a central venous catheter to apply drugs and determine central venous saturation (SVO_2) to assess tissue oxygenation, are recommended (Ibanez et al. 2018a, b; van Diepen et al. 2017). Advanced hemodynamic monitoring using pulmonary artery catheter (PAC) or PICCO system is recommended for differential management of volume and catecholamine therapy, although a general benefit of the systems offers little evidence in terms of patient outcome (IIb B recommendation) (Ibanez et al. 2018a, b). For therapeutic assessment and follow-up of the patient in cardiogenic shock, knowledge of the cardiac output, which is defined by preload, afterload, and contractility, as well as heart rate, is mandatory. Classical clinical signs such as blood pressure, urine output, neck vein filling, skin perfusion and skin turgor do not allow a reliable assessment of the current hemodynamics.

Hemodynamic data from the PAC can characterize the presence and severity of shock, define any right ventricular (RV) involvement, measure pulmonary arterial pressure and PCPW, and determine the vascular resistance of the pulmonary and systemic vascular bed. In addition, a PAC/PICCO system can determine prognostic parameters such as Cardiac Power (CPO) and assess response to therapeutic interventions (Hasdai et al. 2000). Cardiac Power and Cardiac Power Index (CPI) describe the mean hydraulic energy. Univariate and multivariate analysis of the SHOCK trial registry identified a CPO of 0.53 and a CPI of 0.33 as the strongest independent hemodynamic parameter of hospital mortality (Fincke et al. 2004). As a caveat, it is important to note that there are no established cutoffs for target hemodynamic values supported by study data; this is expert opinion. In general, a mean arterial blood pressure of >65 mmHg should be aimed for to ensure adequate perfusion of the organs. Further target parameters of drug therapy according to the extended hemodynamic monitoring are:

- SVR 800–1000 dyn s/cm^5
- CI >2.5 l/m^2
- PCPW 15–18 mmHg
- SVO$_2$ >65%
- CPO >0.6 W (CPI >0.4 W/m^2)

These values should be targeted by minimal use of catecholamines. In general, sufficient organ and tissue perfusion should be serially assessed by integrating hemodynamic variables, arterial lactate concentration, mixed or central venous oxygen saturation, urine volume, creatinine concentration, liver function tests, and the patient's mental status (van Diepen et al. 2017).

3.4 Airway Management in the Cardiac Catheterization Laboratory

Martin Müller

3.4.1 Introduction

Endotracheal intubation remains the gold standard for airway management. If endotracheal intubation is not feasible for whatever reason, the use of supraglottic airway devices (e.g. laryngeal tube) is indicated. If the patient can neither be intubated nor ventilated with a bag and mask in the case of respiratory arrest, or if ventilation via a supraglottic airway device is impossible ("can't intubate, can't ventilate"), an emergency coniotomy must be performed using a coniotomy set designed for this purpose.

3.4.2 Endotracheal Intubation

■ **Material**

An endotracheal tube (ID 7.5–8.5 mm) according to Magill is usually used for endotracheal intubation. The tube should always be fitted with a guide rod, as this makes it possible to give the tube a suitable pre-bend, which facilitates insertion. This is particularly useful in emergency situations. Inserting the guide rod after a primarily unsuccessful intubation attempt leads to an unnecessary loss of time during endotracheal intubation.

Direct laryngoscopy is performed with a Macinstosh laryngoscope. In adults, blades of sizes 3, 4 and 5 (blade lengths 13, 15.5 and 18 cm) are used for this purpose.

Since it may be necessary to remove saliva or gastric contents or blood that have returned to the mouth and throat, a sufficient suction device should be available. It should be noted that the lumen of the suction catheters used must also be sufficiently large. In everyday clinical practice, suction catheters of size CH 16 (orange) have proven successful.

A blocker syringe (10 ml) should be available to block the tube cuff.

After intubation, the stethoscope can be used to verify the position of the tube by auscultating ventilation-synchronous sounds over both lungs.

A resuscitator, preferably with an oxygen reservoir and a ventilation mask of sufficient size, must be available.

All the aids mentioned for securing the airway are part of the standard equipment of a cardiac catheterization laboratory (see also ► Sect. 1.1.2).

3

It is also useful to insert a Guedel tube after successful intubation. This serves as bite protection so that the patient cannot accidentally compress the tube. The tube must also be secured with a suitable fixator so that it cannot slip in or out.

If available, appropriate head support pillows should be used.

Of course, for hygiene reasons, disposable gloves are worn by the treatment team for intubation.

Material for endotracheal intubation:
- Tube (ID 7.5–8.5 mm) according to Magill with guide rod
- Laryngoscope according to Macinstosh with blades sizes 3, 4 and 5
- Suction option (suction catheter >CH 16 orange)
- Blocker syringe (10 ml)
- Stethoscope
- Resuscitator bag O_2-Reservoir and respiratory mask
- Bite guard (e.g. Guedel tube)
- Tube fixation (e.g. Thomas ET tube holder)
- Positioning pillow for the head
- Gloves

■ **Practical Implementation**

The patient's head is positioned in the improved Jackson position. Most patients—assuming sufficient cervical spine mobility—are easier to intubate in this position. For this purpose, the head is carefully hyperextended into the so-called sniffing position.

Next, open the patient's mouth wide (e.g. cross grip thumb to the mandibular border, middle finger to the maxillary border) and remove foreign bodies (dentures, vomit) if necessary.

The laryngoscope is introduced with displacement of the tongue and the tip of the blade is advanced into the epiglottic vallecula.

With traction in the direction of the laryngoscope handle, the epiglottis straightens to reveal the entrance to the trachea.

Then insert the tube under visual control. Most tubes have a marking (black ring) above the cuff. It is advisable to advance the tube only until this marking is at the level of the vocal cords.

The inserted guide rod is removed and the tube must be secured manually during this process.

> **Practical Tip**
>
> The guide rod gives the tube greater strength and better formability, so always intubate with a guide rod. Especially in difficult situations, it can be advantageous to be able to shape the endotracheal tube individually. Make sure that the guide rod or the tube lumen are sufficiently moistened so that the rod can be easily removed after intubation.

The cuff is then blocked and connected to the resuscitator.

Now the tube position is checked. Several methods are used to check the position of the tube.

On inspection, ventilator-synchronous bilateral chest excursions can be perceived.

Auscultatory sounds are heard synchronously over both lungs. Noises when operating the bag over the stomach indicate an oesophageal malposition of the tube. If in doubt, auscultate over the stomach first.

An existing capnography or capnometry should definitely be used. The expiratory return flow of carbon dioxide is a very strong sign of a bronchotracheal tube position (◘ Fig. 3.6).

On the cardiac catheterization table, the tube position can theoretically also be verified radiologically by means of fluoroscopy, since the carina of the trachea is usually clearly visible.

If the inspection and auscultation findings are inconclusive and capnography/capnometry or fluoroscopy are not available, the position of the tube can be checked by direct laryngoscopy.

Now a bite guard is inserted and the tube is fixed. Sufficient tube fixation is absolutely necessary so that the tube cannot dislocate when the patient has to be repositioned.

■ **Tube Malposition**

Basically, there is the possibility of an oesophageal or endobronchial tube malposition. In the case of an oesophageal tube malposition, no ventilation-synchronous sounds above

◘ **Fig. 3.6** Endotracheal intubation. (Medical illustration by Nataša Kaiser)

3

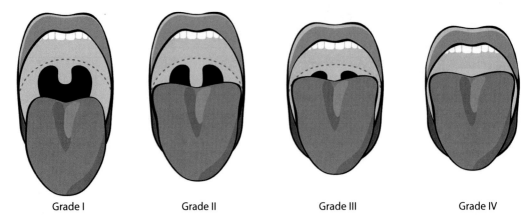

Grade I   Grade II   Grade III   Grade IV

Fig. 3.7 Malampati score. (Medical illustration by Nataša Kaiser)

the lungs and no thoracic excursions can be heard. The CO_2 return flow typical of ventilation is also absent.

If the tube is endobronchial, it has been advanced into the (usually the right) main bronchus. Unilateral ventilation-synchronous sounds above the lung, unilateral thoracic excursions are the result. If the tube is positioned correctly, the marker is 20–22 cm in the corner of the mouth/row of teeth in a normal-sized adult.

■ **The Difficult Intubation**

Predictive factors for difficult intubation include a short, thick neck, restricted mouth opening (Malampati score >3), restricted cervical spine mobility, overbite, large tongue, injuries, and malformations and surgery in the head and neck region (■ Fig. 3.7).

Practical Tip

Even with difficult intubations, quick, efficient work is the order of the day. If there are problems during direct laryngoscopy, analyse them and adapt your procedure accordingly. In most cases, it is not helpful to make multiple intubation attempts under identical conditions. As long as the patient can be ventilated well with bag and mask, there is sufficient time to optimize the conditions for the next intubation attempt. Consider the use of supraglottic airway devices in time.

In the case of difficult intubation conditions, all external circumstances relevant to intubation should be checked (again) and optimised if necessary.

First, the positioning should be optimized. Is the patient's head in the improved Jackson position? Clinical experience shows that patients with significantly reduced reclination ability are sometimes easier to laryngoscope directly if the head is positioned flat and the reduced cervical spine mobility is completely available for reclination.

The mouth should be opened as much as possible and foreign objects be removed. Are the existing teeth really not removable dentures? Vomit and saliva should be completely evacuated.

Furthermore, an attempt can be made to improve the intubation conditions by means of cricoid pressure, the so-called BURP maneuver (backward, upward and rightward pressure). Here, an assistant presses the thyroid cartilage backwards and upwards and, if necessary, slightly to the right. Initially, the BURP maneuver can be performed during direct laryngoscopy with the patient's own free right hand in order to evaluate whether this allows sufficient visualisation of the laryngeal anatomy.

It is also useful to check the size of the blade. Is the blade used sufficiently large? Can the tip of the blade actually be advanced into the epoglottic vallecula?

You can always intubate a "too small" neck with a "too big" blade.

Sedation with medication and relaxation should always be considered. Is the patient still too vigilant despite respiratory and circulatory insufficiency? In clinical practice, prior intravenous administration of Midazolam (bolus 1–2.5 mg) has proven effective in suppressing any myoclonia that may occur during sedation with Etomidate (0.15–0.3 mg/kg).

Propofol (1.5–2.5 mg/kg) provides a well-developed tolerance to pharyngeal and laryngeal stimuli during anesthetic induction.

Practical Tip

A deeply sedated patient is easier to intubate than a patient who is still half awake. Therefore: Dose sedatives for intubation appropriately!

Best intubation conditions are achieved by complete relaxation of the patient. It would be desirable for the relaxation to begin quickly and to be reversed after a short duration (in the single-digit minute range). The only substance that makes this possible is Succinylcholine (0.7–1 mg/kg for intubation). As a depolarizing muscle relaxant, Succinylcholine has side effects and interactions that can be life-threatening. Careful indication is therefore essential.

Non-depolarising muscle relaxants generally have a longer onset time and a significantly longer duration of action. Rocuronium in increased dosage (1 mg/kg for intubation) has a rapid onset of action similar to that of Succinylcholine. The effect of Rocuronium can be rapidly reversed at any time (even immediately after injection of Rocuronium) with the specific antagonist Sugammadex.

3.4.3 Supraglottic Airway Support, Laryngeal Tube

As a supraglottic airway device, the Laryngeal Tube has become more and more popular in recent years. The advantage is the easy handling and the overall good ventilation characteristics even with moderately increased airway pressures under cardiopulmonary resuscitation. The disadvantage is the lack of

Table 3.5 Laryngeal tube sizes

No	Patient height (cm)	Colour coding
3	<155	Yellow
4	155–180	Red
5	>180	Purple

aspiration protection compared to endotracheal intubation.

The Laryngeal Tube consists of a plastic tube with two simultaneously blockable balloons, one of which is placed in the esophageal inlet and the other in the pharynx. Ventilation is provided through openings between the balloons. The Laryngeal Tube is supplied with a bite block, so that an additional bite guard is not necessary. Laryngeal tubes are color coded according to the patient's body size. For adults, the sizes listed in ◘ Table 3.5 can be considered.

A color-coded syringe is used to insufflate the block balloons.

■ **Insertion of the Laryngeal Tube**
The appropriately sized laryngeal tube is inserted through the patient's mouth until the dentition mark applied to the laryngeal tube is aligned with the patient's dentition.

The cuffs are then blocked with the adequate amount of air according to the color coding of the blocker syringe. After connection of the ventilation bag to the laryngeal tube, ventilation-synchronous thoracic cursions and corresponding ventilation sounds above the lungs can be detected. The capnographic/capnometric CO_2 return flow is also an indication of the correct position of the laryngeal tube (◘ Fig. 3.8).

■ **Malposition of the Laryngeal Tube**
Incorrect insertion of the Laryngeal Tube is practically impossible. If the patient cannot be ventilated with a laryngeal tube of the correct size, repositioning is indicated after unblocking. If correct positioning is not possible due to anatomical peculiarities, an alternative form of airway protection/ventilation must be selected (Laryngeal tube in emergency medicine: ▶ www.vbm-medical.de).

◘ Fig. 3.8 Laryngeal
tube. (Medical illustration
by Nataša Kaiser)

3.4.4 Video Laryngoscopy

For some years now, video laryngoscopy has been gaining more and more acceptance in the fields of anaesthesia, intensive care and emergency medicine for securing difficult airways. Via an optical system on the blade tip of a video laryngoscope, image information is fed to a camera and displayed on a monitor. The corresponding S1 guideline (AWMF no. 001/028) of the DGAI assigns an important role to video laryngoscopy for the management of difficult airways (▶ www.awmf.org).

Depending on the manufacturer, blades (e.g. D-Blade, Storz) are available for video laryngoscopes, which can be positioned laryngeally in regions that cannot be reached during conventional direct laryngoscopy with McIntosh blades.

To place the tube under video laryngoscopic view, it should be provided with a guide rod and preformed. It is often convenient to bend the lower quarter of the tube in a "hockey stick" shape. Once the glottis has been passed, the guide rod is removed by an assistant and the tube is advanced at the same time.

If the tube cannot be placed in this way, the following procedure can lead to success: First, under video laryngoscopic control, a malleable guide rod with an atraumatic tip (Eschmann rod, Cook rod) is inserted a few centimeters into the trachea. The guide rod should be at least twice as long as the tube used.

The tube is then inserted into the trachea via the guide rod. To avoid injuries, the guide rod is held by an assistant so that it cannot be pushed deeper into the bronchial system. The tube should be moistened internally with saline solution (NaCl 0.9%) before this procedure. After successful placement of the tube, the guide rod is removed.

3.4.5 Sedation in the Cardiac Catheterization Laboratory

Basically, when performing sedation in the cardiac catheterization laboratory, comparable personnel, equipment and organizational requirements must be provided as in the surgical area. However, some essential points will be discussed in more detail here.

Prior to surgery, a patient is considered fasting if, assuming an undisturbed gastrointestinal passage, he or she has not consumed any clear liquid for at least 2 h and no other food or drink for at least 6 h (▶ www.dgai.de).

With regard to the equipment and medication to be provided, the possibility of securing the airway, including intubation and ventilation, must be given. An adequate supply of oxygen connections as well as sufficient continuous patient monitoring by equipment (ECG, blood pressure, pulse oximetry) must be ensured. The spatial and personnel situation must allow effective cardiopulmonary resuscitation at all times.

The cardiologist working in the cath lab rightly focuses his attention on the intervention to be performed and not on monitoring the patient's vigilance and respiratory activity. It is therefore necessary that a second qualified person, specially trained in monitoring patients who have received sedatives and/or analgesics, reliably performs this task. An anesthesiologist or ICU staff should be consulted for patients with significant medical history or for procedures requiring deep sedation or higher doses of analgesics.

If the cardiologist performing the intervention is the only licensed physician in this situation, he or she is also responsible for the measures to be taken for analgesia and sedation (analgesia: ► www.dgai.de).

■ Conscious Sedation

Conscious sedation is understood to be a level of sedation with a slight impairment of consciousness, preserved sufficient spontaneous breathing and preserved protective reflexes. It is possible for the patient to respond appropriately to verbal requests at any time. The German Society for Anaesthesia and Intensive Care Medicine (DGAI) refers to this sedation level as "Sedation Stage II, Moderate Sedation" (► www.dgai.de).

In principle, this level of sedation can be achieved by intravenous administration of Ketamine, Benzodiazepines, (short-acting) Opioids, and Propofol individually or in combination.

For interventions in the cardiac catheterization laboratory, it should always be critically questioned whether a sedation procedure is necessary. A careful benefit/risk analysis is obligatory.

Consider administering a Benzodiazepine (e.g., 3.75–7.5 mg Midazolam or 10–30 mg clorazepate orally) to patients 30–45 min before a planned examination/intervention

for anxiolysis. This corresponds to the usual premedication for a surgical procedure in routine clinical practice.

If additional sedation is then required, it is to be expected that the drugs used for this purpose will have to be dosed rather low. The substances in question will be discussed in more detail below.

Ketamine: Since Ketamine increases heart rate and blood pressure, it should be used in cardiac risk patients with very strict indications. Because of its psychotropic effects, Ketamine should always be combined with a Benzodiazepine. The isolated S-enantiomer (S-Ketamine or Ketamine-S) has been available for some time. It has a much higher analgesic and anaesthetic potency than the racemate. Furthermore, S-Ketamine is considered to be significantly more controllable.

Midazolam: A long-established benzodiazepine that is usually well-controlled when used for short periods only and produces retrograde amnesia in addition to sedative/hypnotic effects.

Opioids: As centrally acting analgesics, easily controllable, short-acting substances (Remifentanil, Alfentanil) should generally be used for conscious sedation. The specific side effects (respiratory depression, thoracic rigidity), especially in combination with hypnotics, must be taken into account. In interventions with a low pain level and additional local anaesthesia, the indication for opioid administration should be critically reviewed in each individual case.

Propofol: Propofol is a hypnotic without an analgesic component. Due to its rather short plasma half-life it is considered to be well controllable. Side effects are respiratory depression and hypotension.

In clinical practice, Conscious Sedation can be produced by bolus injection of Midazolam (e.g. 1 mg midazolam per bolus) or Propofol (e.g. 10 mg propofol per bolus) under appropriate supervision of equipment and personnel by a specially trained, qualified person. Alternatively, Propofol may be delivered in a low dose using a syringe pump.

The indication for additional opioid administration should be strict.

■ **Anaesthesia in the Cardiac Catheter Laboratory**

If, for whatever reason, anaesthesia is foreseeably required for a cardiac catheter examination, an anaesthetist or intensive care physician must be consulted.

If a patient is brought to the cardiac catheterization laboratory already intubated and ventilated, analgesia is usually established, e.g. from the intensive care unit. It is often necessary to adjust the dosage of the ongoing analgesia upwards for repositioning and for the procedure to be performed.

If a patient requires intubation during an examination, sedation is also required after successful intubation to tolerate the tube and the measures to be performed. In this case, easily controllable substances should be administered via syringe pumps. Usually a combination of a hypnotic (e.g. Propofol 3–8 mg/kg/h) and an opioid (e.g. Remifentanil 0.1–0.5 (1) µg/kg/min) is used. Relaxation is not required for cardiac catheterization. A patient who performs defensive movements during manipulations requires more hypnotic/analgesic, not relaxation.

3.5 Cardiopulmonary Resuscitation in the Cardiac Catheterization Laboratory

Erhard Kaiser

3.5.1 General Remarks and Strategy of CPR in the Cardiac Catheterization Laboratory

Cardiopulmonary resuscitation (CPR) in the cardiac catheterization laboratory does not differ fundamentally from resuscitation performed in intensive care units or chest pain units. As a rule, the same or at least comparable personnel and equipment resources can be used in the cardiac catheterization laboratory compared to both other acute care areas of interventional cardiology. Since in addition to elective catheter-based interventions in a cardiac catheterization laboratory, which is integrated into the acute medical care in its service area, emergency care also takes place regularly, the occurrence of resuscitation situations is part of the work routine. In addition, interventional cardiology is currently developing rapidly, including highly complex catheter-based interventions, so that procedure-related resuscitations are increasingly to be expected. As a rule, cardiac catheterization laboratories, like other facilities or wards, are integrated into the in-house emergency care plan, in which specially trained crash teams are available around the clock to provide rapid assistance.

For CPR in the cardiac catheterization laboratory, the recommendations of the European Resuscitation Council (ERC) (▶ www.erc.edu) apply in the current valid revision from 2021 (Michels et al. 2022). CPR is always performed in a standardized manner. There are special features relevant to the CPR procedure in the cardiac catheterization laboratory, some of which have now been incorporated into the current ERC resuscitation guidelines. The basis for this is the fact that, in contrast to an out-of-hospital cardiac arrest (OHCA) situation, the need for resuscitation in the cardiac catheterization laboratory can always be experienced and observed directly, similar to the situation in an intensive care unit. In both areas, patients are continuously monitored on the ECG monitor. A time delay until the start of the assisting measures can therefore usually be ruled out. In addition, the cause of ventricular fibrillation occasionally lies with the surgeon and not with the patient, or is due to the device and handling. Anticipatory work can help to avoid a protracted resuscitation situation in addition to rapid defibrillation.

If resuscitation is required during a percutaneous coronary intervention in the cardiac catheterization laboratory, CPR and coronary intervention must unfavorably be performed in parallel (Larsen et al. 2010). For the CPR team, the difficult access to the patient's thorax (due to the image receiver of the X-ray equipment) for chest compressions is a particular challenge. In addition, radiation protection aspects must be considered in this context. Close coordination between the surgeon and the CPR team is essential for successful resuscitation and coronary intervention. Ideally, the operator chooses an angulation of the C-arm of the X-ray unit that ensures a sufficient view of the culprit lesion on the one hand, but also provides the CPR team with the best possible access to the thorax for cardiac massage and airway management on the other. LAO or RAO angulations, which can be tilted cranially or caudally, are ideal for this purpose. The PA position, the 90° position and the isolated cranial angulated position of the C-arm should be avoided.

Situations such as the introduction of wires and devices as well as the moment of balloon dilatation and stent implantation require special consideration and consultation. For these moments, cardiac massage must be briefly interrupted on the command of the surgeon.

If a mechanical chest compression aid is available, it should be used (Wagner et al. 2010). Care should be taken to ensure correct positioning of the device (Blomberg et al. 2011). However, limitations in C-arm control and visualization must then be accepted.

3.5.2 Defibrillation Strategy in the Cardiac Catheterization Laboratory

According to the current recommendations of the ERC, we perform a so-called one-shock strategy in the context of CPR outside as well as inside the hospital. In the cardiac catheterization laboratory, however, there are special circumstances and a shockable heart rhythm is often present in the context of an acute myocardial infarction or is iatrogenic (see below). Therefore, the three-shock strategy still applies exceptionally to electrotherapy of a shockable heart rhythm in the cardiac catheterization laboratory. Thus, up to three defibrillations must first be delivered before protracted CPR is initiated (Michels et al. 2022).

3.5.3 Technical Equipment

For sufficient cardiopulmonary resuscitation in the cardiac catheterization laboratory, a minimum of auxiliary equipment must be available. Not everything that is available is helpful. It is more important to perform sufficient CPR quickly and without interruption in addition to causal therapy (PCI). Technical aids for CPR in the cardiac catheterization laboratory are:

- Suction
- Medical oxygen for inhalation and ventilation
- Laryngeal tubes in different sizes
- Laryngoscope with blades of different sizes
- Endotracheal tubes in different sizes
- Guedel tubes in different sizes
- Resuscitator bag
- Ventilator for controlled and assisted ventilation
- Biphasic defibrillator/cardioverter
- External pacemaker

In addition, the usual emergency drugs must be readily available (◘ Table 3.6). Here too, not everything that is available necessarily has

◘ **Table 3.6** Emergency drugs for acute therapy/CPR in the cardiac catheterization laboratory

Analgesia	– Midazolam – Morphine – Remifentanil – Ketamine-S – Propofol
Arrhythmia therapy	– Atropine – Metoprolol – Esmolol – Amiodarone – Verapamil
Circulatory support	– Dobutamine – Epinephrine – Noradrenaline
Anaphylaxis therapy	– Clemastine – Ranitidine – Prednisolone/methylprednisolone

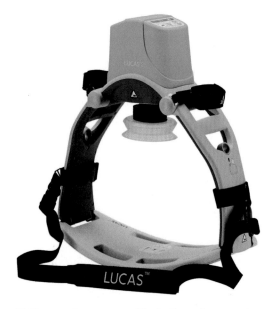

Fig. 3.9 Lucas system (Physio Control company)

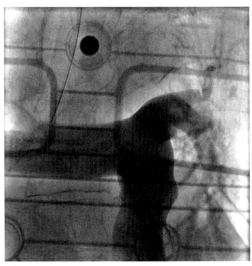

Fig. 3.10 Lucas system in the cath lab for fulminant pulmonary embolism

to be kept on hand. Rather, care should be taken to ensure that known and effective medications are used in the team, the handling and control of which are well mastered. The therapy started in the cardiac catheterization laboratory can and should then be continued and, if necessary, extended in the intensive care unit.

Other, but optional, tools include:
- Intra-aortic counterpulsation (IABP)
- Portable heart-lung machine
- LUCAS system (■ Figs. 3.9 and 3.10)
- Hypothermia system

3.5.4 Staffing

The cardiac catheter laboratory team, consisting of surgeon and nurse, should ideally be supported by the so-called crash team in the event of resuscitation. The crash team includes a physician who is experienced in intensive and emergency medicine and a nurse who is trained in intensive and emergency medicine. The purpose of the support is a division of tasks, because CPR and coronary intervention must be able to continue in parallel. The operator must be supported by the crash team so that he can concentrate fully on his coronary intervention. The cooperation between the cardiac catheterization laboratory team and the crash team should be jointly defined in-house and practiced regularly.

> **Practical Tip**
>
> Team training of emergency situations in the cardiac catheterization laboratory now plays a central role in the quality management of a modern interventional cardiology department. In the virtual cardiac catheterization laboratory, all relevant emergency situations can be trained in a safe training environment using full-scale simulations and endovascular VR simulation, and team performance can be improved as a result (► www.cardioskills.com).

3.5.5 Typical Triggers of Resuscitation Situations in the Cardiac Catheterisation Laboratory

- **Closure of the Coronary Vessel with a Diagnostic Catheter or Guide Catheter**

If the catheter is too large compared to the diameter of the coronary ostium and the vessel occludes, pressure drop and asystole or ventricular fibrillation may occur. Intubation should therefore be performed with the limb of the cockpit open for invasive pressure recording, so that the drop in pressure can be noticed immediately. The catheter must then be withdrawn to restore orthograde flow to the coronary vessel. Consequently, a smaller catheter or a catheter with side holes must be used.

■ **Overinjecting of the Coronary Vessel**

Depending on coronary blood flow, vessel caliber, and the diameter of the catheter chosen to inject the contrast agent, ventricular fibrillation may occur if too much, too fast, or with too high a pressure is injected. Sinus arrest or ventricular fibrillation may also occur if the catheter is misplaced by probing the right coronary artery with injection into the sinus node artery (Kotoku et al. 2007). Therefore, intubation should always be performed correctly and under fluoroscopy, and the first portion of the contrast medium should be applied very carefully as a test dose with very low pressure in order to verify the correct catheter position. Only then should one proceed to the normal injection. The vital monitor must always be kept in view in order to be able to detect and react to arrhythmias immediately.

■ **Coronary Wire Placement**

In particular, the coated coronary wires can perforate the coronary vessel without being clearly felt on the wire. If the coronary wire reaches the myocardium, this tactile stimulus can trigger arrhythmias and even ventricular fibrillation. In addition to rapid defibrillation, the coronary wire must then be corrected/retracted in its position and the coronary vessel angiographically checked for significant extravasation.

> **Practical Tip**
>
> Nowadays, correct catheter handling can be trained very well on the endovascular VR simulator. The handling of devices such as contrast injection pumps can also be trained on the simulator (▶ www.cardioskills.com).

References

Antoniucci D, Valenti R, Migliorini A, Moschi G, Trapani M, Dovellini EV, Santoro GM (2002) Abciximab therapy improves survival in patients with acute myocardial infarction complicated by early cardiogenic shock undergoing coronary artery stent implantation. Am J Cardiol 90(4):353–357

Basir MB, Schreiber T, Dixon S, Alaswad K, Patel K, Almany S, O'Neill Md WW (2018) Feasibility of early mechanical circulatory support in acute myocardial infarction complicated by cardiogenic shock: the Detroit cardiogenic shock initiative. Catheter Cardiovasc Interv 91(3):454–461

Berwanger O (2010) Acetylcysteine for the prevention of contrast-induced nephropathy (ACT) trial: a pragmatic multicenter randomized trial to evaluate the efficacy of acetylcysteine for the prevention of renal outcomes in patients undergoing coronary and vascular angiography, Abstract 21843, Tuesday, November 16, 11:51–12:01. American Heart Association's Scientific Sessions

Blomberg H, Gedeborg R, Berglund L, Karlsten R, Johansson J (2011) Poor chest compression quality with mechanical compressions in simulated cardiopulmonary resuscitation: a randomized, cross-over manikin study. Resuscitation 82(10):1332–1337

Chan AW, Chew DP, Bhatt DL, Moliterno DJ, Topol EJ, Ellis SG (2002) Long-term mortality benefit with the combination of stents and abciximab for cardiogenic shock complicating acute myocardial infarction. Am J Cardiol 89(2):132–136

De Backer D, Biston P, Devriendt J et al (2010) Comparison of dopamine and norepinephrine in the treatment of shock. N Engl J Med 362:779–789

de Waha S, Fuernau G, Eitel I, Desch S, Thiele H (2016) Long-term prognosis after extracorporeal life support in refractory cardiogenic shock—results from a real-world cohort. EuroIntervention 12(3):414

Enright T et al (1989) Ann Allergy 62(4):302–305

Esposito ML, Zhang Y, Qiao X, Reyelt L, Paruchuri V, Schnitzler GR, Kapur NK (2018) Left ventricular unloading before reperfusion promotes functional recovery after acute myocardial infarction. J Am Coll Cardiol 72(5):501–514

Fincke R, Hochman JS, Lowe AM, Menon V, Slater JN, Webb JG, Investigators S (2004) Cardiac power is the strongest hemodynamic correlate of mortality in cardiogenic shock: a report from the SHOCK trial registry. J Am Coll Cardiol 44(2):340–348

Flaherty MP, Khan AR, O'Neill WW (2017) Early initiation of impella in acute myocardial infarction complicated by cardiogenic shock improves survival: a meta-analysis. JACC Cardiovasc Interv 10(17):1805–1806

Gertz EW et al (1992) J Am Coll Cardiol 19(5):899–906

Goss JE et al (1995) Systemic anaphylactoid reactions to iodinated contrast media during cardiac catheterization procedures: guidelines for prevention, diagnosis, and treatment. Laboratory Performance Standards Committee of the Society for Cardiac Angiography and Interventions. Catheter Cardiovasc Diagn 34(2):99–104

Gruberg L, Mintz GS, Mehran R et al (2000) The prognostic implications of further renal function deterioration within 48 h of interventional coronary procedures in patients with preexistent chronic renal insufficiency. J Am Coll Cardiol 36:1542–1548

Harjola VP, Lassus J, Sionis A, Kober L, Tarvasmaki T, Spinar J, Network G (2015) Clinical picture and risk prediction of short-term mortality in cardiogenic shock. Eur J Heart Fail 17(5):501–509

Hasdai D, Topol EJ, Califf RM, Berger PB, Holmes DR Jr (2000) Cardiogenic shock complicating acute coronary syndromes. Lancet 356:749–756

Hintze G et al (1999) Risk of iodine-induced thyrotoxicosis after coronary angiography: an investigation in 788 unselected subjects. Eur J Endocrinol 140(3): 264–267

Hochman JS, Sleeper LA, Webb JG, Sanborn TA, White HD, Talley JD, LeJemtel TH (1999) Early revascularization in acute myocardial infarction complicated by cardiogenic shock. SHOCK Investigators. SHould we emergently revascularize Occluded Coronaries for cardiogenic shocK. N Engl J Med 341(9):625–634

Hochman JS, Buller CE, Sleeper LA, Boland J, Dzavik V, Sanborn TA, LeJemtel T (2000) Cardiogenic shock complicating acute myocardial infarction–etiologies, management and outcome: a report from the SHOCK Trial Registry. SHould we emergently revascularize Occluded Coronaries for cardiogenic shocK? J Am Coll Cardiol 36(3 Suppl A):1063–1070

Hochman JS, Sleeper LA, Webb JG, Dzavik V, Bulle CE, Aylward P, Investigators S (2006) Early revascularization and long-term survival in cardiogenic shock complicating acute myocardial infarction. JAMA 295(21):2511–2515

Ibanez B, Halvorsen S, Roffi M, Bueno H, Thiele H, Vranckx P, James S (2018a) Integrating the results of the CULPRIT-SHOCK trial in the 2017 ESC ST-elevation myocardial infarction guidelines: viewpoint of the task force. Eur Heart J 39(48):4239–4242

Ibanez B, James S, Agewall S, Antunes MJ, Bucciarelli-Ducci C, Bueno H, Group ESCSD (2018b) 2017 ESC Guidelines for the management of acute myocardial infarction in patients presenting with ST-segment elevation: the task force for the management of acute myocardial infarction in patients presenting with ST-segment elevation of the European Society of Cardiology (ESC). Eur Heart J 39(2):119–177

International Collaborative Study of Severe Anaphylaxis (2003) Risk of anaphylaxis in a hospital population in relation to the use of various drugs: an international study. Pharmacoepidemiol Drug Saf 12(3):195–202

Jeger RV, Harkness SM, Ramanathan K, Buller CE, Pfisterer ME, Sleeper LA, Investigators S (2006) Emergency revascularization in patients with cardiogenic shock on admission: a report from the SHOCK trial and registry. Eur Heart J 27(6):664–670

Kane GC, Doyle BJ, Lerman A et al (2008) Ultra-low contrast volumes reduce rates of contrast-induced nephropathy in patients with chronic kidney disease undergoing coronary angiography. J Am Coll Cardiol 51:89–90

Kapur NK, Davila CD (2017) Timing, timing, timing: the emerging concept of the 'door to support' time for cardiogenic shock. Eur Heart J 38(47):3532–3534

Kapur NK, Paruchuri V, Urbano-Morales JA, Mackey EE, Daly GH, Qiao X, Karas RH (2013) Mechanically unloading the left ventricle before coronary reperfusion reduces left ventricular wall stress and myocardial infarct size. Circulation 128(4):328–336

Kar B, Gregoric ID, Basra SS, Idelchik GM, Loyalka P (2011) The percutaneous ventricular assist device in severe refractory cardiogenic shock. J Am Coll Cardiol 57(6):688–696

Katzberg RW, Newhouse JH (2010) Intravenous contrast medium-induced nephrotoxicity: is the medical risk really as great as we have come to believe? Radiology 256:21–28

Kotoku M, Tamura A, Naono S, Kadota J (2007) Sinus arrest caused by occlusion of the sinus node artery during percutaneous coronary intervention for lesions of the proximal right coronary artery. Heart Vessel 22(6):389–392

Kuchibhotla S, Esposito ML, Breton C, Pedicini R, Mullin A, O'Kelly R, Kapur NK (2017) Acute biventricular mechanical circulatory support for cardiogenic shock. J Am Heart Assoc 6(10):e006670

Larsen AI, Hjørnevik A, Bonarjee V, Barvik S, Melberg T, Nilsen DW (2010) Coronary blood flow and perfusion pressure during coronary angiography in patients with ongoing mechanical chest compression: a report on 6 cases. Resuscitation 81(4):493–497

Lembo NJ, King SB 3rd, Roubin GS, Black AJ, Douglas JS Jr (1991) Effects of nonionic versus ionic contrast media on complications of percutaneous transluminal coronary angioplasty. Am J Cardiol 67(13): 1046–1050

Levy B, Clere-Jehl R, Legras A, Morichau-Beauchant T, Leone M, Frederique G, Collaborators. (2018) Epinephrine versus norepinephrine for cardiogenic shock after acute myocardial infarction. J Am Coll Cardiol 72(2):173–182

McCullough PA, Bertrand ME, Brinker JA, Stacul F (2006) A metaanalysis of the renal safety of isosmolar iodixanol compared with lower molar contrast media. J Am Coll Cardiol 48:692–699

Mehran R, Aymong EO, Nikolsky E et al (2004) A simple risk score for prediction of contrast-induced nephropathy after percutaneous coronary intervention: development and initial validation. J Am Coll Cardiol 44:1393–1399

Michels G et al (2022) Guidelines of the European Resuscitation Council on cardiopulmonary resuscitation

2021: update and comments. Anaesthesist 71(2): 129–140

Neumann FJ, Sousa-Uva M, Ahlsson A, Alfonso F, Banning AP, Benedetto U, Group ESCSD (2019) 2018 ESC/EACTS Guidelines on myocardial revascularization. Eur Heart J 40(2):87–165

Nolte MR et al (1996) Prophylactic application of thyrostatic drugs during excessive iodine exposure in euthyroid patients with thyroid autonomy: a randomized study. Eur J Endocrinol 134(3):337–341

O'Neill WW, Schreiber T, Wohns DH, Rihal C, Naidu SS, Civitello AB, Ohman EM (2014) The current use of Impella 2.5 in acute myocardial infarction complicated by cardiogenic shock: results from the USpella Registry. J Interv Cardiol 27(1):1–11

O'Neill W, Basir M, Dixon S, Patel K, Schreiber T, Almany S (2017) Feasibility of early mechanical support during mechanical reperfusion of acute myocardial infarct cardiogenic shock. JACC Cardiovasc Interv 10(6):624–625

Orban M, Mayer K, Morath T, Bernlochner I, Hadamitzky M, Braun S, Kastrati A (2014) Prasugrel vs clopidogrel in cardiogenic shock patients undergoing primary PCI for acute myocardial infarction results of the ISAR-SHOCK registry. Thromb Haemost 112(6):1190–1197

Ouweneel DM, Eriksen E, Sjauw KD, van Dongen IM, Hirsch A, Packer EJ, Henriques JP (2017) Percutaneous mechanical circulatory support versus intra-aortic balloon pump in cardiogenic shock after acute myocardial infarction. J Am Coll Cardiol 69(3):278–287

Pancholy SB, Palamaner Subash Shantha G, Romagnoli E, Kedev S, Bernat I, Rao SV, Patel TM (2015) Impact of access site choice on outcomes of patients with cardiogenic shock undergoing percutaneous coronary intervention: a systematic review and meta-analysis. Am Heart J 170(2):353–361

Pappalardo F, Schulte C, Pieri M, Schrage B, Contri R, Soeffker G, Westermann D (2017) Concomitant implantation of Impella((R)) on top of veno-arterial extracorporeal membrane oxygenation may improve survival of patients with cardiogenic shock. Eur J Heart Fail 19(3):404–412

Parodi G, Xanthopoulou I, Bellandi B, Gkiza V, Valenti R, Karanikas S, Alexopoulos D (2015) Ticagrelor crushed tablets administration in STEMI patients: the MOJITO study. J Am Coll Cardiol 65(5):511–512

Persson BP, Tepel M (2006) Contrast medium-induced nephropathy: the pathophysiology. Kidney Int 69: 8–10

Rab T, Ratanapo S, Kern KB, Basir MB, McDaniel M, Meraj P, O'Neill W (2018) Cardiac shock care centers: JACC review topic of the week. J Am Coll Cardiol 72(16):1972–1980

Rathod KS, Koganti S, Iqbal MB, Jain AK, Kalra SS, Astroulakis Z, Jones DA (2018) Contemporary trends in cardiogenic shock: Incidence, intra-aortic balloon pump utilisation and outcomes from the London Heart Attack Group. Eur Heart J Acute Cardiovasc Care 7(1):16–27

Ring J et al (1985) Prevention of anaphylactoid reactions after radiographic contrast media infusion by combined histamine H1- and H2-receptor antagonists: results of a prospective controlled trial. Int Arch Allergy Appl Immunol 78(1):9–14

Sandler CM (2003) Contrast-agent induced acute renal dysfunction—is iodixanol the answer? N Engl J Med 348(6):551–553

Schonenberger E, Muhler M, Dewey M (2010) Komplikationen durch Kontrastmittelgabe. Was ist gesichert in der Prävention? Internist (Berl) 51: 1516–1524

Schrage B, Ibrahim K, Loehn T, Werner N, Sinning JM, Pappalardo F, Westermann D (2019) Impella support for acute myocardial infarction complicated by cardiogenic shock. Circulation 139(10):1249–1258

Seyfarth M, Sibbing D, Bauer I, Frohlich G, Bott-Flugel L, Byrne R, Schomig A (2008) A randomized clinical trial to evaluate the safety and efficacy of a percutaneous left ventricular assist device versus intra-aortic balloon pumping for treatment of cardiogenic shock caused by myocardial infarction. J Am Coll Cardiol 52(19):1584–1588

Stretch R, Sauer CM, Yuh DD, Bonde P (2014) National trends in the utilization of short-term mechanical circulatory support: incidence, outcomes, and cost analysis. J Am Coll Cardiol 64(14):1407–1415

Tehrani BN, Truesdell AG, Sherwood MW, Desai S, Tran HA, Epps KC, O'Connor CM (2019) Standardized team-based care for cardiogenic shock. J Am Coll Cardiol 73(13):1659–1669

Thiele H, Zeymer U, Neumann FJ, Ferenc M, Olbrich HG, Hausleiter J, Investigators I-SIT (2012) Intraaortic balloon support for myocardial infarction with cardiogenic shock. N Engl J Med 367(14):1287–1296

Thiele H, Ohman EM, Desch S, Eitel I, de Waha S (2015) Management of cardiogenic shock. Eur Heart J 36(20):1223–1230

Thiele H, Akin I, Sandri M, Fuernau G, de Waha S, Meyer-Saraei R, Investigators C-S (2017a) PCI strategies in patients with acute myocardial infarction and cardiogenic shock. N Engl J Med 377(25):2419–2432

Thiele H, Jobs A, Ouweneel DM, Henriques JPS, Seyfarth M, Desch S, de Waha S (2017b) Percutaneous short-term active mechanical support devices in cardiogenic shock: a systematic review and collaborative meta-analysis of randomized trials. Eur Heart J 38(47):3523–3531

Thomsen HS, Morcos SK, Barrett BJ (2008) Contrast-induced nephropathy: the wheel has turned 360 degrees. Acta Radiol 49:646–657

van Diepen S, Katz JN, Albert NM, Henry TD, Jacobs AK, Kapur NK, Mission L (2017) Contemporary management of cardiogenic shock: a scientific statement from the American Heart Association. Circulation 136(16):e232–e268

Wagner H, Terkelsen CJ, Friberg H, Harnek J, Kern K, Lassen JF, Olivecrona GK (2010) Cardiac arrest in the catheterisation laboratory: a 5-year experience of using mechanical chest compressions to facilitate PCI during prolonged resuscitation efforts. Resuscitation 81(4):383–387

Yamaguchi K et al (1991) Prediction of severe adverse reactions to ionic and nonionic contrast media in Japan: evaluation of pretesting. A report from the Japanese Committee on the Safety of Contrast Media. Radiology 178(2):363–367

Zeymer U, Vogt A, Zahn R, Weber MA, Tebbe U, Gottwik M, Arbeitsgemeinschaft Leitende Kardiologische Krankenhausärzte (2004) Predictors of in-hospital mortality in 1333 patients with acute myocardial infarction complicated by cardiogenic shock treated with primary percutaneous coronary intervention (PCI); results of the primary PCI registry of the Arbeitsgemeinschaft Leitende Kardiologische Krankenhausarzte (ALKK). Eur Heart J 25(4):322–328

Further Reading

Analgosedierung für diagnostische und therapeutische Maßnahmen bei Erwachsenen. http://www.dgai.de/eev/EEV_2011_S_121-128.pdf. Accessed on Aug 2012

Fachinformationen zu Clorazepat, Etomidate, Ketamin, Midazolam, Propofol, Remifentanil, Rocuronium, Sugammadex, Tranxillium und Ultiva. http://ch.oddb.org

Gebrauchsinformation Ketanest S. http://static.pfizer.de/fileadmin/pfizer.de/documents/gi/KetanestS_5-5_GI.pdf. Accessed on Aug 2012

Larynx-Tubus in der Notfallmedizin. http://www.vbm-medical.de/cms/files/a5-1.0_06.08-de%2D%2Dweb%2D%2D.pdf. Accessed on Aug 2012

Perioperatives Nüchternheitsgebot bei operativen Eingriffen. http://www.dgai.de/eev/EEV_2011_S_93-94.pdf. Accessed on Aug 2012

Error Management

Kai-Uwe R. Strelow and Erhard Kaiser

Contents

E. Kaiser (ed.), *Complication Management In The Cardiac Catheter Laboratory*,
https://doi.org/10.1007/978-3-662-66093-5_4

4.1   What Can We Learn from Aviation?

Kai-Uwe R. Strelow

4.1.1   Introduction

In the last decade, numerous articles and books on emergency and crisis management in medicine have been published, highlighting the special importance of human factors and human performance as important factors for patient safety. Approximately 70–80% of the problems, events and complications (hereinafter referred to as incidents) that lead to undesirable consequences in the treatment process, to harm or to the death of patients are thereby attributable to human error and negligence (Human Errors). The publication of the Institute of Medicine (IMO) report "To err is human: Building a safer health system" (Kohn et al. 2000) vividly demonstrated the resulting problems and brought the inadequacies in the quality and safety of health care into public focus. It was estimated that 45,000–98,000 deaths per year were associated with medical error.

Transferred to the Federal Republic of Germany, it is estimated that approximately 30,000 deaths per year are attributable to adverse events in German hospitals (St. Pierre et al. 2003). More recent publications assume a mortality rate of 0.1% at German hospitals in this context (Schrappe 2007, 2018). For example, the Scientific Institute (WIdO) of the Federal Association of the AOK assumes for the reference year 2011 that, on the basis of 18.8 million treatment cases, there are approximately 19,000 patient safety-relevant events (PSRE) due to a treatment error that end fatally (AOK 2014).

Thus, measures aimed at reducing the probability of errors and error rates associated with the human factor represent significant potential for improving patient safety. In terms of increasing safety, medicine, particularly in the disciplines of critical care and emergency medicine, is thus in good company with other industries that are considered high-risk or high-reliability industries (HROs), in which the safe and reliable actions of the employee are of particular importance. In addition to aerospace, the air traffic control, nuclear, and shipping industries are particularly noteworthy in this regard and have made great efforts in recent decades to improve and standardize safety through education, training, and development in non-technical skills (NTS) (hereafter also referred to as interpersonal skills). However, Gaba et al. (1994) state in this regard, "Although incidents occur in surgery, intensive care medicine, emergency medicine, and invasive cardiology, none of these specialties has systematically addressed the teaching of incident management." The fact that this circumstance has not fundamentally changed in the Federal Republic of Germany to this day can be seen very well in medical education. Even at universities with established model courses of study, there is no catalogue of learning objectives that systematically addresses the human factors issue or the development of interpersonal skills for safety-oriented behavior. Even the topic of patient safety, which has been of great importance in the public debate on health care for more than a decade, has not yet managed to be established as part of curricular teaching, let alone as a separate topic or health subject.

Therefore, it is obvious, then as now, to orientate oneself on models and concepts from non-medical areas in order to counter the risks in patient care with comparable strategies, concepts and measures as in the other industries listed. Commercial aviation, where the development of interpersonal skills for cockpit personnel has recently become a mainstay of the training concept, is undoubtedly considered exemplary in this regard. The focus of competence development is on so-called Human Performance and Crew Resource Management Seminars (CRM), which are mandatory elements for obtaining and maintaining licenses, both in training and on the job.

The direct comparison between competence development measures for cockpit crews and cardiac catheterization laboratory teams, for example, shows parallels. In interventional cardiology, too, attempts are being made to better prepare the team for the management of incidents with comparable training courses, most of which are offered under the heading of Crisis Resource Management (CRM), using full-scale patient simulators, skills trainers and human factors elements. Surprisingly, these concepts have not become as widespread and established in the past 20 years as they have in commercial aviation. This circumstance is taken as an opportunity to present the different CRM concepts from aviation and medicine and to compare them with each other in order to find insights and clues for improvements and further developments of incident management in medicine.

In the following section, we will first take a closer look at the essential elements of the key skill "interpersonal" in aviation as well as its development over the past decades. This includes consideration of the beginnings of the CRM idea in aviation, the importance of airlines, aviation organisations and authorities in implementing CRM, and the development of CRM training as the essential tool in teaching skills, abilities and attitudes relating to the subject of safety. This is followed by a presentation of the medical variant of CRM, which emerged in the early 1990s following closely the aviation model and remains an essential training element in incident management in various medical disciplines today.

The fourth section seeks to compare CRM concepts between aviation and medicine. Despite similar roots and the common concern to increase safety in the respective professional environment, the didactic concepts have developed very differently over the past 20 years. These differences also apply to their respective status in professional education, training and continuing education. Thus, the comparison and conclusion take a questioning look at the different perspectives of CRM training as well as the importance of safety and promote a changed view of human factors training in medicine as an important employee qualification and an investment in improving patient safety.

4.1.2 History of the Development of Human Factors Training

In the late 1970s, extensive studies by the US space agency NASA (National Aeronautics and Space Administration) established a direct link between aircraft accidents and the behaviour of cockpit crews for both military and civil aviation (Cooper et al. 1980). They identified deficits in communication, cooperation, leadership, and decision-making behavior as contributing factors in the occurrence of crew errors and event sequences with more or less fatal outcomes. Moreover, Ruffell-Smith (1979) showed a positive correlation between crew performance and their ability to effectively use available resources inside and outside the cockpit. Crews that did not do this were judged to perform less well in working together and in dealing with problems and critical flight situations. Thus, the first training concepts developed that specifically addressed the interpersonal aspects (interpersonal) (Helmreich et al. 2004) and thus complemented the traditional training content, which consisted mainly of the technical-procedural components of flight execution (stick and rudder) in addition to building and maintaining the necessary knowledge. In the 1980s, the first basic concepts and training modules were developed, which, as so-called Cockpit Resource Management Seminars (CRM), addressed the deficits in the management of resources and were supplemented by simulator scenarios specifically designed for behavioural aspects (Lauber 1986). However, it took until the 1990s before the training content now known as Crew Resource Management (CRM) gained the necessary acceptance. This development was favoured by the increasing use of electronic flight instrument systems (glass cockpits) and the associated possibilities of automation and the switch to a two-man cockpit. This circumstance changed the demands on pilots and thus also the view of training and instruction. This did not remain without consequences for

4

the CRM programs, which from then on had to increasingly deal with the necessity of changing behavioral requirements and group processes, and in a later development phase also included the evaluation of behavioral aspects (Helmreich et al. 1999). Helmreich et al. describe this phase as five evolutionary stages.

4.1.3   The Five Evolutionary Stages of Crew Resource Management

■ **The First Generation of CRM Training**
Helmreich also refers to the basic concepts mentioned in the previous section, which emerged at the beginning of the 1980s, as the first generation of CRM training. Since, at that time, the occurrence of human errors and misconduct were very strongly associated with personal attitudes, many programs aimed to address safety-related preferences and short-comings of cockpit crews. The focus was on general leadership and management concepts, which were tested in the seminar context through exercises not specific to the workplace. This approach was usually supplemented by practical training in a simulator, which allowed the cockpit crews to apply their interpersonal skills without risk. At the time, however, these seminars and their subject matter experienced a certain reluctance on the part of the participants. From today's perspective, this reticence does not seem entirely incomprehensible, because despite the clear commitment to contribute to error prevention and safety, the seminars and their content and methods primarily focused on aligning the development of the participants with an "ideal image" of personality and attitudes.

■ **The Second Generation of CRM Training**
The experience gave rise to the second generation of training courses, which from the mid-1980s onwards increasingly dealt with group dynamic aspects within the crew and aviation-specific topics, such as error prevention, briefing, general communication, situational

awareness or the topic of decision-making. The major American airlines, in particular, began to conduct introductory training courses throughout the country. These seminars, now further developed under the name Crew Resource Management Training, were also adopted and used outside the USA at the beginning of the 1990s.

As part of the emerging consideration of a comprehensive organizational and safety culture, CRM became an integral part of pilot training in the early 1990s and was further developed into its own area of competence (Non Technical Skills [NTS], Interpersonal).

■ **The Third Generation of CRM Training**
This expansion of the scope of CRM essentially characterizes the third generation of CRM training. In addition to the integration of CRM into technical-procedural training, there were also initial approaches to define effective and safety-oriented behavior for cockpit crews more precisely and to check it in training and check events (CRM assessment). In addition, CRM training was extended to other relevant groups involved in the flight, in particular the flight attendants, the ground personnel responsible for handling, and technical maintenance and repair. In addition to a differentiation of CRM training within the cockpit into initial and recurrent training and special command courses, CRM events were also offered across groups, e.g. as joint cockpit/cabin training.

■ **The Fourth Generation of CRM Training**
A fourth generation of CRM developed largely in parallel with the third generation. As part of the efforts to optimize pilot training as a whole through innovative concepts (Advanced Qualification Program [AQP], Alternative Training and Qualification Program [ATQP] (Strelow and Allgaier 2014) and, above all, to adapt it to the specific needs of flight operations, it became necessary to extend the evaluation of the competencies of the (cockpit) crew to the non-technical area (NTS). This meant that the CRM also had to be defined and trained for non-standard situations (abnormals and emergencies) in order to

be able to evaluate the interpersonal competencies across all flight phases and requirement situations in a common checklist with the technical and procedural competencies.

- **The Fifth Generation of CRM Training**

The development of the Threat and Error Management (TEM) concept, which was developed in the mid-1990s, marks the fifth and, for the time being, last evolutionary stage of CRM. TEM is understood as a collection of countermeasures for the detection and management of threats, hazards, errors and undesired flight conditions as well as the mitigation of the resulting effects. This phase is accompanied by the development of so-called non-punitive reporting systems, which also record events relevant to human factors and are intended to trigger learning processes for the individual and for the organization through permanent communication. In addition, the individual factors influencing performance and misconduct are increasingly enriching CRM training. This includes topics such as fatigue, workload, stress, behavior and reactions in emergency situations, which naturally also represent individual influencing factors in the medical environment.

4.1.4 Legal Basis and Guidelines for CRM Training

The implementation of human factors training in civil aviation was supported and accompanied by the initiatives of the U.S. Federal Aviation Administration (FAA) and the International Civil Aviation Organization (ICAO). For example, in its 1989 implementing regulations, the FAA first defined "CRM training is designed to become an integral part of training and operations." In a 1993 revision, the assessment of behavioral performance was then included for the first time in the evaluation of Line Orientated Flight Training (LOFT, training form in the simulator) and defined as a fixed component of the briefing and debriefing for all training and review events (checks) (Basic Concepts of CRM). LOFT is a form of training in the simulator in which predefined flight routes are flown in which standard procedures (Standard Operating Procedures [SOPs]) for normal and emergency situations are applied and trained.

Largely in parallel, the ICAO also became active, one of whose most important tasks is to develop recommendations, guidelines and binding standards for aviation, which are subsequently adopted in the national aviation legislation of the ICAO member states. In Annex 6 (Operation of Aircraft) of the ICAO International Convention on Civil Aviation, the chapter "Human Factors" was included for the first time, describing training as "knowledge and skills related to human performance" (ICAO 2001; Maurino 1995). This annex was further elaborated, with a comprehensive CRM Training Manual being published as an ICAO document in 1998. This document also described for the first time the need to review the application of the skills taught in CRM training (Helmreich et al. 1995; ICAO 2002). This also paved the way for Europe, which agreed in the European unification process in the early 1990s to harmonize national regulations in European aviation (Regulation [EEC] No. 3922/91). This process was supported by the merger of a large part of the civil aviation authorities in Europe with the establishment of the Joint Aviation Authorities. The primary objective was to unify the safety regulations of the member states through the publication of guidelines (Joint Aviation Requirements [JARs]) and to support and monitor their implementation subject to certain substantive and time margins of the signatory states. With the creation of the European Union Aviation Safety Agency (EASA) (EU 2002, 2018) to establish common rules for civil aviation, the training and licensing of aircrew for the commercial operation of aircraft has recently been harmonised. This includes the content and scope of human factors and CRM training.

4.1.5 Scope and Content of Human Factors Training Courses

According to the European guidelines, the subject Human Performance and Limitations (HPL) comprises a time frame of 40 h in the

4

training to become a commercial pilot. In addition to the classic CRM topics (◘ Table 4.1, first column), the training includes, in particular, the teaching of knowledge of the basic flight physiological and psychological concepts relevant to occupational safety. The human factors training is treated on an equal footing with other theoretical training content such as meteorology, navigation, aerodynamics, etc. and is concluded with a written examination.

If a pilot acquires a type rating after his training in a flight operation, which entitles him to operate a specific type of aircraft, a CRM initial training course must be completed (◘ Table 4.1, second column). This training is intended to familiarise the pilot with the company's safety philosophy and CRM terminology, which includes the procedure and criteria for checking interpersonal skills. In addition, other trainings are scheduled at specific points in career development, as well as annual trainings that require refreshing on a 3-year cycle of the specified topics for license retention.

◘ **Table 4.1** Flight crew CRM training (EASA 2016, p. 112)

CRM training elements	Initial operator's CRM training	Operator conversion course when changing aircraft type	Operator conversion course when changing operator	Annual recurrent training	Command course
General principles					
Human factors in aviation General instructions on CRM principles and objectives Human performance and limitations Threat and error management	In-depth	Required	Required	Required	Required
Relevant to the individual flight crew member					
Personality awareness, human error and reliability, attitudes and behaviours, self-assessment and self-critique Stress and stress management Fatigue and vigilance Assertiveness, situation awareness, information acquisition and processing	In-depth	Not required	Not required	Required	In-depth
Relevant to the flight crew					
Automation and philosophy on the use of automation	Required	In-depth	In-depth	In-depth	In-depth
Specific type-related differences	Required	In-depth	Not required	Required	Required
Monitoring and intervention	Required	In-depth	In-depth	Required	Required

☐ Table 4.1 (continued)

CRM training elements	Initial operator's CRM training	Operator conversion course when changing aircraft type	Operator conversion course when changing operator	Annual recurrent training	Command course
Relevant to the entire aircraft crew					
Shared situation awareness, shared information acquisition and processing Workload management Effective communication and coordination inside and outside the flight crew compartment Leadership, cooperation, synergy, delegation, decision-making, actions Resilience development Surprise and startle effect Cultural differences	In-depth	Required	Required	Required	In-depth
Relevant to the operator and the organization					
Operator's safety culture and company culture, standard operating procedures (SOPs), organisational factors, factors linked to the type of operations Effective communication and coordination with other operational personnel and ground services	In-depth	Required	In-depth	Required	In-depth
Case studies	In-depth	In-depth	In-depth	In-depth	In-depth

There is a consensus in aviation that relevant competencies cannot be built up and maintained through one single training. In addition to a so-called awareness phase and the practical training, the practical phase, a third phase is required that ensures the maintenance and increasing flexibility of the acquired competencies. In the licence-relevant further and advanced training of the pilots, there are therefore also repetition training courses for the CRM area. In order to ensure the best possible adaptation to the needs of flight operations, the legislator allows flight operations a great deal of freedom in the choice of content and method of implementation (☐ Table 4.1, fifth column "Annual recurrent training").

4.1.6 The Assessment of Behavioural Performance in Aviation

As has been made clear above, the evaluation of non-technical behaviour (NTS) is closely linked to the development of CRM seminars. Originally, these assessment concepts pursued the idea of evaluating the training programs and simulator scenarios used. The "University of Texas behavioral markers" marker system, developed jointly by NASA and the University of Texas, is considered to be the first development of the time that allowed reviewing personnel to evaluate behavioral components within the entire flight process (Helmreich et al. 1990) and also to be used in terms of measuring team performance (Helmreich et al. 1999).

In Europe, it was mainly the large national airlines that drove CRM development, which also applied to the introduction of appraisal systems. Flin et al. (2008) mention the "Feedback and Appraisal System" of the Royal Dutch Airlines KLM from 1996 as a precursor, which was already available in a preliminary version (WILSC/SHAPE) in 1992 (Antersijn and Verhoef 1994). Other airlines, such as Swiss or Lufthansa, followed this example and also developed their own evaluation systems. In addition to the possibility of behavioural assessment, these systems also defined what is meant by safety-oriented behaviour in terms of flight operations and formed the basis for the content of CRM seminars and simulator events. The European Aviation Safety Agency (EASA) associated further subsequent objectives with the introduction of the CRM assessment (NPA 16):

- Improvement of the CRM training system and security.
- Embedding the behavioural feedback in an overall assessment, i.e. combined with technical and procedural aspects of flight management in the line check.
- Providing feedback on team performance and allowing for self-criticism in the context of a debriefing on performance in the area of Non Technical Skills (NTS).
- The possibility of an individual feedback by the examiner (Examiner).
- Development of a procedure as well as measures to maintain or ensure the required standards in case of underperformance (incl. retraining).

In order to support the achievement of these objectives, a validated assessment system called Non Technical Skills (NOTECHS) was developed and approved on behalf of the JAA to complement the airlines' own developments (van Avermaete and Kruijsen 1998). The development of NOTECHS is largely based on prior experience of existing marker systems and thus makes use of existing expertise. Thus, van Avermate and Kruijsen (1998) states, "… NOTECHS was set up to build on existing knowledge and solutions."

4.2 Transferability of Human Factors Concepts from Aviation to Medicine

Kai-Uwe R. Strelow and Erhard Kaiser

The human factors topic has been characterized by constant further developments over the past decades. What initially developed from accident research and the initiatives of a few well-known airlines in the late 1970s is now regarded as a model and is exemplary for many other industries. Also due to the stipulations of the legislator, Human Factors concepts have become an integral part of today's training and safety culture in aviation. In particular, interpersonal skills training, which has become known as Crew Resource Management (CRM), has encouraged many industries to draw on aviation expertise when implementing safety concepts.

According to Gaba et al. (1994), the measures used in aviation to increase performance, reduce the likelihood of errors and incidents, and optimally manage safety-related situations are also essential for the field of medicine. Among others, the following are mentioned here

- the development and use of checklists for the prevention of incidents,
- the definition of a standardised approach to specific situations and incidents,
- the development of standards in communication, cooperation and decision-making within the team, and
- the systematic practice of incident management.

The current literature also shares the view of Gaba et al. (1994) that these concepts have not yet become sufficiently established in medical safety culture and in education, training and continuing education. The fact that implementation is a development process that takes time and is not free of implementation problems can also be observed in other industries. Even the "success story" of aviation has evolved over more than two decades and required several stages of development to reach today's level of standardization and training quality in terms of Human Performance and CRM seminars, reporting systems of Human Factors relevant events and systems for the evaluation of NTS. A transferability of Human Factors concepts from aviation to medicine is possible and already happens today, not least due to many parallelisms of both fields and the demand for a maximum of safety.

4.2.1 Crisis Resource Management (CRM) Seminars

A starting point for the development of medical CRM seminars was research conducted by the Laboratory for Human Performance in Health Care in Stanford, California (USA) on the thought and analysis processes of anesthesiologists (► http://med.stanford.edu/VAsimulator/acrm).

The results of the studies from the late 1980s showed that there were performance limitations in recognizing and responding to unexpected situations and conditions regardless of the anesthesiologist's experience. These situations were further prone to problems in working with surgeons and nursing staff, as a result of which medical problems could also not be addressed in a timely manner by anesthesiologists. The results revealed significant gaps in incident management, leading to the realization that a well-trained or experienced physician was far from being a good incident manager and that no systematic training existed until then (Gaba et al. 1994). Thus, the first catalogues and publications of incidents in anaesthesia with medical backgrounds and

concrete instructions on how to proceed were produced. However, only partial success was achieved with the training courses tailored to this, as deficits in case management continued to emerge that lay outside medical knowledge and proposed procedural applications and were due to a lack of resource management.

As in comparable studies in aviation (Ruffell-Smith 1979), the conclusion was also reached in medicine that incident management depends on the good interaction of various competencies and the use of available resources. Based on experience in aviation, the content and methods from cockpit training were adapted for a comparable training course entitled "Anesthesia Crisis Resource Management" (ACRM) (Howard et al. 1992). The key feature of this seminar concept to date is the use of fullscale patient simulators. In addition to the teaching of case-specific and general action concepts (checklists), basic concepts for communication, teamwork, leadership and decision-making behavior are also trained in preparation for the implementation of exercise scenarios on the simulator. In debriefings, the exercises are usually processed using video recordings.

4.2.2 CRM in Medical Education and Training

What originated as ACRM in continuing education and training in anaesthesiology has also been adopted as CRM in other medical disciplines, especially in the dynamic and complex working environments shaped by medical technology, where the management of complications and incidents is an expected part of medical action. It is important to mention interventional cardiology as one of the disciplines currently developing most rapidly in this respect (for more on this, see also ► Chap. 5).

In the medical training of some universities, but also of training centres independent of universities, Crisis Resource Management seminars are usually offered in connection with compulsory modules in the clinical study section of human medicine, which take place

4

within the framework of a training course of several days in acute, emergency and intensive care medicine. The aim of the course is to enable trainee doctors to recognise incidents and initiate adequate treatment. In addition to consolidating theoretical principles and clinical case discussions that address the nature of the incident and the associating factors, but also the presentation of standards in incident management, there is the opportunity to work on skill trainers or full-scale patient simulators in a practical and realistic manner. However, reviews of the defined learning and training objectives are still rare, for example through the acceptance of a written paper and/or a practical examination in the sense of an OSCE (Objective Structured Clinical Evaluation/Examination). In the context of an OSCE, the practical skills of the test person, the mastery of medical routines and the adequate handling of the patient can be tested in addition to the theoretical knowledge. To ensure the learning success, the results and possible improvement potentials are discussed in a debriefing.

4.2.3 The Importance of Simulation for CRM in Medicine

Since the use of full-scale patient simulators or similarly suitable medical training devices (▶ www.laerdal.com, ▶ www.gaumard.com, ▶ www.meti.com) is an integral part of the CRM concept, the development of simulation technology also has a not inconsiderable influence on the spread and quality of CRM in medicine.

As early as 1963, an early version of the patient simulators in use today was available, equipped with accurate human anatomical features for relevant medical concerns. The SimOne, by Denson and Abrahamson, served as an anesthesia and emergency trainer for anesthesiologists. The goal back then was to be able to practice as realistically as possible and to depict problems in treatment. Today's full-scale patient simulators (e.g. from Gaumard, Laerdal or Meti) make it possible to represent even complex emergency situa-

tions very realistically and precisely in detail. Today, the physiological reaction to administered medication is just as much a standard feature of a full-scale patient simulator as the ability to communicate verbally with the patient. Due to the high acquisition costs and the very limited mobility of the devices at that time, the distribution of simulators and CRM was initially limited to university institutions and specialized training centers. This changed with the further development of the devices and computer technology, which, in addition to more mobility, above all brought expanded application possibilities. In particular, the mobility of the current generation of devices (wireless) opens up completely new possibilities for conducting CRM training in a more realistic and flexible manner. In addition to the execution of standard scenarios, input functions also enable the trainer to influence ongoing scenarios, so that the level of difficulty can be reduced or increased at any point in the training scenarios. The comprehensive storage of data and the diverse possibilities of presentation also support the evaluation and debriefing of the scenarios in the debriefing.

4.2.4 The Evaluation of Behavioural Performance in the Context of Crisis Resource Management

When the first ACRM was created and implemented in 1990 (Howard et al. 1992), the behavioural requirements were defined in addition to the incidents depicted for the simulator scenarios. The following ◻ Table 4.2 shows the key points of the interpersonal areas that were identified as relevant in advance by investigations.

These were overarching themes such as decision-making behaviour, teamwork and resource management, which were introduced as part of the CRM course introduction in 1990. Where the areas and behaviours were relevant to the exercise delivery, these were picked up for exercise assessment during the exercise debriefings.

▪ **Table 4.2** Key points of the ACRM (Fish et al. 2001)	
Points regarding	**Relevant key points**
Decision making and cognition	– Know the environment – Anticipate and plan – Use all available information and – Cross check – Prevent or manage fixation errors – Use cognitive aids
Teamwork and resource management	– Exercise leadership and followership – Call for help early – Communicate effectively – Distribute the workload – Mobilize all available resources for optimum management

▪ **Table 4.3** The ANTS system—categories and elements (Flin et al. 2008)	
Category	**Elements**
Task management	– Planning and preparing – Prioritizing – Providing and maintaining standards – Identifying and utilising resources
Team working	– Coordinating activities with team members – Exchanging information – Using authority and assertiveness – Assessing capabilities – Supporting others
Situation awareness	– Gathering information – Recognising and understanding – Anticipating
Decision making	– Identifying options – Balancing risks and selecting options – Reevaluating

Following the example of aviation, behavioural criteria and evaluation systems were also further developed in medicine for the assessment of behavioural performance in simulation exercises. The aim was to better record and describe the performance of individuals and teams in the field of NTS as well, and to address and report back during exercise debriefings. Thus, a marker system based on NOTECHS called ANTS (Anaesthetists' Non-Technical Skills) was developed and validated in 2003 (Fletcher et al. 2003; Flin et al. 2008). ▪ Table 4.3 shows the four behavioural domains of the ANTS, which are further described by 3–5 items. A manual on the use of the ANTS system describes the categories and elements in more detail. This is done in particular by presenting behaviours that can be assessed as good and not so good lived practice (► www.abdn.ac.uk).

An adaptation of the ANTS system to the field of work of surgeons (Non Technical Skills for Surgeons [NOTSS]), for example, shows that the requirements in the field of NTS certainly differ in the various disciplines. For example, the topic of leadership was included as a separate category and provided with its own elements. Due to the particular importance of communication for error prevention, this area of behaviour was also included and presented as a joint category with the topic of teamwork (► www.abdn.ac.uk).

The ICL (Interpersonal Competence List) concept, which was also initially developed for cockpit personnel based on NOTECHS 2001 (Strelow and Allgaier 2012), takes a different approach. ▪ Figure 4.1 below shows the medical version of ICL (Strelow 2019), which defines the relevant training content and behavioural objectives for developing the different competencies and is used as a marker system for assessing behavioural performance in CRM training. The ICL concept assumes that the overall requirements for the safety-oriented behaviour of responsible personnel differ only insignificantly in principle across different high-risk industries. In addition to the same categories and elements, it is industry-specific differences within the elements that need to be considered. The ICL concept is currently also applied in CRM training with interventional cardiologists (► www.cardioskills.com).

ICL - Interpersonal Competence List

0 hazard and error management

0.1 Principles		0.2 Individual work behaviour	
1	Acts in accordance with the safety culture	1	continuously monitors and controls
2	works according to valid standards	2	reports and reacts to special features
3	prepares and uses tools	3	acts and decides in a safety-oriented manner (safety first)
4	checks boundary conditions of the order	4	respects its own constitution
5	discusses relevant details in the briefing / debriefing	5	respects constitution of others
6	has a proactive attitude towards hazards	6	uses all technical and human resources
7	reacts immediately to errors & undesirable conditions	7	leads and uses necessary documentation

1 Situational attention

1.1 Information sources		1.2 Information Processing	
1	Documentation, handover information	1	systematically observes
2	Workplace and technical systems	2	recognizes the importance of the information
3	Patient	3	concludes comprehensibly
4	Activities of the employees and work processes	4	takes necessary measures
5	resource availability	5	takes into account alternative developments and scenarios
6	other constraints	6	controls and verifies desired changes

2 Decision-making behaviour

2.1 Preparation		2.2 Execution	
1	recognises the need for action / to intervene	1	makes safety-oriented decisions, preserves safety margins
2	analyzes and verifies the causative factors	2	communicates the decision
3	sets goals and priorities	3	distributes tasks and responsibilities
4	collects facts and possible actions	4	Executes and reports back
5	applies regulated procedures	5	checks the result against intentions and plans
6	uses FORDEC in analytical situations	6	informs all persons and bodies concerned

3 Management

3.1 Anticipation & Planning		3.2 Workload	
1	plans ahead and keeps plans	1	prioritizes
2	pays attention to influencing factors & threats	2	delegates tasks appropriately
3	actively involves others in the planning	3	Provides sufficient time to complete tasks
4	operates realistic time planning	4	tracks the actions and progress of others
5	sets interim targets and ensures that they are met	5	avoids the negative effects of stress
6	avoids distractions and time pressure	6	manages errors, undesired conditions and effects

4 Leadership

4.1 Authority		4.2 Assertiveness	
1	fills his role	1	takes responsibility when the situation demands it
2	takes the initiative	2	contributes knowledge, expertise, information and suggestions
3	chooses a leadership style appropriate to the situation	3	speaks one's mind appropriately
4	instructs, controls and corrects in an appropriate manner	4	Urges clarification of concerns
5	recognises disruptive factors in cooperation and addresses them	5	ensures compliance with SOP's, intervenes in case of deviations
6	advises, supports and coaches	6	maintains a businesslike attitude

5 Teamwork

5.1 Cooperation		5.2 Interpersonal relationships	
1	adheres to work concepts, SOPs and agreements	1	actively offers help
2	encourages cooperation and actively involves others	2	motivates others, recognises the behaviour of others and reinforces
3	Exchange of plans and intentions	3	pays attention to social and cultural aspects of cooperation
4	ensures alignment of mental models	4	is open to feedback and criticism
5	takes into account workload and attention load of others	5	intervenes effectively
6	examines the effectiveness of cooperation	6	manages conflicts

6 Communication

6.1 Information exchange		6.2 Atmosphere	
1	informs in time and completely	1	communicates in a situationally adapted and recipient-oriented manner
2	communicates clearly and uses standard phraseology	2	promotes an open exchange and encourages input
3	is factual	3	pays attention to social and cultural aspects of communication
4	listens actively	4	Does not take feedback and criticism personally
5	confirms that information has been understood	5	gives feedback and criticism objectively
6	asks if anything is unclear	6	takes non-verbal signals into account

ICL 2.1 med 5-2008 dt.doc

■ Fig. 4.1   Interpersonal competence list. (Copyright: K.-U.R. Strelow; with friendly permission)

The dissemination of marker systems for the evaluation of behavioural performance in CRM seminars is still comparatively little established in medicine. The first training providers are now beginning to specifically use marker systems such as ANTS or ICL in CRM seminars in order to also evaluate the training measures from the point of view of NTS. Although evaluating NTS and addressing the issue is an essential part of debriefing, it often does not follow a defined set of criteria. It would also be desirable to precede the use of criteria catalogues with training that explains the benchmarks to the CRM participants and the CRM instructors so that the behavioural performance of the simulation can be observed, evaluated and fed back in line with the criteria.

4.2.5 Error Culture Versus Blaiming Culture

The implementation of simulator training in structured medical education, whether through the use of skill trainers to improve technical skills or through the use of full-scale patient simulators, opens up entirely new possibilities for continuing medical education and training compared to the way medicine has been learned and taught in the past. However, the use of simulators and the application of concepts, as described in detail above, also poses a significant challenge to the medical community. This is because, contrary to previous training and teaching models, simulation deliberately offers the opportunity to make mistakes in a safe training environment and to learn from these mistakes through structured reappraisal (debriefing). It formally promotes the playful but constructive handling of the same. In addition to getting individuals accustomed to this new learning methodology in medicine, there needs to be a broader social acceptance of this method. In aviation, we have had this societal acceptance for many years and see simulation training as a natural part of the effort to ensure the highest possible flight safety. As explained above, it must logically follow that medicine must follow suit

here. Since the technical development of both skill trainers and full-scale patient simulators is already so far advanced that, embedded in the appropriate curricula, they are hardly inferior to reality, it must probably also be due to the human factor in this context that the possibilities are not yet exploited to the last consequence.

The point is to create a teaching and learning atmosphere parallel to technical progress that allows mistakes to be made without sanctions, perhaps even establishing a completely new mood and attitude towards mistakes in medicine—an error culture. Because we know from our own experience of more than 19 years in working with cardiac catheter laboratory teams in the context of full-scale simulation training in the cardiac catheter laboratory that there is still a blaming culture, the existence of which is unfounded in the matter, but traditional—and indeed widespread. Fear of sanctions often plays a decisive role here, as do encrusted, hierarchical structures. This is where CRM in medicine comes in. Praiseworthy approaches to cultural change with the implementation of non-punitive reporting systems in clinics can fortunately be observed and must urgently be further promoted and cultivated.

4.2.6 Influences on the Implementation of CRM from the Aviation Perspective

After the essential elements of CRM seminars from aviation and medicine have been outlined in the last sections, some selected similarities and differences will now be considered. Derived from this, we will conclude with some comments on possible changes and innovations that appear necessary in medical education, training and continuing education in order to further minimize the influence of people as a risk factor in patient care in a similar way by promoting interpersonal skills.

The fact that, from today's perspective, CRM concepts in aviation appear so differentiated compared to other industries can be

4

explained, among other things, by the fact that aviation began much earlier to investigate more intensively the effects of human actions on the safety of flight performance and to derive and consistently implement measures to improve human performance. In the introduction of training standards in the field of NTS, the role of aviation authorities is particularly important. Derived from the experience of aviation companies (best practice), the findings of research, and the recommendations and guidelines of a wide variety of aviation professional and interest groups, international and national legislation now largely defines the training and assessment standards for the field of NTS. Similar regulations are currently not found in medicine, so that a comparison of NTS standards between aviation and medicine is only possible to a limited extent. However, there are first approaches to implement simulation training in the continuous, medical education and training (▶ Chap. 5) and through the Masterplan Medizinstudium 2020 (BMBF 2017) fundamental changes also appear within reach for medicine. For example, the introduction of the National Competence-Based Learning Objectives Catalogue for Medicine (NKLM) (MFT 2016) defines new medical training requirements that go far beyond what was previously covered in the interpersonal competence area only by the topic of communication and the doctor-patient conversation. It can be assumed that the NKLM will also be supplemented by the specific requirements of the learning objectives catalogues of the Action Alliance Patient Safety (APS 2014) and the Society for Medical Education (GMA 2016). Thus, it is currently largely the responsibility of university hospitals, training centres for medical professions and training providers of CRM seminars to define and promote the content, methods and boundary conditions of education, training and continuing education for the field of NTS in medicine. This development is comparable to the one in aviation, because in the 1980s (in the USA) and in the 1990s (in Europe), NTS standards were mainly shaped by the major airlines' own initiatives. Regardless of the initial legal situation, which undoubtedly

improved and encouraged the standardization and implementation of NTS concepts and training, the differences in CRM concepts between aviation and medicine can be well explained by the different understanding of the letter "C" in the CRM term. Although both approaches pursue the goal of managing incidents in a safety-oriented and effective manner by using all available resources, aviation, not least due to its three-stage training concept, first relies on extensive teaching of basic NTS knowledge in the training of the student pilot and the novice in flight operations. This is followed by applications of what has been learned in practice, which includes the integration of training on procedure trainers, simulators and the aircraft. In-service recurrent training ensures further maintenance, consolidation and deepening of the CRM concept and interpersonal skills (Strelow 2013).

Comparable systematic approaches to the development of NTS competencies are rarely found in current Crisis Resource Management (CRM) concepts. The learning and application of NTS in medicine largely corresponds to the form of the first CRM generation in aviation (▶ Sect. 4.1.3). Here, difficult treatment situations are usually presented in a very practical manner through the use of skill trainers or fullscale patient simulators, in which the participants are expected to manage the tasks appropriately. Even though incident management is supposed to include behavioral tools in the sense of non-technical skills (NTS), it is often observed that these are treated as secondary to medical knowledge and procedures.

Frequently Encountered Indicators in the Implementation of Crisis Resource Management (CRM) Trainings Are (Strelow 2013)

- Lack of previous training in the field of Human Factors (HF)/NTS
- Missing learning objectives/markers for the HF/NTS area
- Short time frame for the presentation of HF/NTS content

- Presentation of only general HF/NTS content
- Preferably case studies from other industries (e.g. aviation, nuclear industry, …)
- Implementation by non-specialist HF/NTS "experts" (e.g. pilots)
- Lack of transfer of HF/NTS content into the medical working environment
- Low connection of the HF/NTS topic and the learning objectives to the practical exercises (e.g. on the skill trainer, on the patient simulator, …)
- Problems in the design and implementation of HF/NTS relevant simulation exercises
- Lack of standard in the assessment of HF/NTS in the practical exercises (assessment/debriefing)
- Heterogeneous composition of participants, who focus on the medical aspects of the exercise in the debriefing (e.g. different clinics, different hierarchical levels, professional experience, …)

4.2.7 Routine Situation Versus Incident

Since the medical CRM training courses focus primarily on incident management, the behavior practiced in these situations is usually also perceived as special and deviating from the routine. Accordingly, participants are also confronted with difficult treatment situations at an early stage in the practical exercises. In contrast, the focus of practical NTS application in the aviation simulation environment is primarily on the reliable handling of routine situations. As accident investigations have shown, standard situations, easily manageable problems or deviating flight conditions can "mutate" into serious incidents due to crew misconduct or inadequate management. This is why it is so important that competencies in the interpersonal area are built up systematically and sustainably. Necessary learning and adaptation processes to the behavioural requirements should be taken into account in

such a way that the pilot has sufficient time to acquire the competencies. In addition, the pilot is given the opportunity to learn and practice the behavioral requirements in the professional environment on procedure trainers, simulators or on the aircraft. In contrast to common medical CRM programs, aviation first focuses on the management of normal operating situations before the behavioral tools are applied in deviating operating conditions (abnormals). It is assumed that the application of correct and systematic behavior in incident management is more likely to succeed if this behavior is anchored and tested in the routine and in cooperation with others.

For the current training situation in interventional cardiology, see below in ▶ Chap. 5.

4.2.8 Team and Interfaces

As described in ▶ Sect. 4.2.1, CRM concepts in aviation were extended in the 1990s to other relevant groups involved in the flight (third generation). Here, the legislator took cabin crew into account, but also technical maintenance, servicing and handling. The aim was to sensitize as many people as possible involved in the process to the issue of safety and to ensure that the same "language" is spoken at the safety-relevant interfaces.

In terms of medicine, non-physician groups, such as nursing staff and other groups involved in the treatment process, should also be trained in the basic principles of NTS. In crisis resource management training, joint training of physicians with cardiac catheterization laboratory and nursing staff, e.g. of chest pain units, is therefore a good way to train incident management in normal team compositions. Practice shows that this participant composition is more likely to succeed in trainings where all CRM participants come from one hospital. In medical education, the Masterplan Medizinstudium 2020 (BMBF 2017) also points out the particular importance of teamwork. Increased interdisciplinary and interprofessional training in the medical-practical areas should take this concern into account in the future.

4.2.9 Aviation: A Perfect Example of CRM?

Despite extensive human factors training, flight accidents from the recent past show that, despite all precautions, cockpit behavior is not always optimal, especially when it comes to controlling unusual flight conditions under unfavorable boundary conditions. A study at the end of the 1990s showed that unregulated problems in flight execution in combination with human error contribute to an increase in flight risk, especially when there are also problems in the cooperation of the cockpit crews (Müller 2003). Routine situations can thus develop into highly dynamic and complex situations within a few moments, with fatal consequences as a result of an incorrect assessment of the situation, an incorrect start to problem solving or deficiencies in cooperation. In this respect, the Crisis Resource Management approach of training more specifically for incidents that deviate from routine under difficult boundary conditions also has its advantages. Here, despite intensive training of the "abnormals" in incident management, aviation is very much focused on the processing of standard procedures (Standard Operating Procedures [SOPs]). Re-evaluating situations and actions in the event of a crisis with a critical attitude, despite the use of checklists that are believed to be safe, poses great challenges even for pilots who have been tested in simulations, where well-developed interpersonal skills and recourse to the resources of the team can become a significant factor for a safe landing.

In this respect, aviation is not a perfect example in terms of CRM and safety, but is itself an industry that is constantly trying to maintain and improve the state of safety with its resources. Schrappe (2018) also states that this has been achieved far better in aviation than in medicine over the past two decades, and that he sees hardly any demonstrable success in improving patient safety despite a wide range of efforts in medicine. For example, the preventable mortality rate in the Federal Republic of Germany is estimated at 0.1%, even 20 years after the publication of the IMO Report (Kohn et al. 2000). With an estimated 420,000 deaths in German hospitals in 2016 (Federal Statistical Office 2017), one in 20 deaths can thus be classified as avoidable and attributable to errors.

Due to this situation, the Patient Safety Action Alliance proposes to orientate itself less on solutions of other industries in the future, but "…*to focus more on industry-typical circumstances*" (Schrappe 2018, p. 37). This also implies a move away from the concepts of aviation, whose focus from a medical perspective was often in the areas of safety culture, the establishment of reporting systems and the introduction of checklists. The fact that the friendly aviation specialists with some directions and good stories from aviation did not help can be acknowledged as a late and also correct insight. However, this path was thus no less successful than the measures taken by a healthcare industry driven by the idea of quality, which has so far failed to train staff in such a way that they can be relied upon to perform safety-relevant tasks at the "sharp end" of the organisation on a permanent and successful basis, in the sense of Flin et al. (2008). Thus, the analysis of preventable adverse events in patient care shows that errors are predominantly due to human or interpersonal factors, but the measures introduced are predominantly of an organisational-institutional nature. A targeted quality, risk and error management can therefore be expected to address these problems and the associated lack of attitudes, skills, abilities and deficits in action through appropriate competence-promoting (training) measures in order to compensate for or eliminate them (Strelow 2019).

References

Antersijn P, Verhoef M (1994) Assessment of non-technical skills: is it possible? In: McDonald N, Johnston N, Fuller R (eds) Application of psychology to the aviation system. Avebury, Aldershot

AOK (2014) Krankenhausreport AOK 2014: Wege zu mehr Patientensicherheit. http://aok-bv.de/imperia/md/aokbv/presse/pressemitteilungen/archiv/2014/krankenhaus_report_2014_pressemappe_210114.pdf. Accessed on 18 Oct 2019

APS (2014) Wege zur Patientensicherheit—lernzielkatalog für Kompetenzen in der Patientensicherheit, May 2014. Aktionsbündnis Patientensicherheit e.V., Berlin. https://www.aps-ev.de/wp-content/uploads/2016/09/Empfeh lungAGBuT_Lernzielkatalog_Wege_2014_05_14_neu.pdf. Accessed on 10 Oct 2019

BMBF (2017) Masterplan Medizinstudium 2020. Beschlusstext. Bundesministerium für Bildung und Forschung. https://www.bmbf.de/files/2017-03-31_Masterplan%20Beschlusstext.pdf. Accessed on 20 Oct 2019

Cooper GE, White MD, Lauber J-K (1980) Resource management on the flightdeck. In: Proceedings of a NASA/industry workshop (NASA CP-2120), Jun 26–28, 1979. NASA-Ames Research Center, Moffett Field, CA

EASA (2016) Acceptable Means of Compliance (AMC) and Guidance Material (GM) to Annex III—Part-ORO consolidated version including issue 2, Amendment 6, Feb 2016. https://www.easa.europa.eu/sites/default/files/dfu/Consolidated%20unofficial%20AMC%26GM_Annex%20III%20Part-ORO.pdf. Accessed on 18 Oct 2019

EU (2002) Amtsblatt der Europäischen Union. Verordnung (EG) Nr. 1592/2002 v. 15, Jul 2002. https://eur-lex.europa.eu/legal-content/DE/TXT/PDF/?uri=CELEX:32002R1592. Accessed on 18 Oct 2019

EU (2018) Amtsblatt der Europäischen Union. Verordnung (EU) 2018/1139 v. 4, Jul 2018. https://eur-lex.europa.eu/legal-content/DE/TXT/PDF/?uri=CELEX:32018R1139&from=IT. Accessed on 18 Oct 2019

FAA (1989) Crew resource management training. Advisory Circular No. AC 120-51. US Department of Transportation, Washington, DC

FAA (1993) Crew resource management training. Advisory Circular No. AC 120-51 b. US Department of Transportation, Washington, DC

Fish JK, Gaba DM, Howard SK, Smith BE, Swob YA (2001) Simulation-based training in anesthesia crisis resource management (ACRM): a decade of experience. Simul Gaming 32(2):175–193

Fletcher G, Flin R, McGeorge P, Glavin R, Maran N, Patey R (2003) Anaesthetists' non-technical skills (ANTS): evaluation of a behavioural marker system. Br J Anaesth 90(5):580–588

Flin R, O'Connor P, Chrichton M (2008) Safety at the sharp end. A guide to non-technical skills. Ashgate, Farnham

Gaba DM, Fish KJ, Howard SK (1994) Crisis management in anesthesiology. Churchill Livingstone, New York

GMA (2016) Der Lernzielkatalog Patientensicherheit für das Medizinstudium – ein Positionspapier des Ausschusses für Patientensicherheit und Fehlermanagement der Gesellschaft für Medizinische Ausbildung. GMS J Med Educ 33(1). https://www.egms.de/static/pdf/journals/zma/2016-33/zma001009.pdf. Accessed on 20 Oct 2019

Helmreich RL, Wilhelm J, Gregorich S, Chidester T (1990) Preliminary results from the evaluation of cockpit resource management training: performance ratings of flightcrews. Aviat Space Environ Med 61:576–578

Helmreich RL, Butler RA, Taggert WR, Wilhelm JA (1995) Behavioral markers in accidents and incidents reference list. Technical report 95-01 Austin Texas. NASA/University of Texas FAA Aerospace Crew Research Project. homepage.psy.utexas.edu/homepage/group/HelmreichLAB/…/564.doc

Helmreich RL, Merrit AC, Wilhelm JA (1999) The evolution of crew resource management training in commercial aviation. Int J Aviat Psychol 9(1):19–32. (UTHFRP Pub235)

Helmreich RL, Musson DM, Sexton JB (2004) Human factors and safety in surgery. In: Nora PF (ed) Surgical patient safety: essential information for surgeons in today's environment. American College of Surgeons, Chicago

Howard S, Gaba D, Fish K, Yang G, Sarnquist F (1992) Anesthesia crisis resource management training: teaching anesthesiologists to handle critical incidents. Aviat Space Environ Med 63(9):763–770

ICAO (1998) Doc 9683 AN/950—human factors training manual. ICAO, Montreal

ICAO (ed) (2001) Annex 6 of the convention on international civil aviation—operation of aircraft, part 1 international commercial air transport—aeroplanes, 8th edn. ICAO, Montreal

ICAO (2002) Doc 9803. AN/761—Line Operations Safety Audit (LOSA)

KLM (1996) Feedback and appraisal system. Amsterdam (Internal paper)

Kohn L, Corrigan J, Donaldson M (2000) To err is human: building a safer health system. National Academy Press, Washington, DC

Lauber J (1986) Cockpit resource management: background and overview. In: Orlady H, Foushee H (eds) Cockpit resource management training (NASA Conference Publication 2455). National Aeronautics and Space Administration, Washington, DC, pp 5–14

Maurino D (1995) ICAO annex amendment introduces mandatory human factors training for airline flight crews. ICAO J 50(7):13, 24–25. http://www.icao.int/anb/humanfactors/ICAO_annex_amendment_1995.pdf

MFT (2016) Nationaler Kompetenzbasierter Lernzielkatalog Medizin (NKLM). Medizinischer Fakultätentag der Bundesrepublik Deutschland e.V., Berlin. https://gesellschaft-medizinische-ausbildung.org/nklm/nklz/nklm.html. Accessed on 13 Oct 2019

Müller M (2003) Soziale Intelligenz und Kompetenz: Ein Werkzeug für das Risikomanagement und Fehlervermeidung. Z Allg Med 79:345–350. https://www.online-zfa.de/fileadmin/user_upload/Heftarchiv/ZFA/article/2003/07/10.1055-s-2003-41913.pdf. Accessed on 20 Oct 2019

Ruffell-Smith HP (1979) A simulator study of the interaction of pilot workload with errors, vigilance, and decisions. NASA TM-78482, Moffett Field

Schrappe M (2007) Agenda Patientensicherheit 2007. Aktionsbündnis Patientensicherheit e.V. Witten/ Herdecke, Witten. http://www.aps-ev.de/wp-content/ uploads/2016/10/Agenda_2007_mit_Titelblatt.pdf. Accessed on 19 Oct 2019

Schrappe M (2018) APS-Weißbuch Patientensicherheit. Sicherheit in der Gesundheitsversorgung: neu denken, gezielt verbessern. Medizinisch Wissenschaftliche Verlagsgesellschaft, Berlin. http://www.aps-ev.de/wp-content/uploads/2018/08/APS-Weissbuch_2018.pdf. Accessed on 19 Oct 2019

St. Pierre M, Hofinger G, Buerschaper C (2003) Notfallmanagement—human factors in der Akutmedizin. Springer Medizin, Berlin

Statistisches Bundesamt (2017) Diagnosedaten der Patienten und Patientinnen in Krankenhäusern (einschl. Sterbe- und Stundenfälle) 2016, Fachserie 12, Reihe 6.2.1

Strelow K-UR (2013) Zwischenfälle als Folge komplexer medizinischer Behandlungssituationen—trainingsmöglichkeiten und Handlungsalternativen. In: Heimann R, Schaub H, Strohschneider S (eds) Entscheiden in kritischen Situationen—neue Erkenntnisse und Perspektiven. Verlag für Polizeiwissenschaften, Frankfurt a.M., pp 225–248

Strelow K-UR (2019) Risiken und Nebenwirkungen: Der Faktor Mensch. In: Oubaid V (ed) Der Faktor Mensch—personalauswahl und Risikomanagement im Krankenhaus. MWV-Verlagsgesellschaft, Berlin, pp 61–88

Strelow K-UR, Allgaier S (2012) 10 jahre interpersonal competence list (ICL). In: Felsenreich C, Waleczek H (eds) Teamkompetenzen und sicheres Handeln. Verlag für Polizeiwissenschaften, Frankfurt a.M., pp 179–202

Strelow K-UR, Allgaier S (2014) Alternative Trainings- und Qualifizierungsprogramme (ATQP) als Maßnahme zur Steigerung betrieblicher Resilienz in der Luftfahrt. In: Bargstedt U, Horn G, van Vegten A (eds) Resilienz in Organisationen stärken—vorbeugung und Bewältigung von kritischen Situationen. Verlag für Polizeiwissenschaften, Frankfurt a.M., pp 327–352

van Avermaete J, Kruijsen E (1998) NOTECHS. The evaluation of non technical skills of multi-pilot aircrew in relation to the JAR-FCL requirements. Final report NLR-CR-98443. National Aerospace Laboratory (NLR), Amsterdam

Further Reading

Adaption des ANTS-Systems an den Arbeitsbereich der Chirurgen. https://research.abdn.ac.uk/wp-content/uploads/sites/14/2019/03/NOTSS-Handbook-2012.pdf

Handbuch zum Gebrauch des ANTS-Systems. https://research.abdn.ac.uk/wp-content/uploads/sites/14/2019/03/ANTS-Handbook-2012-1.pdf. Accessed on 2 Mar 2020

https://med.stanford.edu/anesthesia/education/residency/simulation.html. Accessed on 2 Mar 2020

http://www.abdn.ac.uk/iprc/documents/Development_of_a_rating_system.pdf. Accessed on 2 Mar 2020

http://www.cardioskills.com. Accessed on 2 Mar 2020

Interpersonal Competence List (ICL). https://www.unimedizin-mainz.de/lernklinik/startseite/human-factors-interpersonelle-kompetenzen-behandlungs-und-patientensicherheit/lehrveranstaltungen/interpersonelle-kompetenzentwicklung-als-gegenstand-der-medizinisch-praktischen-ausbildung-041073245-wf.html. Accessed on 2 Mar 2020

NPA 16 (modification/creation of JAR OPS 1.940, 1.945, 1.955, and 1.965). http://www.raes-hfg.com/reports/npa-16.pdf. Accessed on 2 Mar 2020

Error Management in Interventional Cardiology

Erhard Kaiser

Contents

5.1 Education and Training Situation in Interventional Cardiology

Erhard Kaiser

Training and continuing education for cardiology in Germany is a matter for the states and ultimately not implemented uniformly throughout Germany (◻ Fig. 5.1). The training course and the training content are fixed in the state-specific further training regulations and are regularly revised. The basis for this is provided by the international scientific community and, on a recommendation basis, by the German Society of Cardiology (DGK). In Germany, as in many other countries, there often is no dedicated training curriculum involving simulations for interventional cardiologists. Rather, the cardiology training regulations already contain components of interventional cardiology, but remain incomplete. Based on this circumstance, e.g. the DGK has established a curriculum for the acquisition of the qualification "Interventional Cardiology" DGK, in order to take into account the rapid and continuous development of the subject and the associated

quality requirements for interventional cardiologists. A great responsibility for the quality of training and continuing education nowadays lies with the hospitals authorized to provide training. They must meet the training and continuing education requirements and guarantee a uniformly high standard of quality. This requirement is made more difficult by the time and cost pressures in today's hospital landscape as well as the personnel shortage that can be observed throughout the medical and non-medical sectors.

A clear lack of detailed description of the training content and a complete lack of management of procedural and periprocedural complications are evident here. It is unnecessary at this point to reiterate the importance of these topics. The same problem can be observed at the European level. Here, too, there is no dedicated training regulation for (European) interventional cardiologists; rather, the training recommendation, the so-called core curriculum, already contains components of interventional cardiology (◻ Fig. 5.2). However, it too remains incomplete and falls short of the requirements for modern training in interventional cardiology and does not

State Medical Association of Hesse Corporation under public law			**12.3.5 Internal medicine and cardiology**							Guidelines on the content of further training (as of 01.07.2008)

Further training content Knowledge. Experience and skills in	Remarks by the training officer *	Knowledge. Experience and skills acquired Date / Signature of the WB Authorized Person
the interdisciplinary indication and assessment of nuclear medical examinations as well as surgical treatment procedures		
the basic intensive medical care		

Examination and treatment methods	Reference number	**Annual documentation according to § 8 WBO ***						Knowledge, Experience and skills acquired Date / Signature of the WB Authorized Person
		Date:	Date:	Date:	Date:	Date:	Date:	
Echocardiographies, of which - Street echocardiographies - Echo contrast examinations - Doppler / Duplex examinations of the heart, the veins close to the heart	500 100 50 100							
transesophageal echodiography	50							
right heart catheter examinations including stress if necessary	100							
Spiro-Ergometne	10							
Left heart catheter examinations including the corresponding left heart angiocardiographies and coronary angiographies	300							
Long-term investigation procedures, z. ... ST-segment analysis, heart-rate variabillity... Late potentials	300							
Application of pacemaker probes	50							
Pacemaker Controls	100							
Controls of internal cardioverters or defibrillators (ICD)	10							

further comments from the training officer(s), if applicable:

◻ **Fig. 5.1** Further training regulations in cardiology, Hesse State Medical Association

The ESC Core Curriculum
for the
General Cardiologist

Prepared by the Education Committee of the European Society of Cardiology

ESC Education Commitee 2006-2008

Peter Kearney,Ireland

Chairman of the ESC Education Committee

Jean-Pierre Bassand. France
Carina Blomström-Lundqvist. Sweden
Martin Cowie,UK
Filippo Crea,Italy
Frank Flachskampf,Germany
Dan Gaita,Romania
Lino Goncalves,Portugal
Roger Hall UK
Erhard Kaiser,Germany
Jose Luis Lopez-Sendon,Spain
Jean Marco,Monaco
IraklisMavrakis,Greece
Peter Mills,UK
Tomasz Pasierski, Poland

Peter Polak, The Netherlands

Juerg Schwitter, Switzerland

Other contributor
Don Poldermans, The Netherlands

ESCStaff

Keith McGregor,France

Claire Bramley,France

Dominique Poumeyrol - Jumeau,France

EUROPEAN
SOCIETY OF
CARDIOLOGY

☐ **Fig. 5.2**   Cover core curriculum

include error and complication management. It would be desirable for the impulses coming from the professional societies to find their way consistently and quickly into the further training regulations of the federal states and, ideally, for there to be a uniform regulation of further training throughout Germany.

In contrast, the current approach of the German Society for Vascular Surgery and Vascular Medicine (DGG) to offer innovative and contemporary continuing education must be explicitly praised. In addition to the classical surgical training course, a systematic training and continuing education recommendation is offered here, which enables optional subspecialization in endovascular techniques and explicitly welcomes simulator-based training. Complication management is also explicitly addressed and called up as training content—a novelty that must serve as an example for the other endovascular disciplines of cardiology, radiology and angiology today.

Corresponding training offers are available, for example, at the Vascular Academy Frankfurt am Main and enable complete further training to become an "Endovascular Surgeon DGG" and "Endovascular Specialist DGG". This optional further training is no longer part of a traditional university education, but takes place in close cooperation with university centers (▶ www.vasa-ffm.com).

5.2 Optimization of Procedural and Periprocedural Complication Management in the Cardiac Catheterization Laboratory

Erhard Kaiser

5.2.1 Technical Skills Training

Today, technical skills training is, in a sense, the foundation of interventional cardiology practice. Until now, it has always been difficult for the physician in training to close the gap between theoretical learning based on literature studies and clinical work and the first own invasive procedure on the patient. Today, this gap can be closed by standardized technique training on the endovascular VR simulator. By periprocedural determination of measured values such as consumption of X-ray contrast medium, delivered X-ray radiation, procedure duration, measurement of friction of devices and anatomical structures and documentation of the procedure success, training can be carried out until the procedure is performed without errors (Hsu et al. 2004; Gallagher et al. 2006; Patel et al. 2006; Chaer et al. 2006). In addition, most endovascular VR simulators are mobile and robust, allowing training to take place in clinics.

Examples of Techniques That Can Be Trained on the Simulator
- Radiological techniques
- Seldinger technology
- Wire handling
- Diagnostic catheter handling
- Guide catheter handling
- Balloon dilatations
- Stent implantations
- Left ventricular angiograms
- Complex aortic interventions
- Complex interventions for structural heart disease
- Procedural complication management
- Special techniques, e.g. bifurcation interventions
- Electrophysiological mapping procedures and ablations
- And much more (◘ Fig. 5.3)

Training

The purely technical training of endovascular, catheter-based procedures can now be trained including procedural complication management on the endovascular VR simulator. Appropriately certified training curricula already exist and are routinely applied in a standardized manner (▶ www.cardioskills.com).

5.2.2 Non-technical Skills Training, Emergency Management

Non-technical skills training is now of central importance in interventional cardiology, as it has been observed that teams whose individual members had good technical skills ultimately failed as a team or at least made

◘ Fig. 5.3 Endovascular simulator, example: Mentice VIST-Lab

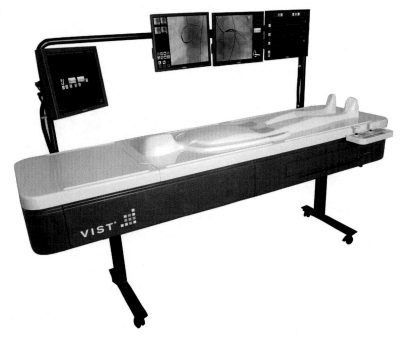

mistakes that they would not have been expected to make. The soft skills were lacking. The quality of the technical skills is often in great contrast to the soft skills/non-technical skills. Ultimately, however, only both skills contribute to optimal patient care and only together guarantee a high level of patient safety, especially in complex procedures or in emergency situations. Even if interventional cardiologists are not directly comparable with the pilots mentioned above, there are commonalities in the requirements profile for both occupational groups as well as similar behavioral expectations despite different training courses.

Similarities in the Requirement Profile Between Cardiologists and Pilots
- Acting in a complex working environment
- The perception of the situation and its changes
- The fulfilment of high communication requirements
- Cooperation with others
- Making decisions
- The consistent use of standards
- Managing resources

While pilots have been training in (full-flight) simulators for decades, neither basic skills training nor emergency management for interventional cardiologists is part of their training, licensure or even licensing. This is all the more astonishing as non-technical skills training in interventional cardiology using endovascular VR simulators and full-scale patient simulators is very effective and efficient. There is a high level of self-commitment among physicians in cardiology training, which makes it clear that the need for simulator-based training in interventional cardiology continues to grow steadily with the complexity of procedures possible today.

There is now more than 20 years of experience in conducting non-technical skills training with cardiologists in the virtual cardiac catheterization laboratory (◘ Fig. 5.4). And during this long time, the training physicians and teams have shown repetitive behavioral patterns that have often stood in the way of successful, error-free patient care.

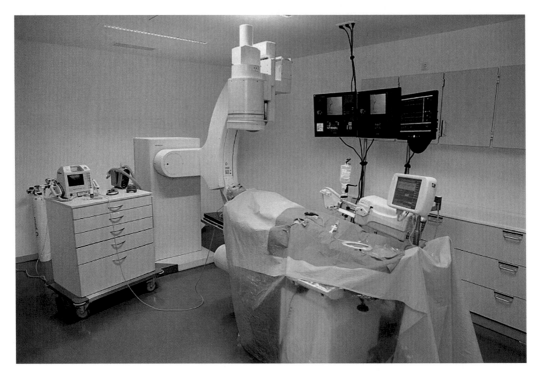

Fig. 5.4 Virtual cardiac catheter laboratory in the Cardioskills Simulation Center Frankfurt am Main with endovascular simulator and fullscale patient simulator

> **Behavioural Patterns of Cardiological Teams Leading to Errors in Non-technical Skills Training**
> - Not a good briefing before the procedure
> - No clear division of tasks
> - No clear responsibilities
> - Self-underestimation
> - Lack of perception of facts
> - Lack of questioning of circumstances
> - No good decision making in the decision making process
> - Hierarchy problems
> - No support of the other
> - Imprecise communication
> - No constructive error management in the team
> - No debriefings

These behavioral patterns are immediately apparent to the trainer observing the training scenario, but can be used through the use of video debriefing systems in semi-open debriefings to engage in constructive error management with the participating physicians (Hoff and Adamowski 1998). The combination of endovascular VR simulation and fullscale patient simulation offers the possibility to train all common emergency situations and potentially complication-prone situations with the physicians.

> **Topics That Are Trained in a Standardized Manner Within the Framework of Emergency Management Simulation Training in the VR Cath Lab**
> - Acute coronary syndrome
> - NSTEMI
> - STEMI
> - Cardiogenic shock
> - Rhythm problems
> - Anaphylactic reaction
> - Sedation issues
> - Cardiopulmonary resuscitation
> - Acute pulmonary artery embolism

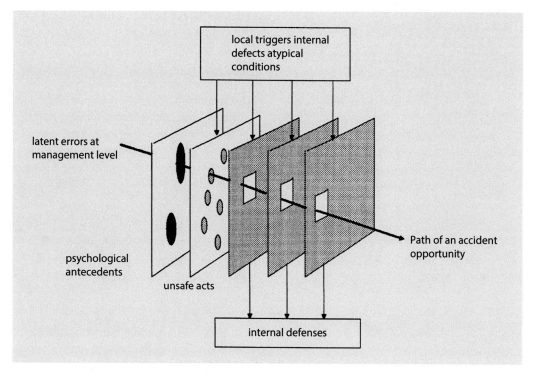

local triggers internal
defects atypical
conditions

latent errors at
management level

Path of an accident
opportunity

psychological
antecedents

unsafe acts

internal defenses

◻ Fig. 5.5 Swiss cheese model. (From St. Pierre et al. 2005)

- Neurological complications
- And much more

It is also important to understand that, even in the cardiac catheterization laboratory, it is always a chain of unfavorable circumstances that leads to a major error or even a loss in the end. Sometimes protective mechanisms, which should always be incorporated into a work process, also fail to take effect. The so-called Swiss Cheese model by James Reason (◻ Fig. 5.5) illustrates this relationship very vividly using the example of a Swiss cheese with holes in it (Reason et al. 2000). Only if safety checks, perhaps also supported by checklists, are established and effective can undesirable treatment outcomes be actively prevented in the best possible way.

Thus, it must also be the task of a cardiology education and training specification to support the learning physician and the teams in the best possible way through appropriate training recommendations. The proximity of

interventional cardiology to aviation is also evident in the concrete situation of a decision-making problem in the cardiac catheterization laboratory. Especially for younger and inexperienced operators, the problem arises of making the right decision in highly complex situations. In addition to delegating parts of the activity in the specific situation, it has proven helpful to use decision-making models in the team in order to make the right decision despite opaque circumstances. Medicine today can also learn from firefighting, for example. ◻ Tables 5.1 and 5.2 list decision-making models for this purpose (Benner 1975; Hörmann 1994, 1995).

Both decision-making models support the operator in the cardiac catheterization laboratory, but also the entire team in decision-making. The collection of facts always takes place jointly, but the decision is then the responsibility of the team leader, i.e. as a rule the operator as the hierarchically highest-placed personality. A steep hierarchy helps to work faster and more effectively in critical situations, while a very flat hierarchy should

Table 5.1 DECIDE model

D	etect	Perception that the current course deviates from the norm
E	sti-mate	Does the change have any significance for the course of events?
C	hoose	The coming decision will be taken from the point of view of safety
I	den-tify	Option with the best prospects of success and lowest risks is chosen
		Framing of alternatives
D	o	Concrete planning and execution of the measure
E	valu-ate	Checking the result. Does it fit the plan?

Table 5.2 FORDEC model

F	acts	What is the situation? Is there a need for action?
O	ptions	What are the options for action?
R	isks and benefits	Assessment of risks and uncertainty factors
D	ecision	Option with the best prospects of success and lowest risks is chosen
		Framing of alternatives
E	xecution	Concrete planning and execution of the measure
C	heck	Checking the result. Does it fit the plan?

be chosen as the basic working model to create a team-friendly working atmosphere characterized by mutual respect. In both decision-making models, the final review of the action, i.e. the "C", is of crucial importance. If the result of the executed action does not match the initial plan, it may be that the wrong facts were assumed or that circumstances have changed in the meantime. So the whole team has to mentally and collectively go back to the beginning of the algorithm and perform a new evaluation.

Training

Team training of emergency situations in the cardiac catheterization laboratory now plays a central role in the quality management of an interventional cardiology department. In the virtual cardiac catheterization laboratory, all relevant emergency situations can be trained in a safe training environment using full-scale patient simulations, and team performance can be measurably improved, among other things by applying decision-making models (▶ www.cardioskills.com).

Cardiology training and continuing education can be given a completely new impetus if influences from outside the field are transferred into cardiology and the realism of the training is adapted. For example, non-technical skills such as communication, situational awareness, stress management and teamwork can be trained specifically and effectively in the Boeing 737 style cockpit simulator (◘ Fig. 5.6) (▶ www.cardioskills.com).

Here, the parallelisms (◘ Table 5.3) between a Boeing 737 style cockpit and a cardiac catheterization laboratory are used to train physicians and then to transfer what they have learned back to their actual working environment, the cardiac catheterization laboratory.

In the course of three standardized training runs, this training method can be used to measurably optimize the non-technical skills of teams in the cardiac catheterization laboratory. A similar approach from Stanford also showed good results in the field of laparoscopic surgery. Here, surgeons were allowed to warm up with video games before performing laparoscopic surgery on a simulator (Plerhoples et al. 2011). Warming up with video games before laparoscopic surgical procedures on the simulator significantly reduced procedural errors and tissue injuries.

◘ **Fig. 5.6** Boeing-737 style cockpit simulator in the CardioSkills Simulation Center Frankfurt am Main

◘ **Table 5.3** Parallelisms between a cardiac catheterization laboratory and a Boeing-737 cockpit

Boeing 737 cockpit	Cardiac cath lab
Watch flight displays	Monitor patient vital signs
Communication with PNF (Pilot Non Flying)	Communication with assistance
Work off checklist	Standardized work
FORDEC in case of emergency	FORDEC in case of emergency

5.3 Outlook

Erhard Kaiser

From the above it must be concluded that standardized simulation training in basic technical skills and non-technical skills should be further and consistently integrated into cardiology education and training. Various efforts in this direction have already been made and will be continued. For example, the working group "Simulation and Virtual Reality" (founded by the editor in 2004) of the German Society of Cardiology (DGK) in cooperation

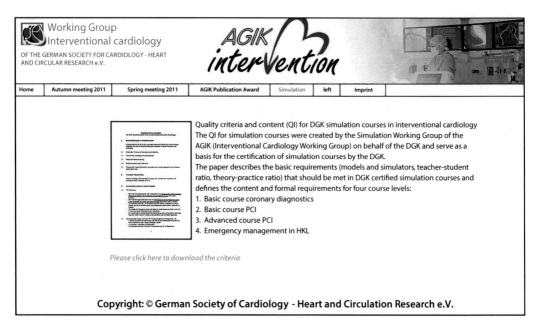

Fig. 5.7   Quality criteria simulation courses DGK

with the working group "Interventional Cardiology" of the DGK was able to publish training recommendations and quality criteria for simulator-based training in interventional cardiology and to comment on the requirements for simulation devices to be used (▶ www.agikintervention.de/Simulation).

These quality criteria (❏ Fig. 5.7) form the basis for DGK-certified training using simulations.

Conclusion

Cardiology must continue to learn from the lessons learned in aviation. Pilot training and error management and the use of simulators in regular training of standards and complex situations helps to minimize errors and losses. It must be recognized that training must keep pace with the current very rapid development of endovascular therapeutic options, and it must take advantage of the fact that state-of-the-art training models can help improve patient safety and training. In addition, it must be the goal of all societies, boards, and individuals involved to create a shift away from a blaming culture toward a culture of error. Non-punitive reporting systems should be implemented in every interventional cardiology department to contribute to error prevention and patient safety.

References

Benner L (1975) L.D.E.C.I.D.E. in hazardous materials emergencies. Fire J 69:13–18

Chaer RA, DeRubertis BG, Lin SC et al (2006) Simulation improves resident performance in catheter-based intervention: results of a randomized, controlled study. Ann Surg 244:343–352

Gallagher AG, Renkin J, Buyl H, Lambert H, Marco J (2006) Development and construct validation of performance metrics for multivessel coronary interventions on the VIST virtual reality simulator at PCR2005. EuroIntervention 2:101–106

Hoff LA, Adamowski K (1998) Creating excellence in crisis care: a guide to effective training and program designs. Jossey-Bass, San Francisco

Hörmann H-J (1994) Urteilsverhalten und Entscheidungsfindung. In: Eißfeldt H, Goeters K-M, Hörmann H-J, Maschke P, Schiewe A (eds) Effektives Arbeiten im team: crew resource management-training für Piloten und Fluglotsen. Deutsches Zentrum für Luft-und Raumfahrt, Hamburg

Hörmann H-J (1995) FOR-DEC: a prescriptive model for aeronautical decision making. In: Fuller R,

Johnston N, McDonald N (eds) Human factors in aviation operations. Avebury, Aldershot

Hsu JH, Younan D, Pandalai S et al (2004) Use of computer simulation for determining endovascular skill levels in a carotid stenting model. J Vasc Surg 40:1118–1125

Patel AD, Gallagher AG, Nicholson WJ, Cates CU (2006) Learning curves and reliability measures for virtual reality simulation in the performance assessment of carotid angiography. J Am Coll Cardiol 47:1796–1802

Plerhoples TA, Zak Y, Hernandez-Boussard T, Lau J (2011) Another use of the mobile device: warm-up for laparoscopic surgery. J Surg Res 170(2):185–188

Reason J et al (2000) Human error: models and management. BMJ 320(7237):768–770

St. Pierre M, Hofinger G, Buerschaper C (2005) Notfallmanagement. Springer, Berlin

Further Reading

www.cardioskills.com. Retrieved 07.09.2012

www.vasa-ffm.com. Retrieved 07.09.2012

www.agikintervention.de/Simulation. Retrieved 07.09.2012

www.cardiovascular-complications.com (under construction)

www.failureculture.com (under construction)

After the Cardiac Catheterization Laboratory

Contents

Patient Follow-Up

Torsten Konrad and Erhard Kaiser

Contents

E. Kaiser (ed.), *Complication Management In The Cardiac Catheter Laboratory*,
https://doi.org/10.1007/978-3-662-66093-5_6

Patient follow-up after diagnostic or therapeutic cardiac catheter examinations is always standardized and is characterized by the aspects inherent to the procedure. During the patient follow-up, clinical and laboratory results are obtained and, if necessary, additional tests are performed (e.g. color-coded duplex sonography, see ▶ Sect. 2.1.1). In addition, the therapy started in the cardiac catheter laboratory is of course continued. This concerns both the medication, such as dual platelet aggregation inhibition, or circulation stabilizing drugs up to further intensive medical therapy.

However, even after an uncomplicated intervention or purely diagnostic procedure, follow-up measures are necessary, which ultimately also involve the general practitioners who continue to treat the patient. This poses a particular challenge to all involved practitioners, and it has been shown time and again that only through optimal communication with each other can adequate therapy adherence be guaranteed for patients.

6.1 Removing the Intra-arterial Sheath and Closing/Pressing the Puncture Site

Torsten Konrad and Erhard Kaiser

6.1.1 Access via the Groin, Puncture of the Common Femoral Artery

The intra-arterial sheath should be withdrawn as soon as possible, depending on the anticoagulation chosen (◻ Fig. 6.1). In purely diagnostic cardiac catheterizations without standard heparin administration, the intra-arterial sheath can therefore be pulled directly in the cardiac catheterization laboratory. For organizational reasons, however, there is no reason why trained personnel should not pull the intra-arterial sheath in the normal ward.

In patients anticoagulated with heparin, the intra-arterial sheath is ideally pulled under ACT control. Clinically, it is common to pull

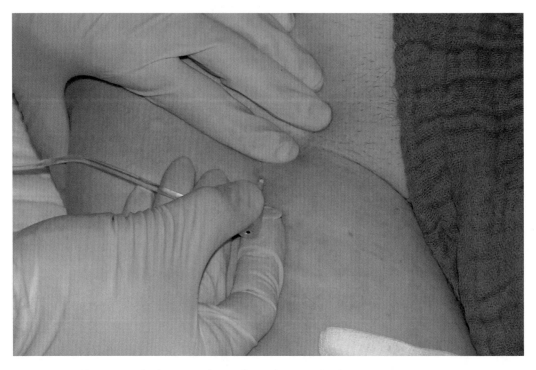

◻ **Fig. 6.1** Pulling the sheath after puncturing the femoral artery. (Thanks to R. Schräder)

the sheath at an activated clotting time of less than 175 s. Often, however, the sheath is pulled simply on the basis of the time (e.g. 2 h after the last heparin administration).

After removal of the intra-arterial sheath, manual compression of the puncture site should be applied for about 5–10 min, but in any case until spontaneous bleeding from the puncture site stops. Compression of the puncture site is strong and punctual (◘ Fig. 6.2).

A flat and not punctual compression, for example by using the fist, should be avoided, as the pressure exerted directly on the puncture site is too low. Mechanical compression aids, such as the FemoStop system or a compression stamp fixed to the patient's bed, can also be used and are effective. In very obese patients, manual compression without mechanical aids should always be preferred (◘ Fig. 6.3).

After the bleeding has stopped safely (check over several seconds!), a strong pressure bandage with a small pressure mediator made of Styropur is applied. In order to avoid accidental bleeding post puncture, in addition to all the measures already mentioned, it is of great importance to inform the patient of the importance of not bending the leg on the punctured side, as otherwise the pressure would be taken off the pressure dressing and the risk of renewed arterial bleeding from the puncture canal would increase. In the case of restless patients or incompliance, the use of a closure system is recommended (◘ Fig. 6.4).

The duration of bed rest depends on the French sizes of the sheaths used and the amount of anticoagulation applied. As a rule, strict bed rest lasts between 2 and 6 h. In special constellations, however, a longer period of bed rest may be necessary. The patient should then take it easy for two days, avoid heavy lifting and exercise.

If arterial closure systems have been used, the further procedure can be adapted to the manufacturer's instructions.

After removal of the pressure dressing and before discharge, the puncture site should be checked by inspection, palpation and auscultation. If abnormalities such as a flow noise, a large hematoma or pronounced pain are

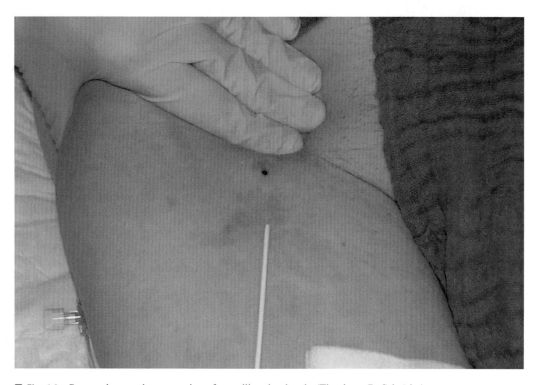

◘ **Fig. 6.2** Punctual manual compression after pulling the sheath. (Thanks to R. Schräder)

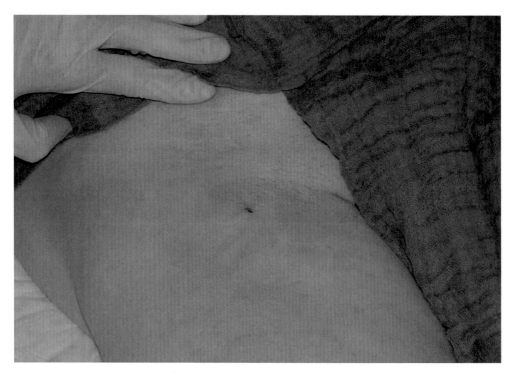

◘ Fig. 6.3 Stopping the bleeding after punctual impression. (Thanks to R. Schräder)

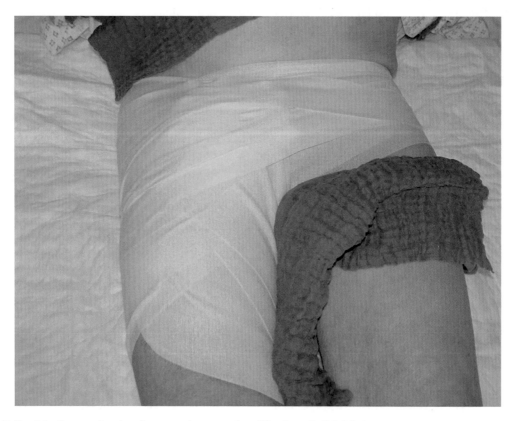

◘ Fig. 6.4 Pressure dressing after manual compression. (Thanks to R. Schräder)

found, immediate duplex ultrasound control of the punctured vessel is indicated. Particularly in the case of back or flank pain and a relevant drop in hemoglobin, the highest level of attention is required and an immediate diagnosis of the presence of a retroperitoneal hematoma is indicated (see also ▶ Sect. 2.1.1).

6.1.2 Access via the Arm, Puncture of the Radial Artery

The advantage of puncturing the radial artery over the femoral approach, namely the good compressibility and rapid mobilization of the patient, is immediately apparent in the post-procedural procedure. The arterial sheath is pulled immediately after cardiac catheterization, even after previous heparin administration. The puncture site is then either manually compressed or compressed with a mechanical compression system, such as the TR-BandTM (Terumo Interventional Systems Company). The advantage of this system is the simultaneous visibility of the puncture site under compression. Alternatively, folded compresses can be placed on the puncture site (sparing the ulnar artery) and wrapped with an elastic bandage. After removal of the sheath, the hand should be monitored closely to note paresthesias of the fingers or malperfusion. However, temporary paresthesias of fingers I–III may also be due to local anesthesia in the area of the puncture site. After removal of the pressure dressing/compression system, the puncture site should again be clinically checked for sensitivity, perfusion and motor function of the hand.

6.2 Monitoring After Coronary Angiography and Coronary Intervention

Torsten Konrad and Erhard Kaiser

The necessity for post-procedural continuous circulatory monitoring results from the respective examination circumstances and the procedures performed. Post-procedural monitoring always continues the monitoring started in the cardiac catheterization laboratory, sometimes without interruption (patient transport, patient transfer). This can be done in the intensive care unit, the intermediate care unit or in the normal ward with telemetry stations.

After elective diagnostic cardiac catheterisations, bland balloon dilatations and stent implantations, continuous ECG monitoring is not required. Rather, a normal 12-lead resting ECG is routinely written after about 4–6 h and the arterial blood pressure is documented non-invasively at regular intervals by the nursing staff. The ordering of this is the responsibility of the operator, who will order the further procedure in his report of the cardiac catheterization. If the arterial sheath is removed on the normal ward, this is a moment that requires special attention, since vasovagal reactions with bradycardia relevant to the circulation can occasionally be observed under the strong pressure on the femoral artery. Because of this, intravenous volume administration or atropine administration is occasionally necessary after the arterial sheath is pulled. The peripheral venous access cannula should therefore only be removed after the arterial sheath has been withdrawn.

In contrast, patients who have already had circulatory problems in the cardiac catheterization laboratory and who may have shown arrhythmias (short VT, atrial fibrillation, etc.) require special attention. Depending on the equipment available for monitoring, continuous ECG registration with arrhythmia detection is then also carried out in the normal ward with telemetry facilities or in the intermediate care unit. In addition to ECG monitoring, this group of patients also undergoes closer non-invasive blood pressure measurement in the first hours after the procedure and, if necessary, additional blood samples are taken for supplementary laboratory chemistry tests.

> **Patients Who Need to Be Monitored in an Intensive Care Unit**
> - STEMI, NSTEMI and acute coronary syndrome
> - Condition after cardiopulmonary resuscitation
> - Circulatory unstable patients
> - Ventilated patients
> - Patients after high-risk interventions
> - High-risk patients for bridging to surgery
> - Patients with catecholamine requirements
> - Patients who have had procedural complications, if applicable
> - Patients who have had periprocedural complications, if applicable

Interdisciplinary intensive care units or pure cardiac care units offer a variety of monitoring and therapy options in addition to the first-mentioned possibilities, so that high-risk patients in particular are monitored and treated post-procedurally here.
- Continuous, non-invasive and invasive circulatory monitoring
- Continuous respiratory monitoring
- Controlled and assisted ventilation
- Controlled mild hypothermia
- Mechanical circulatory support such as ECMO, heart-lung machine
- Different forms of anaesthesia
- Complex drug therapies via syringe pumps

- Echocardiography, duplex sonography and TEE
- Defibrillation, cardioversion and pacemaker therapy
- Intensive nursing and medical care

6.3 Outpatient Follow-Up Examinations After Cardiac Catheterisations

Torsten Konrad and Erhard Kaiser

After cardiac catheterization and especially after coronary interventions, outpatient non-invasive follow-up should be performed. As a rule, you yourself or the cardiologist who is continuing your treatment will see your patient again immediately and then again after 4–6 weeks post procedural in the practice/outpatient clinic in order to then carry out a complete non-invasive follow-up.

> **Examinations in the Context of the First Non-invasive Follow-Up**
> - Physical examination and follow-up history
> - Special inspection, palpation and auscultation of the punctured groin/wrist
> - 12-Lead resting ECG and rhythm ECG
> - Color Doppler Echocardiography
> - Possibly stress ECG (climbing level according to Kaltenbach, ergometer, treadmill)
> - Checking and adjusting the medication taken
> - Determination of the further treatment strategy and the further examination intervals

6.4 Conclusion

In addition to all medical aspects of the therapy, it is also psychologically important for the patient to have a reliable, friendly and knowledgeable companion in his treating cardiologist during the course of his disease.

Printed in the United States
by Baker & Taylor Publisher Services